ONE FRONT ACROSS THE WORLD

Books by Douglas Hyde

—

I BELIEVED
THE ANSWER TO COMMUNISM
RED STAR VERSUS THE CROSS (*With Francis Dufay*)
ONE FRONT ACROSS THE WORLD

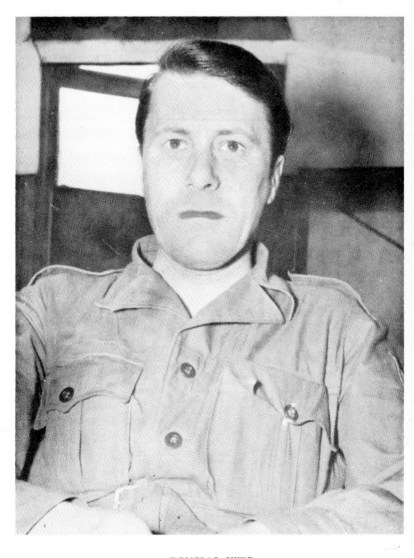

DOUGLAS HYDE

"ASSIMILATED RANK, MAJOR ACTING COLONEL U.S. ARMY;" UNIFORM
BRITISH, BUT STILL EVERY INCH A CIVILIAN

ONE FRONT ACROSS THE WORLD

by

DOUGLAS HYDE

THE NEWMAN PRESS
WESTMINSTER, MARYLAND
1956

Printed in the United States of America

DEDICATED TO THOSE HUNGRY
SHEEP IN ASIA WHO LOOK UP AND ARE
NOT FED

CONTENTS

CONTENTS

ILLUSTRATIONS

A*

I

WHY I DID IT

IN a clean, white factory in the heart of Africa, a man who just four months earlier had been a tribesman in the bush sat working at a conveyor belt. As the cigarette packet reached him he took it with one hand, deftly turned it from side to side on the inked forme, then put it back on the belt with the other. The whole operation took only a few seconds. In that time the packet changed from one of plain white card into one bearing a name and trade mark known throughout the world.

His movements, as he worked, would have interested a motion-study expert. He sat on a wooden bench, and as he took the packets with one hand and replaced them with the other he swung unceasingly, rhythmically, backwards and forwards, almost touching the bench on either side with his elbows as he did so. It was a new African dance, belonging half to the primordial jungle of yesterday and half to the new world of industry of tomorrow, a dance which lasted, with only a brief break, for eight hours a day, from the time the factory whistle called him to it in the morning to when it shrilly told him to go back to his hut again at night.

Stuck in his machine was his time card, on which were recorded the hours he had worked and the output bonus he had earned during the past month. Any problems which arose during the course of his work were taken up with the management by his departmental shop steward. He was represented by fellow Africans on the works committee and the joint production committee.

"Come and see our model canteen," said the works manager.

We walked across to an adjoining building, even whiter and cleaner than the works itself. The menu for the day—and every day—was a simple one, for it was of necessity based upon the traditional diet of the tribesman now turned factory worker. There was a choice of boiled bananas or boiled beans.

The time sheet of the man I had seen printing cigarette packets showed that he had earned one hundred and twelve shillings so far that month. "More money than he had ever seen in his life until he came here four months ago," said the manager. "And we provide him with his house, which is far better than anything he ever had, into the bargain."

Since the man at the machine was barefooted and, very sensibly, dressed only in a shirt and shorts, and unlikely to wear anything else, I asked what there was left for him to buy with his one hundred and twelve shillings. "How do they spend their earnings?"

"How would you expect? Booze and women. There's nothing else."

I wondered just how much better off, in terms of the things that really matter, he was now than he had been when he was still 'in the bush'. My question met with a shrug, and then:

"Some of them come and work on contract for a couple of years, save all they can, then go back, buy some cows and use them for the bride price with which to get a wife. But more and more are staying, and the more industry we have here the more they will be likely to remain. Soon the big hydro-electric scheme will be operating and then they will come crowding in and we shall have a settled industrial population here instead of the constantly changing one we have now."

That was in December, 1953, in Uganda, a mile or two from where the Nile leaves Lake Victoria to set out on its long journey to the edge of the once dark continent. From the great new Owen Falls electricity plant would soon be going out all over Uganda and, given more settled conditions, all over Kenya, too, the power of the mighty Nile. Wherever it went, new factories would spring up. Already they were beginning to move in.

More tribesmen would come from the surrounding bush, and from beyond the great forest, exchanging the easy life on the shamba among the banana trees for eight hours a day among the conveyor belts in the bright new factory.

The dissolution of the old life is already under way; the new one, approached in a state of total unpreparedness by all concerned, has begun.

Industrialisation for Africa, Asia or anywhere else means education of the type required to produce men who can be clerks, managers, executives. That means the acquiring of some sort of a Western outlook, Western ways of thought and, in time, largely Western forms of existence.

That same process, to a greater or lesser extent is going on all over the world today. The more we become conscious of the evils and dangers of having two thousand million people living on the verge of starvation, the more we develop the undeveloped areas, the more quickly will that process spread. It is true of Africa. It is true of Asia, too.

Those continents in a generation's time will be quite unlike what they are now.

It is not sufficient to say that as yet the change of life and thought touches only a minority, that for the millions who till the soil life will go on as it has done since time immemorial. Those affected are the new proletarians and the intellectuals. They are the pioneers of the new life, the natural leaders of the masses in the modern world. They can be decisive in a modern community. And what they think and do is today given a political content and significance by the spread of resurgent nationalism and Communism.

Industrialisation, whether we like it or not, means some sort of Westernisation. The new life takes on a pattern which was made in the West. The new outlook adopted, the political philosophies acquired, were made in the West, too. They may be given African or Asian forms, but they had their origins in the West.

The West has itself been through the process. The new wealth which came with merchant capitalism and the new revolutionary inventions which followed gave rise to new values. The old way of life and the old Faith were forgotten or rejected. An unthought-out, creeping materialism slowly gained domination over the life of the faith-less masses. Then Communism came along to fill the spiritual vacuum.

True, Communism has organised only a small section of the masses. But the Communist does not need majorities. He is interested in the moulding and training of a minority ready and able to grasp the opportunity when it comes. After the seizure of power the masses, too, are moulded according to the Marxist pattern, not then so that they shall revolt, but in order that they may be brought to acquiesce.

The spiritual consequences of Western industrialisation in practice have, so far, been the growth of materialism and, out of that, Communism, which is materialism in its most highly organised form.

The spread of Westernism to Asia and Africa, which is something we cannot prevent even if we would, has, demonstrably, led also to the spread of materialism and the springing up of Communist movements. The dangers which come from the existence of an organised, determined Communist minority in the West are nothing as compared to those springing from its existence in lands where the spiritual vacuum is made far more complete, education is more superficial and hunger more widespread.

Communism in less than forty years has conquered a quarter of the world. It rules over more than one in four of the human race. The process which made that possible has enormously speeded up since the end of World War II and is likely to snowball during the next quarter of a century.

If the development of the world's hitherto 'backward' areas leads only to the spread of materialism, then, taking the long view—but it will not be very long, for all that—the possibilities of a Communist world will enormously increase, not decrease, as the years go by. It threatens to undermine everything we do for the defence of what we euphemistically call 'the West'.

Put at its very lowest—at the level of the materialistic West itself—the millions of dollars we spend on arms, and even on economic aid, too, will all go down the drain unless we stop the process whereby the development of a society along modern lines leads almost inevitably to the creation of faithless millions.

But there is hope. For it has still to be settled whether that

Western way of life which the vanguard in the East must be expected in the coming years to assume will be the one which too many in the West now follow, or whether they can be guided into taking the way which so many people of the West have themselves already forgotten. The mistakes made in the centuries which preceded the Industrial Revolution do not necessarily have to be repeated. Indeed we might say that we have a moral obligation to assist those about to follow the same course to avoid the errors we made, which lie at the root of the modern problem.

That, as I see it, is, in broad outline, the background to the battle of our time. That battle is one for men's hearts and minds. That is true of the West. It is equally true of the East. Upon its outcome hangs the fate of mankind.

The fight is a spiritual one, a fight of faiths. That is why it is only partially true to say that it is a conflict between materialism and religion. Materialism is not a faith. It does not win a man's heart and mind—it only rots them. Men need a faith, and that is where Communism comes in. In that sense, it is between the Communist man and the man of God.

The decisive sectors of the world battle today are Asia and Africa. The colonial front is the active, fighting front. In the West, Communism is for the moment consolidating its position. In the East, it is still actively pushing forward. In Africa and other colonial and semi-colonial areas, it is probing around looking for the opportunity of a break through.

It happens that the colonial countries are also the mission countries. There, the missionary, and the Communist confront each other. It is the job of each to wrestle for minds and hearts in those great, rapidly changing areas of the world. Hearts and minds are, generally speaking, more open to be won there than here. New ways mean new thinking, new beliefs. The Communist and the missionary are both there to try to steer its course. The missionary and the active Asian layman are front-line fighters in the battle of our time just as much as are the trained cadres of Communism. Upon the outcome of their activities an enormous amount depends.

The missionaries' is not a political, still less a military, job.

That is something which cannot be over-emphasised. Their task is a spiritual one. But if the basis of our present ills is spiritual, then the repercussions of their work must go widely into other spheres, for our spiritual ills colour the whole of life and threaten our very existence.

This is not rendered less true by the fact that they, if they are attending to their business, are mainly concerned with men's hearts, minds and souls. Nor is it made less true because many of them are hardly conscious of the battle in which they are involved, or have only recently been made aware of something of its nature by, for example, the disappearance of China, one of the major mission fields of the Church, into the camp of atheistic Communism.

For twenty years I was a Communist. As a writer, I assisted in the work of Marxist mind-moulding. As an active party leader and one of its tutors, I helped to train its front-line fighters. I know the strength of the Communist 'steel-hardened cadres', who are the same wherever you go. They know what they want, where they are going and how they are going to get there. Their strength has been demonstrated in almost every country of the modern world. I know their calibre, their qualities. They are formidable.

But after more than six years with the Faith, I wanted also to know something of the calibre and qualities of the front-line fighters of the Faith. Conscious of the enormous and almost unrealised importance to our time of the colonial mission lands, I wanted to know more about the men working in them and the consequences of their work.

What manner of men are they? How far are they equipped for their work? With what success are they meeting? And what sort of people are they attracting and holding?

The Communists profess a contempt for them, but, in fact, as the experience of China, Korea and Vietnam goes to show, they take them very seriously indeed.

In particular, it seemed important to know what was happening in Korea, which is the one country on earth whose people have tasted Communism, known something of the consequences of Communist rule and have been rescued from it.

Korea is of unique importance in the battle in two ways. Firstly, we may there see the reactions of a pagan people who have experienced Communism. Secondly, the West, with all the Orient watching with intense interest, went into Korea professedly to make a stand against the spread of Communism. That stand clearly, sooner or later, had to be made somewhere. It was by an accident of history that it occurred in Korea. But that did not make the protracted war any less unpleasant for the Koreans.

The West is now tending to lose interest in the fate of battered Korea and to wish that its irritating ruling politicians would let it decently forget the country, its people and their problems altogether. In fact we can't decently forget, because it would be indecent to do so.

The West made Korea its guinea-pig for military resistance to Oriental Communist aggression. We owe it to the Koreans now to make it our guinea-pig for peaceful development. We owe it to those of our own people who died there in the fight against Communism to protect it from the infiltration of Communist ideas and influences.

Certainly, the East does not forget Korea. There are too many other countries in Asia which might be 'other Koreas' for that to be possible. They are anxious to know whether what happened and is happening to Korea is the worst thing that can happen to a nation, or is it the best?

I tried to learn more about Asia's front-line fighters, and particularly those in Korea, from my work as a journalist, meeting men home from the Orient and through my association with many men and women from the East who are now working or studying in the West. But the more I saw of them the more necessary I realised it was that I should go there. I had been to Africa, now I wanted to see how the battle was going in Asia, too.

So I went there and, for a period, travelled among, lived with and shared the minds of the missionaries and their charges. In particular, I associated with the members of a missionary body about whose work I already knew a good deal, the Society of

St. Columban, which has its men all over the Orient. At its headquarters you may, if you have the background and training, learn more of the East from people who have lived *in* it, and made themselves *of* it, than anywhere else I know.

In the Society's houses in Tokyo, Seoul and remote Asian villages I lived with men whose whole life is bound up with that of the people. Their relationship to them is quite unlike that of the Western business man, or soldier, or tourist, who observes the life of the common folk from without, detached from it physically and, still more, psychologically.

The Society has a record second to none. Providentially, it came into existence at approximately the same time as the birth of the first Communist State in Russia. It has been in the front line ever since. Its men have been wherever Communism was most active in the East. They were contending with Asian Communism almost before the rest of the world was conscious of its existence.

Because I believe that in the last analysis the battle for men's hearts and minds is between the man with the Communist faith and the man with the Faith, I have narrowed down my picture in the main to those two figures who confront each other so dramatically all over the Orient today. And, so that it shall be of human beings, and not just 'isms', that I write, I have pinpointed it in particular, although not by any means exclusively, upon Columban Fathers active in the field.

There will, I know, be some who will disagree with my main thesis as to what the battle is about and who, in the last resort, are the decisive men in it. But even those who disagree should know something of this sector of the front. They should have some knowledge of these men whose activities, on any reckoning, may clearly have a great bearing on the future of nations now awakening to a new life and of the battle in which they are involved.

II

PHILIP CROSBIE'S STORY

(1)

EACH evening, as I came downstairs from my study, Philip Crosbie would put on the new long-playing record of Tchaikovsky's Pianoforte Concerto No. 1, which he had brought back from London one day as a gift for the family. He never seemed to grow tired of hearing it. To this day I cannot play it without being reminded of him.

When supper was over, we would go back to the lounge for coffee and I would choose something of Bach's, usually one of the Brandenburgs. It was becoming a sort of ritual. Yet all the time he knew, and I knew, that the purpose of his stay in my home was not just to play our favourite gramophone records to each other.

He had come so that I might get his story from him. As a journalist I had realised from the moment that I had met this quiet, diffident, unpretentious man that it would not be easy, that this was, in fact, going to be one of my most difficult assignments. For his was a story of incredible suffering and, since it was still only a week or two behind him, and since men of his type talk least freely about what means most to them, it was, I knew, quite useless to expect to get from him anything more than the scraps which had already appeared in the newspapers if I tried to rush him.

I wanted him to tell me his experiences in detail. But I wanted also to get to know just what he thought and felt when he was thrown into the Korean Communist jail, whilst he was on that appalling 'Death March to the Yalu River', and whilst he was whiling away the demoralising months and years in idle captivity up there on the fringes of the Communist world.

For he was one of the relatively small number of men who were, if my reading of the situation was correct, right in the front line of the battle of our time. If, in the last resort, that battle, which is one for men's hearts and minds, has to be fought between the Communist élite on the one hand and those with the Faith on the other, and if Asia is at this moment the most active front, and might prove to be the decisive one, too, then it was important to know something of the motives, preparation, calibre and quality of front-line fighters like Philip Crosbie.

My years in the Communist Party had taught me just how toughened and tempered were Stalin's 'men of a special mould.' They, I knew, were put through the same training, given the same indoctrination, shared the same philosophy, learned and practised the same strategy, tactics and techniques.

But how, I had been asking, about the front-line fighters on the other side—our side? How did they measure up to the job, not simply of combating Communism, for that was not directly their business—or at the most was certainly only one small part of it—but of providing a living, positive alternative to it which would, almost incidentally as it were, ensure that the spiritual defences of Christendom would stand firm against the Red onslaught?

So far we had hardly mentioned the things which were most in our minds. I was waiting for the opportunity to come naturally so that I could get something more than just yet another newspaper story about the already much-publicised Death March.

I didn't play one of the Brandenburgs that night. Instead, I put on something quite short, Bach's "Mortify us through thy grace", which through the medium of wordless instruments tells unmistakably of man's suffering and of the mercy of God as well.

As the record finished and its message still hung in the air I asked him casually, "Where were you born? In Sydney?"

"No, in Victoria—way back in the wilds."

Then I saw how the job could best be done. If I could get him to talk about how and when and why he decided to go to Asia and what happened to him when he got there, telling his story chronologically and in his own way, I would get the whole thing in time.

"Was it a nice place?"

"No. My people were trying to farm land up-country from Melbourne. There was practically no water there, no irrigation scheme. The place was almost a desert as a consequence."

"Well, how on earth did you come to think of becoming a Catholic missionary, and in particular of joining the Society of St. Columban and going to Asia?"

He thought for a minute or two. How and why *does* one make the decisions that determine the course of one's life? Most often they are the ones which men analyse least. I doubt if in his case he had ever put the question to himself just like that. His first answer merely skimmed the surface.

"I guess I would have roamed away from home whatever happened. I wasn't the sort to settle quietly and never move away."

"Yes, but why be a missionary? You might have gone abroad and made a mint of money. Did you hear a lecture or meet some missionary from some romantic-sounding place?"

Again he thought for several minutes. Then, as was typical of him, he came out with a short answer which told the whole story.

"No, I never heard any lectures or met any missionaries. I suppose I got the idea from reading the Society's magazine. I thought I had a vocation, which meant that I would be a priest in any case. And if I was going to be a priest and give up so much, I might as well give it all up and have done with it."

And that was that. No embroidery, no frills, certainly no dramatics.

From there we moved on to his days at seminary, to his life after he set out for an Asia in turmoil, his work in a parish straddling the 38th Parallel in which half of his people were already inaccessible because their part of Korea had already come under Communist rule.

But getting his story was hard work all the way. Everything was put into a minimum of words. Every event in which he was personally concerned was written down, told absolutely flatly. He embellished nothing. He would have broken the heart of any journalist who was thinking only in terms of sensational headlines and arresting adjectives.

I would spend a whole evening prompting and coaxing, almost prising the words out of him. It was not that he was deliberately unco-operative, although I confess that at times I secretly felt so exasperated that I almost believed that this was so. Then I would see what it was costing him: how, despite the fact that he gave the appearance, at first glance, of having come out of his sustained ordeal in extraordinarily robust condition, he would darken under the eyes, his face would grow lined and he would show signs of strain as I urged him on.

His reticence was partly due to his natural disinclination to talk about himself and to see himself and his life as of any possible interest to anyone outside his own little circle. It was partly, also, due to the fact that he felt quite genuinely that he had done no more than anyone else would have done in the circumstances. He had done what he had to do, what in conscience he was obliged to do. When he had first set out for troubled Asia he had known that he was likely sooner or later to be in danger. So why make a fuss about it when it happened?

And, of course, his reticence sprang also from the fact that the experiences which had so recently ended in Moscow were of a type that a man wants to forget. He had no desire to re-live them, not even in imagination, sitting in a comfortable chair in a London suburb.

This last point was emphasised by the way in which my questioning unsettled him. He was clearly finding it difficult to readjust himself to normal life in any case. At the end of an evening's discussion he would be left restless. Late at night we would go upstairs to bed, but as I lay thinking over what he had told me I would hear him go quietly into my study and soon he would be urgently typing letters about which, I knew quite well, there was no real urgency at all.

"I don't need much sleep and there are jobs which must be done," he would say by way of excuse when I told him next day that I had heard him working until three or even four o'clock in the morning.

But as he told his story, the very flatness of its telling became impressive. It was *pianissimo* all the way—and all the more convincing for that very reason. Certainly one could be sure that there were no exaggerations.

Nor was there any question of his modesty being just a turn put on for the occasion. He was one of the most natural and lovable people I have met.

Five minutes after his arrival from the airport he had made himself quietly and, Australian-fashion, informally at home. In not much longer he had his Roman collar off and was going around the garden in open-necked shirt and light shoes. Without any apparent effort, and without conforming to any conscious pattern of behaviour, he became part of any company by just remaining himself.

He was now in his late thirties or early forties but at first glance he looked much younger. He was, I would judge, about five and a half feet in height with the build, carriage and wiry toughness of a cross-country runner. He had an open, almost boyish face, with frank blue eyes, small nose, pink complexion and a permanently puckered forehead. His Irish origins showed themselves in the reddish tint in his fair hair, to which recent events had added some silver.

The presence of those white hairs, about which he showed some embarrassment, for he resented, I think, anything which suggested that his experiences had been in any way exceptional, were easily accounted for when he told his story.

When first he learned that he was being sent by the Society of St. Columban to Korea he was bitterly disappointed. He knew little about the country and what he knew was unattractive. Before he joined the Society he had been hardly conscious of its existence. In thinking of the various Asian mission fields to which he might, as a newly-ordained priest at a missionary college, be sent, Korea had never entered into his calculations.

Like most young men who joined the Society of St. Columban at that time he had thought in terms of China, for it was there that the Society had started, still had most of its men and had collected most of its proud crop of martyrs. To this day, incidentally, even after the total conquest of China by Communism, the Society is still known in Ireland, where it began, as the Maynooth Mission to China.

He had known in any case that he would be travelling into trouble; China had meant precisely that for the Society from the day it started way back in 1918. When he got his Korean assignment, World War II had already begun. Korea was part of the Japanese Empire and as such was already involved in the China 'incident'. It was clearly only a matter of time before she would be in the world war too. He was there for just twelve months before Pearl Harbor, then he was immediately interned.

Japan had for long been preparing to come into the war, and as a natural consequence foreigners' activities had been watched with suspicion the whole of the time. Every Westerner was seen as a potential spy. And that was the way he, and all the other Columban Fathers arrested with him, were treated in jail. This was his first taste of life in a Korean prison—but not his last. He was arrested in Hunchon, where he was then assistant priest, but was taken over the mountains to the jail in Chunchon, some twenty-five miles away.

Conditions in Chunchon were bad. Koreans have entirely different standards of comfort from those of the people of the West and even the most comfortable Korean home falls far short of the minimum requirements of Westerners. There are, for example, no chairs. The polished floors provide the only seating. There is little or no furniture. Sleeping on the floor, large numbers of people can and do occupy a remarkably small amount of space. It is hardly surprising in the circumstances if Korean prison standards are far below our own.

There was no polish, only filth, on the floor of the ill-lit and badly ventilated cell into which fourteen priests, all members of his Society, were put. But it was on that floor that they had to sit and sleep. On the walls could be seen traced in dirt the dark outline of other prisoners who in the past had, like them, sat for hour after hour, day after day, with nothing to do but sit and sit.

Into the missionaries' single cell was also put a Korean woman convict. Whether this was done out of malice or was just someone's idea of a joke was never clear. Her presence was not appreciated.

Another 'guest' in the cell was a more welcome one. He was the Korean who had been house-boy to one of the 'old Korea hands', Fr. Brian Geraghty. When Brian Geraghty was arrested, the boy insisted on coming too. After much pleading and persuasion, the Japanese guards granted him permission to prepare the food for the employer he loved, and the other missionaries as well, since this would save themselves work.

After some three months the Columbans, thin and bearded, were all released together. After a period of house arrest all those classed as enemy aliens, Philip Crosbie among them, were repatriated. The Irish, as neutrals, were permitted to remain behind, but their every move was watched and the next four years were difficult ones for them.

Back in Australia, Fr. Crosbie was put to teaching at his Society's house of studies. He would have preferred to spend some of his time studying the Korean language, but had no text-books. Then in 1947 he was sent back to Korea, to go as parish priest to Hunchon, where he had previously been assistant.

He found that the half of his parish which was situated above the 38th Parallel was now sealed off behind the Bamboo Curtain. This was a result of the country's arbitrary division which had been agreed to at the end of the war, and which left one half of Korea in the hands of the Russians, the other in those of the Americans.

So once again he started to study Korean whilst at the same time having to give most of his time and thought to other matters. "Let the parish go for the moment and concentrate on the language," he had been told, but although he now had a Korean priest as assistant, he was drawn into more and more activity and in practice had little time for study. It was one hundred miles from the mission house to the farthest point in his parish, with mountains all the way.

Spurred by his restless itch for action, he quickly began to make changes in the Hunchon compound. Because the water supply was erratic he erected a pump. Korean vegetables grown under Korean conditions have a habit of giving typhoid to those not brought up to them—the result of using insufficiently composted 'night soil' (human excrement) as manure. So he started a vegetable plot of his own. One achievement of which he was particularly proud was the cement-walled cellar which he constructed under his Korean-type house. He planned to store vegetables there during the hard winter months and hoped that in time some of his ideas might be taken up by his Korean parishioners, who lived on pickled turnip for most of each winter.

He was planning, too, to build a church hall in which, if he could beg a projector from someone back home, he would show films which would make his Christians realise that, although they might be but a small minority in Korea, they were in fact part of a great, world-wide body four-hundred million strong. The Koreans who had helped build the church would construct the hall, too, under his supervision.

Life in a parish straddling the Parallel was, during those uneasy years, never without its excitements. There was much clandestine coming and going by North Korean Communists who were busy infiltrating the South. Occasionally, too, Catholics from behind the Curtain would make their way southward across the border to places where they could practise their religion.

There were frequent armed skirmishes. The silence of the night would be broken by gunfire, and even in broad daylight there were sometimes short, sharp raids from across the Parallel.

It was almost impossible to tell who was on the side of the Communists and who was not. The Communist Party had its following among workers in the towns and had attracted some members of other classes too, notably the intellectuals. From Fr. Crosbie's own area one day a group of Korean soldiers, led by an officer, made a sudden dash for the North. At first it was thought that they had gone on a raid in retaliation for those from the North. But soon it became clear that they—or at any rate those in charge of the party—had been Communists who were going over to the other side, taking arms and vehicles with them.

Superficially, life went on as though the people of Hunchon were not living on the edge of a volcano. But as he started each new project Philip Crosbie wondered whether he would ever see its completion.

"What do we do if the balloon goes up?" he and his colleagues from other parishes would ask when, on rare occasions, they met at Chunchon, their diocesan centre, on some ecclesiastical business.

"Youngsters with no knowledge of the language get out. So must those too old to take whatever may be coming. Assistant priests also should leave. The rest stay at their posts and see if it is possible to carry on under Communism," their 'boss', Monsignor Thomas Quinlan, the Prefect Apostolic, told them.

Thomas Quinlan had no illusions about Communists and Communism. He had been in China in the early days of the Society and had seen them at work there. Many of the young men who went out with him were jailed by the 'Communist bandits' at one time or another, others died at their hands. Nor was he ignorant of prison life. He had been in the Japanese jail with Fr. Crosbie and the rest and, as an Irishman, had lived under house arrest after the British and Americans had been repatriated. He knew that the missionary in Asia was a front-line fighter and as such must be prepared to take risks. And the order he gave was one which he intended obeying himself.

The name of Thomas Quinlan meant little to anyone outside the Society of St. Columban and his own parish of Chunchon in those days. Three years later his picture was to appear in papers throughout the free world as the hero of the Death March to the Yalu River. But from the start those who worked with him knew that the big, smiling man with the Tipperary brogue was exceptional in his combination of generosity, kindness, humility, intelligence and courage.

For years, though ranking as a prelate, he had lived like a Korean peasant, sleeping on the floor of his little house beside the church on the hill. At that precise moment he was dreaming of the day when the Cathedral on which he and his parishioners were working would be completed. Building it there just below the Parallel, at that moment, expressed his own approach to the situation. He knew that if war should come it would inevitably be destroyed, for Chunchon stands at important cross-roads from the North, but it was not for him to delay his work for God because of the folly of man. His job was to build and, if the worst came and all was lost, to build again if necessary. And that was what his priests should do too.

(2)

It started on Sunday, June 25, 1951. Philip Crosbie had gone over to Chunchon for the day and was unaware that the gunfire meant anything more than just yet another, perhaps rather larger, raid from the North. When he got back to Hunchon he realised that this was something more; it was a large-scale, highly organised, carefully prepared invasion.

The local Christians came to him and urged him to make for safety. "You are a foreigner and a priest," they said, "and you will be in trouble right away. We'll carry on without you." His assistant, a young Korean, in accordance with the general instruction, got into mufti and disappeared.

Philip Crosbie remembered Mgr. Quinlan's words: "Those in care of souls stay at their posts." He resisted his parishioners' offers of help and just carried on. Three days later, on June 29, Hunchon fell.

He was in his garden when the first soldiers from the North arrived. "They were not particularly hostile," he told me in his usual flat way. "They took away my gramophone, radio, some ball-pens, the chickens from the garden, the food supplies from the cellar I had built, some candles from the church and various bits of personal gear. Those were just things which attracted them and which they saw as the spoils of war. They didn't strike me as particularly bad men. But I was interested in the fact that, although they were Koreans all right, they clearly had never lived in Korea. Some had come from Manchuria, where they had been part of the Korean *émigré* community, and some seemed to be Koreans from Russia."

Again, more urgently, Korean Catholics urged him to get away before it was too late. Already many people were preparing to leave for further south. "I'll stick it out," he told them.

"Then if you stay, we stay too," said his Korean housekeeper, carpenter and 'outside man'. And, with the loyalty which is one of the Korean's outstanding qualities, they did, willingly taking the risks that that involved. Already it was becoming apparent that this war, like all civil wars, was going to be one where little mercy was shown by either side.

On Wednesday, July 5, a detective came to the house. As he searched the premises a crowd of the local Party members and hangers-on, led by a tough-looking woman Communist, gathered at the gate. Remembering how in sermons he had warned his people of the evils of Communism, he anticipated that he was in for trouble, but the woman told the detective: "This man is all right," and others joined in with: "He does no harm. He minds his own business."

He realised that he had probably been helped by his inadequate knowledge of the language, for at a public meeting he had once declared that if the Communists came it would be bad for them and he had said that they should stand together in defence of their Faith against Communism. Perhaps, he ruminated, his Korean had been so bad that no one had understood what he was saying. Or perhaps he was helped by the fact that at that same meeting he had condemned the South Korean police methods, too. "Rough-neck methods learned from the Japs will get you nowhere," he had said. But he was not sure they had got that point either.

"That North Korean detective was a nasty guy," he told me. "And the interesting thing was that, unlike the soldiers who had come on the first day, he really was a North Korean, not an *émigré*."

He guessed that Communist policy was hardening, and in

the wrong direction. He guessed also that that would mean that he would be confined, although he assumed that it would take the form of some sort of house arrest.

He was right in his first assumption but not in his second. Next day the security police arrived, arrested him and at midday, after ransacking the place, took him to the local lock-up. The security men were hardened Communists and made no attempt to conceal their hostility. "I felt that the critical time would be the first few minutes after they got me to the police station, when they would decide whether I should be executed or just interned," he said.

In fact, they told him that he would be repatriated as soon as the whole country had been over-run, which would be very soon.

The police chief came to see him in his cell. Philip Crosbie demanded to know why he had been arrested.

"Communism has no place for religion," he was told.

The police chief tried to argue with him. "Do you know what religion really is?"

"I should do, as a minister of the Gospel."

"What do you think is the most effective weapon the West has against Communism?"

"The atom bomb, I suppose."

"No, religion is the West's most subtle and important weapon against us. That is why you are here."

At seven in the evening he was taken in a truck filled with guards and Red soldiers on the twenty-five-mile journey through the mountains to Chunchon. There he was put into the local penitentiary. He had done that same journey, to the same destination, under the Japanese only a few years earlier.

The cells, which were in groups of four, were built of heavy wood; they were some nine feet by twelve feet, and for most of the time each accommodated approximately a dozen people. When Philip Crosbie was put into his it was still not full, but through the gloom he could see some half-a-dozen Korean soldiers and civilians sitting against the wall. The South Korean police had emptied the cells before they left and so both prisoners and guards were new to the place.

Some time after his arrival, as he sat wondering what had happened to the other Columban Fathers of the area, a guard came down the corridor taking the roll call. "It was a pleasant surprise," he said, "to hear the names of two old friends, Mgr. Quinlan and Fr. Frank Canavan, called out and their familiar voices replying through the darkness—pleasant, that is, for my sake, not theirs."

Every day new prisoners of the Communists were brought in, and every night others were taken away—to be shot, according to the reports that filtered through.

Then, on the Sunday night, he heard Mgr. Quinlan and Fr. Canavan taken away. In the absence of any news he assumed that they, too, had been executed. For the next two days he lived in expectation of immediate death, just waiting for the guards to come. He prepared himself to die as a Christian should.

How, I asked him, did he feel during that period when he believed himself to be within hours, if not minutes, of death?

"It's grim facing that sort of thing alone," he answered. "But the thought that others whom I knew were in it too made me feel different, although I would have preferred to have actually been with them."

He thought for a minute, then added: "It is the loneliness of preparing for death which is the worst thing about it."

But instead of the guards coming to take him to the firing squad, an unusually tough-looking Communist officer came into his cell and told him that the missionaries were all to be repatriated. He, too, like the officer in Hunchon, wanted to talk about religion and tried to draw him on the subject.

"There is no such thing as spirit," he declared provocatively.

Philip Crosbie tried to think of a line that would pierce the other's Marxist armour.

"Is your mother dead?"

"Yes."

"Do you think that when she died she was finished, just like an animal?"

"Yes."

"I was staggered by such an answer from a Korean," Fr.

Crosbie told me, "for they are ancestor worshippers and in Korea men go into mourning for three years for their parents." It was clear, he decided, that this was a case-hardened Communist. He later had good reason to know that this was so.

A week after the departure of Mgr. Quinlan and Fr. Canavan he, too, was taken out of his cell. More exciting, he was taken not to his death, but out of the jail. At the main gate he met the other two. They, like him, had no idea of where they were going or what was going to happen to them. But at least he was no longer alone.

They were taken to the station and bundled into a freight truck, in which they travelled by fits and starts all night long. They had been told they were not to talk, but when the train was noisily rattling along in one of its rare moments of activity Mgr. Quinlan whispered to him: "I think Tony's dead." Tony was Fr. Anthony Collier, a young Irishman, also of the Society of St. Columban, who had had his own little place on the other side of Chunchon from the Monsignor's. He had built himself a little house and was just about to start on a church when the invasion from the North began. Mgr. Quinlan had then invited him to join him, but he had said he preferred to stay with his people. Fr. Crosbie had been wondering why he was not with them. Now the reason was clear. It was not until three years later, after he had at last reached the free world, that he learned the story, which a local pagan boy who was an eye-witness of the young priest's death told some local Christians.

Fr. Collier had, in fact, been arrested along with Gabriel Kim, a young lay catechist. The boy saw them being led along the road, tied together. He heard two shots, then some more. Then the soldiers left the two for dead and went away. But Kim had been protected by the body of the young priest and, though badly wounded and taken by the Red soldiers for dead, was able later to crawl away and was nursed back to health.

When daylight came, the three priests discovered that the train had taken them down to Seoul, the South Korean capital. There they were sent to a building which had been a police barracks and was now serving as an overflow jail. They were put into a basement packed to suffocation with a mixed crowd of foreigners and Koreans.

Among the former were the sick sixty-two-year-old Bishop Patrick Byrne, Apostolic Delegate to Korea, and his secretary, Father William Booth, both Americans of the Maryknoll Missions. There were the two old brothers Gombert, seventy-seven-year-old Father Antoine and seventy-five-year-old Father Julien, and Father Celestine Coyos, all three of the Paris Foreign Missions. They were soon joined by feeble, eighty-two-year-old Father Paul Villemont and frail Mother Beatrix, aged seventy-six, Provincial Superior of the Sisters of St. Paul of Chartres. Other nuns among the prisoners included a group of Carmelites, among whom was the blind Sister Marie Madeleine. The Carmelites, living in the cloistered seclusion of their silent convent, first knew of the war when they heard the big guns roaring in the streets of Seoul.

Interrogation and indoctrination of prisoners went on all day. The Koreans were questioned in the cell, foreigners in another room. Those interrogated would be with the guards for, perhaps, hours on end, then return to their corners sick and shaken, sit down and begin to write confessions. The food consisted of boiled barley wrapped in newspaper. "Pretty grim," was how Fr. Crosbie described it to me. "It was like eating dry, unflavoured rice."

The room was some twenty-feet square, and at times there were up to two hundred people crowded into it. All the Koreans were opponents of the régime whose 'reform' was being achieved by third degree.

Upstairs was a room where Korean women were interrogated and from it night and day came the sound of screams. "There wasn't much in the way of raping, though," Fr. Crosbie told me. "The Communist guards were a pretty disciplined lot in their own way, or were kept well in hand."

He was, he said, "tremendously impressed" by the zeal shown by the Communists for their unpleasant work. They would interrogate for hour after hour for days on end, attempting to exhaust their victims and exhausting themselves as well in the process. Often, in the middle of questioning a prisoner, one

B

of them would just put his head on the desk and fall asleep from sheer exhaustion.

All the jailers appeared to be hardened Communists, grimly convinced of the necessity of what they were doing. They saw the Korean supporters of Syngman Rhee as people who served the capitalists and the Western imperialists, and therefore as traitors.

One night the jailers came and took a young Korean away; he was bent backwards, his wrists tied to his ankles and then questioned. Hours later, when he came back, he wrote no confession. Next night he was taken away, and trussed up again in the same way. This time the questions were accompanied by kicks in his groin as he lay on the floor. Again he refused to 'confess'. When he was brought back to the cell and his feet untied he tried to stand but collapsed in a heap. The torture continued until in the end he was taken out for execution, still refusing to give the answers that the Communists for some reason wanted from him.

After several days in Seoul the three Columbans, along with a party of other foreign missionaries, who included Bishop Byrne and some of the nuns, were put into a goods truck. For thirty-six hours their train slowly made its way north, standing in sidings by day and moving only after dark. For the first twenty-four hours all the prisoners were without water or a drink of any sort. One Carmelite nun, a lay sister, broke down under the strain. Bishop Byrne became ill and appeared to be going down fast. Then they reached Pyongyang, some seventy miles north of the 38th Parallel.

"What," I asked Philip Crosbie as he sat telling his story in my Wimbledon home, "were your reactions to being taken right into the heart of the Communist territory?" His answer was a typical understatement.

"It was a very discouraging thing. We had heard that the United Nations were coming to the aid of South Korea, and had thought that it would soon be over. We didn't know of the unpreparedness of America. In fact, we assumed that they had all the men and materials they needed in Japan. Bishop Byrne, who was an American, in particular was convinced that the victory would come quickly. Being taken north damped our hopes a lot."

They were marched through the streets of Pyongyang to a school house, four miles outside the town, and put into a large room, to which they were confined. There they met for the first time Commissioner Lord, of the Salvation Army, Father Hunt, an Anglican from Seoul, and a party of British diplomats. In an adjoining room were some of the staff of the French Consulate, along with a French journalist, Maurice Chanteloup. Soon they were joined by a fresh group of prisoners, which included the Anglican Bishop Cooper and an Anglican nun. Within a few days there were in all sixty-three foreigners, including some White Russians and Turks, among whom were women and small children. The diplomats were segregated from the rest and appeared to be regarded as of greater usefulness as hostages. They were therefore given slightly better treatment. Food was both bad and scarce, conversation restricted and exercise impossible.

"The biggest problem, since we lived under those conditions from July 20 to early in September, was one of boredom," Philip Crosbie said. But Mgr. Quinlan helped to end it by giving his two fellow Columbans, Frank Canavan and Philip Crosbie, lessons in Korean.

In those six weeks Fr. Crosbie, like the others, was interrogated half-a-dozen times. The main purpose of the questioning seemed to be to attempt to extract evidence which could be used to prove that they were spies. He refused to speak except through an interpreter—a position given to Commissioner Lord —lest through his inadequate knowledge of Korean he might say some word which would incriminate himself or one of his colleagues.

On September 6, they were all taken to the station and, whilst waiting for a train, heard the tramp of boots. Soon nearly seven hundred American prisoners of war had joined them. They had been captured in the front line. Their wounded, they said, had been shot by the Communists. Some had been beaten up and others threatened with death. All were in a wretched state. Their grim story gave the missionaries and other civilians an idea of what they might expect.

For the next couple of months, whilst the outcome of the war seemed to hang in the balance, they were shifted about from place to place, transported in overcrowded trains which travelled only by night to avoid attack from the air, housed in schools and similar buildings, and given talks on Communism. Then they began to see Chinese supply wagons and troops making their way south, and realised that China had come into the war. That meant that it might now very well become a long one, the outcome of which was by no means so certain as it had once seemed. The weather turned cold, the guards became more aggressive and morale dropped visibly. Some forty or fifty of the G.I.s were sick, two of the nuns had already had pneumonia and were weakened as a consequence. The very old, who included the brothers Gombert, and the very young, among whom was a Turkish boy of twelve months and a White Russian of two years, began to show signs of suffering from the strain.

An officer came one day and said that once again they would have to move on. Shortly afterwards the soldiers who had been their guards were replaced by a mixed force of police and prison warders. The man who was in charge of them at once came to the group of civilians, singled out the three Columban Fathers and greeted them with: "I've met you before. Do you remember me?" He was the Marxist prison officer who in Chunchon jail had told Philip Crosbie that he believed that when his mother died she was finished, "just like an animal." Before long this man had earned himself the name of The Tiger.

He lined up the mixed bag of prisoners, aged priests and nuns, mothers with young children at the breast, sick and well, diplomats and missionaries, and told them that from now on they must march in military formation. They must obey orders or take the consequences.

"But we have old people, sick women, mothers with children here," Commissioner Lord protested.

"Then let them march until they die," was the answer.

The G.I.s moved off, then the supply wagons, the civilians brought up the rear, the whole fantastic column proceeding at brisk military marching pace. They marched until eleven o'clock at night, then were told to sleep, in the freezing cold, at the side of the road. Throughout the day, for most of the way, Mgr. Quinlan was helping to half-carry the eighty-two-year-old French priest. Fr. Crosbie was supporting Mother Thérèse, an aged French Carmelite nun, still weak from pneumonia.

At four next morning they were given a meal of boiled unground corn ("rather hard on the stomach" as Fr. Crosbie put it). In fact, it led to large numbers, particularly the old or already sick, developing dysentery, which weakened them with every hour.

After breakfast, The Tiger told the group leaders who had been appointed that it was their job to see that no one fell out. Anyone who collapsed must be carried. Then the march started. Before long some of the G.I.s, many of whom were clearly quite unfitted for the privations they were enduring, could go no further. The group leaders asked the guards what should be done with them and were told: "Leave them at the roadside. They will be picked up later." But when The Tiger learned that they were not being carried he called the group leaders together and furiously demanded to know why his orders had been disobeyed. Disregarding their pleas that they had done only what the guards had suggested, he singled out the man responsible for the group in which most had fallen out, a Lieutenant Thornton.

"What shall we do with a man who defies orders?" he called to the guards.

"Shoot him," came back the answer.

So there, in front of the whole civilian group, Lieutenant Thornton, an American of great courage, was blindfolded and shot through the back of the head by The Tiger himself. Some of the women became hysterical, a party of G.I.s dug a shallow grave into which the body was thrown, and the column, frightened, silent and conscious that it was more than just plain bullying with which they now had to contend, moved off.

"We knew that we were in the hands of rather a grim type," Philip Crosbie told me.

They marched without food until four that afternoon. Then,

whilst boiled corn was being fetched, an American officer came to the little group of priests and in whispers revealed that he was a Catholic. He said that he and other Catholic G.I.s would like to go to Confession. As they moved off again Bishop Byrne gave them an abbreviated general absolution. As far as they could judge, there were at least one hundred Catholics among the American prisoners of war.

That day, weak from the bad and inadequate food, and the dysentery and digestive disorders caused by it, they marched twenty miles. Mgr. Quinlan was still supporting the old French priest ("I never saw Quinlan when he wasn't carrying some-one, the whole of the way. He was magnificent," the Anglican Bishop Cooper was later to tell me in Seoul). Fr. Crosbie half-dragged along an ailing nun. Almost everyone was helping someone else.

Under such conditions small things became large. One of Philip Crosbie's troubles was that when he had been arrested he was wearing light Korean shoes made only of rubber. Mgr. Quinlan's, also rubber, and one with a worn sole, were too small. So they made an exchange. But still each had shoes that pinched and became more uncomfortable with every mile they walked over the rough and stony roads. One Carmelite nun was in cloth slippers. Some of the G.I.s had bare feet.

"But soon you ceased to be concerned for yourself," Philip Crosbie told me. "You were so tired and had seen so much that you did not get worried or excited any more. You were just numbed."

The great thing was to keep your feet moving. To begin to drag them meant either that others would have to carry you or, if that were not possible, that you would be shot.

"The G.I.s on the whole were a fine, cheerful lot," Fr. Crosbie said, "but among them were some young boys hardly out of their teens who had learned to drink and have a good time over in Tokyo, but had neither the training nor the mentality to face great trials. Their morale broke quickly. Many of them collapsed and were shot, or just had not the will to carry on and so deliberately dragged their feet in order to get the bullet that would end their troubles."

Late at night, foodless, they again settled down to sleep in the open. The prisoners of war made fires, but by next morning at least ten of their number had died from exposure and exhaustion. Others were unable to go on. As the party moved off again they heard the guards telling a farmer how to dispose of a number of bodies. The figure given was that of those already dead plus the sick they were leaving behind. They knew then that the sick, who had been promised treatment in the 'People's Hospital', were being executed.

(3)

The full horror of what they had endured was brought home to me when Philip Crosbie came in his story to the night when, after eighteen miles' hard marching, this army of broken men and women, who knew that to spend the hours of cold and darkness in the open was to increase enormously the chances of swift death, were told that as many as possible should get into a small school house; the rest would have to remain outside.

The women and the diplomats were put into little anterooms. The missionaries were allotted a corner in the main school-room and then the G.I.s were told that those who could find a place on the floor should do so. There was a mad rush. Men began to pack in. They covered the floor, they stood around the walls. And still more tried to force their way in. At all costs they must have a roof over their heads and some warmth for their chilled and exhausted bodies. Without that they would be frozen by the morning, dying by the wayside as so many of their colleagues had already done, or falling sick and being shot like wounded animals. There was pandemonium. Quarrels broke out. The mass desire to survive suddenly broke down all the reserves and restraints of civilisation. There were blows on all sides. Every man was fighting for himself.

The guards rushed to the doors, threatening to spray them with their tommy-guns. Everywhere there was cursing and swearing. Men collapsed on to others and were cursed for doing so. A dying man would fall forward and the one on to whom he fell would smash a fist into his face, hastening him on the way to enternity. Some died on their feet and the crush was such that their corpses still continued to stand among the living long after they had grown cold. During a break in the noise, the voice of the mortally sick Mgr. Byrne could be heard weakly pleading that he was being crushed to death. By then the space allotted to the missionaries had been reduced to an eighth of its original size.

"That was certainly a tough night," said Philip Crosbie.

And so his story went on, for hour after hour, a story of appalling suffering and inhumanity, of heroism and self-sacrifice. We reached the beginning of his account of the Death March at nine o'clock one evening. He was still telling me about it at two next morning. It is a story which has since been told by Philip Deane, of the London *Observer*, in his book *Captive in Korea*, by Maurice Chanteloup, the French journalist, by Fr. Crosbie in *Pencilling Prisoner*, and by others who were also on the March. But it took on a particular poignancy and significance as this quiet-voiced man with his fantastic under-statements told of the things they had suffered together.

Mgr. Quinlan, Fr. Crosbie and an aged and dying French priest saying the Rosary together as they dragged themselves along, hanging for support on to each other's shoulders. . . . Fr. Canavan, himself already doomed, helping to carry the sick. . . .

The Tiger standing on a box telling his victims that it was all being done for their good, that the sick were being put into People's Hospitals and were well looked after. . . .

Commissioner Lord, and a stout old White Russian woman of seventy years of age tied to his waist by a rope he had plaited from rice straw, stumbling up a mountain side together until even with that aid she could go no further, fell out and was never heard of again. . . .

Mother Eugenie, a French St. Paul of Chartres nun with never a thought for herself, caring day and night for Mother Beatrix, aged seventy-six, of the same Order, who was tuber-culous, sick with pneumonia and spitting blood. . . .

The old nun, at last unable to go any further, dropping out

and being shot by the guards through the back of the head
. . . Sister Eugenie going on alone. . . .

Winter had come, snow was falling and it was mountains all
the way, which meant climbing day after day over steep passes.
Often they marched on empty stomachs or at the best after only
a meal of roasted coarse-ground grain which none could digest
("Not a particularly satisfying meal," as Philip Crosbie put
it.)

One morning the column was straggled over a mountain side
for a distance of two or three miles, winding up and up. The
G.I.s were ahead and as the civilians came along at the rear they
heard shots. Soon they came upon sick and exhausted young
American soldiers sitting at the roadside with guards standing
over them. When they got round the bend they heard more
shots and knew that the Communists were executing those who
had fallen out. Breakfastless they marched on up the mountain
with the guards speeding up the pace, snow on the ground,
blood on the snow, death everywhere. Twenty-two fell out that
day and were shot like dogs. Eighteen had been executed the
previous day.

"Perhaps," they whispered to each other, "they have nowhere
to take us and will keep us going like this until orders come
through. Or perhaps they intend to keep us marching on and
on until there is no one left." That seemed quite a possibility
and it clearly would not take long in its final stages.

(4)

They came at last to a temporary stop, in a remote village high
up in North Korea, close to the Manchurian border. Sister
Mary Clare, the Anglican nun, died the night they arrived.
During the seven days' halt G.I.s were dying every day. Some
one hundred—one in six of the total—had died or had been shot
on the one-hundred-miles march. The place where they were
quartered was cold and draughty. Half-starved, exhausted,
filthy and verminous, their resistance to disease was down to

B*

zero, and one after another they contracted colds which quickly got out of hand. To add to their troubles, The Tiger decided that the best way to keep them warm was to make them all do physical jerks each morning before breakfast.

So the day began with the macabre spectacle of this band of sick, exhausted and dying men, women and children, longing above all for rest, but lined up in temperatures far below zero doing vigorous exercises around their prison yard. The seventy-seven-year-old Fr. Antoine Gombert was sent out one morning, took a few paces, collapsed and was dead by next day. He outlived his seventy-five-year old brother by just twenty-four hours. They had given their years and their lives for Korea.

There was no rest for those who remained. After a week they were moved on to Ha Chang Ree, a village five miles away on the Yalu River. They arrived at midnight and were left standing in the cold by the side of their ice-covered ox-carts for three hours. The whole place had been taken over for them and they were installed in the Korean peasant houses, with fifteen to twenty people crowded into rooms of some nine feet square.

Life became monotonous, but all through this hard winter, when for weeks the temperature was thirty below, the Death March continued to take its toll. Eleven of the fifty-seven members of the civilian party died. Among them were Bishop Byrne; thirty-five-year-old Father Frank Canavan (who had been just one class behind Philip Crosbie at the Columbans' college at Navan in Ireland); two more French missionaries, leaving only one of their original group alive; two of the Carmelite nuns; and the Anglican Fr. Hunt.

For most of the time civilian captives of the Communists were fed on boiled millet twice a day, with the American soldiers doing the cooking.

"The food improved around Christmas time," Philip Crosbie told me. "We got one meal of rice a day. That meant a lot to us in those days." But even then the deaths continued. Every day there were burials; during one day alone in the New Year ten G.I.s died.

(5)

The little band of priests felt utterly frustrated in the presence of so much sickness and death. They helped, when they were fit enough, with the burials each day. But they were priests. Something more was needed. They had something more they longed to give. Here every day were men going to eternity, yet between the missionaries and the majority of those who died was an impenetrable curtain of indifference and unbelief. They longed to give them spiritual aid but felt completely helpless. On such matters these men who had shared so much suffering had no common language.

Once, on the Death March, Fr. Crosbie had come across a young boy sitting waiting to be shot. A soul was within seconds of going to its Maker. He felt he must attempt to help.

"God is good," he whispered as he passed. "Ask Him to forgive you your sins."

Dully, uncomprehendingly, the boy looked up.

"Have you got a cigarette?" he said.

But there were some things they could do. On the march, and after, Mgr. Quinlan, in particular, put up a fight for, and won, the right to give a Christian burial to the Catholics who died.

But the chances of doing any active work of conversion were few, except in so far as they set an example by their whispered recitation of the Rosary as they marched along. There were rare occasions when, along with Catholics among the American soldiers, they would, under cover of darkness, say their beads or whisper a hymn together. When they settled on the Yalu they got together nightly for a while, quietly saying the Rosary, with some of the G.I.s creeping in to join them. But then one day all the civilian prisoners were suddenly moved to some Korean houses about a mile away from the American P.O.W.s. It was believed that this was because their nightly prayers had been reported and the Communists separated them for fear that the Christians' influence would make their own attempts at the Marxist indoctrination of the American soldiers still less successful.

Most of the time, both on the march to the Yalu River and during the years of captivity which followed, the best they could hope to do was to give themselves to others and to be as generally helpful to everyone as they could in the ordinary day-to-day things. And for this Monsignor Thomas Quinlan continued to build up the reputation for Christian kindness which he had from the start gained, quite naturally and without show.

"The Monsignor was a tower of strength," Philip Crosbie told me. "He was appointed as a group leader. As such he was responsible for organising fatigues, but he never asked anyone to do anything he wouldn't do himself, and if those to whom he gave jobs did not respond he went out uncomplainingly and did them for them. Up on the Yalu River, although he had had beri-beri and his legs were still badly swollen, he worked from morning till night at loading wood for the fires, carrying water and doing anything that needed doing for the comfort of the rest."

"During the Death March, swollen by beri-beri, his bare feet grotesquely distorted by frost-bite, he carried the sick, the weak," wrote Philip Deane in an Irish paper after their release. "His blue eyes still smiled. They were the only pair that did. 'Sure we'll be out,' said this perfect saint.

"He worked for us, tended our wounds and ailments, gave up his tobacco for others, went out in seventy degrees of frost to bury the dead, grew down to a shadow, and still he smiled. . . . 'Sure we'll be out, please God.'

"And at the sound of his brogue, at the sight of his indomitable figure, the bent-down heads lifted, the glassy eyes brightened and hope followed. He was our banner, and in a group of remarkably selfless, heroic people—the missionaries of Korea—Thomas Quinlan was, without trying, the most remarkable. A saint came to be with us in our hours of trial. To meet him it was worth being interned, and having met him you could not lose hope."

That winter, when so many were sick, Mother Eugenie, too, came to be seen by the rest as a ministering angel. She worked with them all day and for them all night. When the old French priests, Bishop Byrne and others were sick with uncontrollable diarrhoea she would bathe them, then take their clothes, thick with bloody excrement and lice, and disappear into the freezing night. For hours on end, whilst others rested she would wash the fouled garments in a little bowl of icy, reeking water, then contrive to dry them by morning. There was never a word of complaint. Her Order, the Sisters of St. Paul of Chartres, which had built the first orphanages in Korea and ran dispensaries and hospitals for the sick and suffering, had taught her to be selfless. Now, in this atmosphere of incredible misery, she turned selflessness into the hallmark of saintliness in the eyes of men without belief.

Sister Marie Madeleine, the French Carmelite nun, was also an inspiration to all who saw her on the March and in the camp on the Yalu. They saw her, but she did not see them. For she was the blind nun.

As a young girl she attended a Catholic teachers' training college, but gave up the practice of her Faith and became an agnostic. She graduated and started teaching. She met a young man with whom she fell deeply in love. When they became engaged she was happier than she had ever been before. Then suddenly he disappeared. She was heart-broken. Her dream of a happy home ended. She started attending church again, but in a rebellious, doubting mood. There she met a young widow who, although she had just lost her husband, was still completely resigned and fervent in her Faith. Struck by the contrast between her own rebelliousness and the submission of her new friend, she began to pray again and she came back to the Faith.

She joined a Catholic Action group for professional girls, began to write poetry and prose for their magazine and her writing attracted wide attention. A huge fan mail came in and she sat up late at night straining her eyes to reply to each letter. She was happy again.

But, she asked herself, what right had she to such happiness and success when she had wasted years as an agnostic? She gave it all up, became a Carmelite, taking the name of Marie

Madeleine. In 1938, in response to an appeal from a bishop home from Korea, she left France to establish a Carmelite foundation in Seoul. There she became mistress of novices, responsible for the instruction and training of the young Korean girls who streamed into the Order. This meant doing a great deal of reading, translating—and eye strain. Doctors warned her that she must use her eyes as little as possible. But she carried on. By 1948 she was totally blind.

On the Death March she was dependent for every moment of her time upon another's aid—that of lay sister Bernadette, who had been taken with her and now led her from place to place, cooked her food and did everything she could for her. Sister Marie Madeleine was delicate, for months on end she had dysentery, and, to add to her troubles, she broke her dentures—a small but devastating thing, for she could no longer chew the hard and indigestible grain they were given to eat. But, like Mother Eugenie, she was never heard to complain despite all the hardships of the March, which were added to immeasurably by her helplessness, and in camp she impressed everyone not only by her patience, but by her cheerfulness, too.

The missionaries of all denominations might not be able to do active 'work for souls', but they could, and did, set an example of Christian faith, hope and charity.

(6)

Their captivity continued for more than another two and a half years. The Tiger went, Chinese guards took over and the fanatical cruelty was replaced by attempts at indoctrination. Life on the Yalu River became easier, even though they longed for liberty. The Death March still continued to claim its victims. The boredom, and the difficulty of living at close quarters over a long period with people between whom there was little in common called for its own type of heroism.

Then, at last, during March and April, 1953, came release. The British and French diplomats and journalists, the Protestant missionaries, the nuns, Mgr. Quinlan, the American Mary-

knoller, Fr. Booth, were all fitted out with new clothes, taken
to the North Korean capital and then home through Siberia and
Moscow. "I found heaven in Moscow," Mgr. Quinlan told
surprised reporters who met him in London. He was referring
to the fact that in an Embassy chapel he was able to say his first
Mass for three years. In Berlin, Paris, London there were
friends and admirers waiting for them.

Of the group who had been together for so long and shared
so much in the way of suffering, only Philip Crosbie was left.
Wistfully he watched the others go, then settled down to life
with the White Russian and Turkish prisoners, who were the
only civilians left. His departure was delayed because there was
no means of rendering the name Crosbie into Korean and the
one under which it appeared was unrecognisable to anyone in
the West. For this reason he had long since been listed as
missing, presumed dead, and whilst ambassadors and ministers
were negotiating with Molotov and other leading Communists
for the release of the rest, less was done on his behalf. It was
only when the others got back and the position had been
explained that things began to move and he was finally released
late in May.

He came back along the same route as the others, taking seven
days to travel from Manchuria via Siberia to Moscow. But he
travelled alone. In Moscow he shaved off his beard, was shown
the usual sights, then flew by Soviet plane to East Berlin and,
soon after, on to London, and so to St. Columban's at Navan in
Ireland.

III

FRONT-LINE FIGHTERS

WELL, that was Philip Crosbie's story. He finished telling it in the early hours of the morning. I spent a sleepless night—or what remained of it—pondering the things he had endured and of which he made so little. He went to my study and for hour after hour I could hear the tap, tap, tap of the typewriter. It was clear that telling the story had brought it all back to him again and there was to be no sleep for him that night. But in the letters he typed he told his friends that, as soon as he had rested up, he would go back again to Korea.

What picture of the Communists and Catholics engaged in the Korean sector of the battle for men's hearts and minds had emerged from his story?

On the one hand there were the Communists. As everywhere, there was their élite, the hard core of fanatical, dedicated men, made and moulded by Marxism, ruthless, pitiless where the enemies of their Communist dream were concerned, yet as hard on themselves as they were on others.

Around them were their less well-instructed supporters and hangers-on, some in it for what they could get out of it by way of power, privilege or profit. Others, probably the majority, believing in what they conceived to be the Communist ideal, which fired their imagination with its promise of a better life.

The Communists were fighting the battle consciously, deliberately aiming at men's hearts and minds, appealing to both their emotions and their reason, knowing that a military victory was not enough and so seeking painstakingly to indoctrinate even the most unlikely of their prisoners.

On the other there were the missionaries—the other élite, Mgr. Quinlan, Bishop Byrne, Mother Eugenie, Sister Marie Madeleine, Fr. Crosbie, and the others of various Christian denominations. They had no guns with which to fight. Their only weapon was the sword of the spirit. But from Philip Crosbie's story it seemed plain that they had acquitted themselves well even though they did not consciously see themselves, as the Communists did, as playing an important rôle in the decisive fight of our time.

Certainly that was not how Fr. Crosbie saw himself or his job. He had been born and baptised into his Faith. His priestly vocation was not something of his seeking, but, having got it, he had more or less consciously decided to go where things were tough. As he put it, if he was going to give up so much he might as well give up everything. And, having done so, he just got on with his job, wherever his Society chose to send him, conscious of his weakness and inadequacy.

His Irishman's *wanderlust* and love of adventure had, as it were, been 'baptised' and harnessed in his decision to join a society which was notorious for its record of being in the trouble spots of Asia. He saw nothing heroic in his rôle, did not dramatise himself or the part he was called upon to play. There was no cult of toughness about him, nor for that matter was there anything of the 'cissy-pious type' either. He wore his Faith as naturally as he wore his open-necked sports shirt and rather more naturally than his Roman collar.

So far as the fight for men's minds was concerned, he would be the last man to call himself an intellectual and so he had not consciously participated in it as the Communists did. He had done something to prepare the minds of the simple people for whom he was responsible, but he was too new to the fight to do much. His knowledge even of the language of his flock was so meagre that, even had he wished to, it is doubtful whether he could at that stage have trained them as leaders in the social sphere, able to provide Christian alternatives to the reforms promised by the Communists. If he was a front-line fighter, it was certainly something of which he was not conscious. And even if he were told that this was so, he would see himself as no more than one of God's less consequential foot-sloggers.

How far, I wondered, was he typical of others engaged in the same work?

.   .   .   .   .

From Fr. Crosbie I heard that a member of a very different religious Order, Fr. Egbert Dorfler, a German Benedictine expelled from North Korea, was in London. I was interested to meet him, get his story and see what manner of man he was. In due course he, too, came to my home.

It was fascinating to compare this other missionary from Korea with Philip Crosbie. They could not have been less like each other.

Fr. Egbert was an older man; he had spent a quarter of a century in Korea. With his square, shaven head, his stiff carriage and his dignified bearing he might have stepped straight off a Potsdam barrack square, except for the fact that there was no trace of arrogance about him. He was 'correct' in every way. One could not imagine his ever getting out of his priest's uniform. His exquisite manners, his slightly stiff, but none the less charming, courtesy were, to an Englishman used to mixing among people who delight in informality, something almost from another world.

He had come from Bavaria, but a lifetime spent in Asia did not prevent him from being German to the very finger-tips. I felt at the time that he must surely have made a tremendous mark upon the people among whom he worked, and I was to discover later, in Korea itself, that that was true of the German Benedictines there as a whole. Talking to him I realised what very different human qualities can be sublimated for work in the missions. If it was the Irishman's *wanderlust* and desire for adventure which were baptised in Philip Crosbie, it was the German's sober sense of duty and military necessity which had been baptised in Fr. Egbert Dorfler. He was a very German soldier of the Church, but a very impressive one, too.

When I asked him whether, after years of hard work, capped by long months in a Communist jail, he would now remain in the West, Fr. Egbert replied firmly yet with no sort of histrionics: "I do not wish to die in the West. I wish to die in Korea, where I spent so many years." It was as though he had said: "I wish to die on the field of battle, commanding my troops." In different circumstances he might, for that matter, have said: "I want to die for Germany."

The years in the prison camp had left their mark upon him. He was a big man, tall and broad, but quite clearly not a fit one. After an hour of questioning and discussion he was drained of energy, his eyes became dark, his face drawn. Sweat ran down his forehead. After a meal together he revived, but another hour's questioning so clearly exhausted him that it seemed neither wise nor charitable to continue with it.

He was a member of the Benedictine Congregation of St. Odile, which had foundations in Korea and Manchuria, and was composed of Germans, Swiss and just two or three Americans. They established an abbey in Seoul in 1909, and eleven years later got permission to go up to Wonsan in the North, and then right to the Russian frontier of Manchuria to work amongst the Korean *émigrés* who lived there.

Fr. Egbert had been in Britain as a prisoner of war in 1918 and 1919. In 1925 he went to Seoul. The following year he was sent thirty miles across the border to work among the Koreans in Manchuria, whilst keeping in close touch with the abbey at Wonsan. His abbey was near the Soviet frontier, and so he had for years had reason to be conscious of the close proximity of Communism.

With the end of the war in the Pacific, Manchuria came under Communist rule. Ten days later the Communist Government was proclaimed, the Russian Army which had occupied it withdrew and the new régime, run by Chinese and Korean Communists who had been trained in Russia, came into existence. Another ten days later all Fr. Dorfler's community were arrested and put into jail. There they were kept packed in small cells along with Chinese political prisoners and criminals for several months. Then they were sent to a village on the Korean-Manchurian border, where they lived under house arrest and were given the poorest-quality food. They were kept there for two years, then permitted to return to their original mission. But their church had been destroyed, they were all confined to a little house and mission work was made impossible.

Persecution of Catholics was general throughout the country by 1947 and, indeed, every religion was attacked in the

Communists' propaganda. Many Catholics were threatened with death unless they renounced their Faith, but none yielded and many were executed in the first days. Then the Communists saw the unwisdom of making martyrs and so tried new tactics. The Catholics were told that unless they gave up their practice of the Faith their loved ones would be killed. This led to their weakening for the moment, although many later came back secretly when they had the opportunity to do so, as Fr. Egbert found when he first returned from jail.

Out of an original Christian population of some six hundred soon only fifteen to twenty old men and women were openly going to church, and they were under constant threat of imprisonment. By that time the majority of the remainder had made their way down to North Korea or, where they could afford to do so, to South Korea. It was not long before the Communists had thus created a situation where no purpose was served by so many Benedictines remaining there, and in January, 1951, Fr. Egbert, along with others, got out of the country, leaving just seven priests to carry on.

At Wonsan in North Korea there were flourishing communities of priests and nuns. They had nearly a dozen mission stations, large schools, dispensary, trade school, a seminary for Koreans and big farm. They became famous throughout Korea and Manchuria both for their agricultural methods, the training in craftsmanship which they gave their pupils, and for their generally high standards of education. The Wonsan abbey, with its wide variety of activities, became probably the greatest civilising influence in Korea—and its influence was felt throughout the land. Perhaps that was why the Communists hated it so.

In March, 1949, the whole of the more than forty German and Swiss priests, a dozen lay brothers, nearly a score of Korean sisters and at least a dozen German ones were arrested. The Communists came at night and took all the community away in lorries, no one knew where. But when the American forces drove north in October, 1950, they picked up the first news of them. Some, they found, had already died of starvation in jail. Others were being used as slave labour. Later, when the survivors were repatriated, it was learned that nearly twenty had died in captivity. Of the flourishing community and its buildings nothing remained. Its civilising mission was blotted out. Superficially, at any rate, nothing remained at all.

What did Fr. Egbert Dorfler, who had himself suffered imprisonment and had seen the work of the two great Benedictine centres destroyed, have to say about his future? Did he wish never to go back, to try to forget all the years of work which had apparently been thrown away?

"I wish to die in Korea, where I spent so many years," he said. And even then, whilst the last of the survivors of his community were still being traced, he was planning to get back again.

If Fr. Egbert Dorfler was very, very German in appearance, Fr. Celestine Coyos was unmistakably French. I talked to this member of the Paris Foreign Missions, who had shared the experiences of the Death March with Mgr. Quinlan and Fr. Crosbie, over lunch at the Falstaff, in London's Fleet Street.

He was in early middle age, of medium height, had his hair close-cropped, French-fashion, wore a beret, and when he talked his hands were as busy as his tongue.

Fr. Coyos first went to Korea in 1934, was there for two years, then fell sick with tuberculosis and returned to France for treatment. He went back to Korea in 1950 to take up a position in his Society's major seminary in Seoul. But it was a troubled Korea, very unlike the Japanese-ruled country he had been obliged to leave years before.

Communist influence in those days, he said, was strong in Seoul, particularly among students and intellectuals, less strong among the workers, the majority of whom were employed in small workshops. Russian propaganda against 'capitalism' was skilful. The South Korean Government's methods against Communism and the Communists, on the other hand, lacked all subtlety. It struck out wildly, ruthlessly, at the Party, seeing it, quite rightly, as a Fifth Column in its midst and revealing by its behaviour its fear of what the Communists might achieve. But, for want of cash or want of will, it did little to help the people; black-marketing, corruption, unemployment were widespread—and were all useful combustible material for the Communists to work with.

In one high school run by the Paris Foreign Missions the Communist 'anti-imperialist' influence became so strong that the headmaster himself could not go out into the playground because of the hostile attitude of the students, who would boo him and abuse him if he appeared outside the classroom.

Fr. Coyos was in Seoul on June 28, when the capital was taken by the Communists. He had then been back in Korea just three months. He was put in jail, taken north and found himself on the Death March to the Yalu River. For two months after the March he was desperately ill.

In the bitter cold and discomfort of the prison camp his throat and lungs began to trouble him again. He received no medical attention from the doctors who by then had been brought in, but instead one doctor, a Communist, would come to him from time to time and sneer: "Now let's see if his God will heal him. If He does not, it will not matter, for then he will go to paradise, which is what he wants." Typically, Fr. Coyos did not condemn him. "His lack of kindness and consideration came straight from his Communism," he told me.

At the end of the March, The Tiger made him do physical jerks in the open each morning, right through his illness, even when he was in danger of death. Six Paris Foreign Missionaries started out on the Death March. He was the only one who was alive when freedom came. In all, thirteen members of his Society were arrested in Korea—the other seven were taken in Taejon—and of them all only Fr. Coyos survived. Martyrdom in Korea was not a new experience for the three-hundred-and-fifty-years-old Paris Foreign Missions. Its members were the first Europeans to enter the 'hermit kingdom' in 1836, and only did so at the cost of many martyrs.

"Our Society has lost by violent death more than one hundred and fifty missionaries since 1940—all in Asia," Fr. Coyos told me. "Most of our men have been jailed by Communists at one time or another. There are still some left in China. One is in jail there at this moment. He had already been condemned to death on an earlier occasion by the Japanese. He was my friend. He has had a hard life."

Our lunch at the Falstaff was notable for Fr. Coyos's light-heartedness and gaiety, despite the fact that even then he was still a sick man, in process of recovery from his experiences in Korea. Indeed, one might say that it was that French gaiety in him which was 'baptised' and which sent him off to the other side of the world to share it with those whose paganism seemed to him to be such a pitifully pessimistic thing.

What did he propose doing as soon as he was well? "I'm looking forward to going back to Korea next year, as soon as I am strong enough," he told me. He went on to tell what an exciting place it now was, with converts coming in as never before. "The possibilities there today are tremendous. Even at that school where they used to shout down the headmaster things have changed. The whole pro-Communist mood of the students has gone since they saw the North Koreans in action and realised that the cruelty and suffering they brought with them were the result of their Marxist totalitarianism. Many of the six hundred students are now Catholics, the school is run by Korean laymen instead of foreign priests and its Christian influence is spreading every day."

In such circumstances it seemed obvious to him that he should go back to the land where he had twice had tuberculosis, had endured the horrors of the Death March and years of captivity.

"Why, yes, of course," he said, "I shall go back. Why not?"

It was in Limerick, in Ireland, that I first met Mgr. Thomas Quinlan. Meeting him was like meeting an old friend. It was not simply that I had already read so much about this hero of the Death March in the press and in Philip Deane's book, and heard so much about him from Philip Crosbie; it was his manner, his kindly, twinkling eyes and his friendly Irish voice that put me at my ease from the very start. Since his return to Ireland he had been fêted and written up wherever he had gone, despite all his efforts to avoid publicity. "Let's just get away from everyone and have a quiet chat," he said.

Mgr. Quinlan was a big man, tall and broad, but, as a consequence of his recent experiences, without an ounce of spare flesh on him. His face, in that summer after his release, was so thin that one got the impression that his cheek and jaw-bones were almost thrusting themselves through the skin. Like the others, he too was showing signs of recent strain, which was hardly surprising since he was a much older man and, according to all accounts, had carried more than his share of the burden through all the days of trial.

For thirty-three years he had been on the Far East missions, joining the newly-formed Society of St. Columban in 1918. He was in China from 1920 until 1933. In 1934 he went to Korea, being among the Society's first missionaries to go there, and for years tried to build up the missions, despite all the difficulties put in their way by the Japanese who ruled the country. He was interned by them during the Pacific War. By the time the Communist forces crossed into the South he was Prefect Apostolic (Bishop) of the Kang-Won-Do region, with a parish in Chunchon, which stretched across both sides of the 38th Parallel.

When first the Communists began to threaten South Korea, Thomas Quinlan thought to himself: "I've been here before." For, having gone to China in 1920, he had seen Asian Com-munism at work from its earliest days. Russia was at that time profoundly influencing Kuomintang policies, and Borodin, the Russian Communist leader, whom he saw many times, was the strong man behind the scenes. The young Fr. Quinlan was with Fr. Tierney, the Society's first martyr—the first of many, when he was arrested. Chou En Lai, at that time unknown outside his own circle, was leading the raid. "The men we regarded as bandits in those days, and who captured so many of our Fathers, now rule China," he told me wistfully.

As we chatted together in Limerick, neither of us mentioned the Death March or the years of captivity. His story had already been told in the press, on the radio and elsewhere, making it unnecessary for me to burden him with the unpleasant task of recalling his experiences yet again. And he showed no desire to talk of it either.

Instead he talked to me about Korea and the Korean people. His was a very different picture from that painted by most of the war correspondents and returned Service men. His was of a lovely land and a lovable people, blessed with more than the average share of natural virtues. And they were a people who were increasingly attracted to the Church. "We were making good headway when the invasion came," he said, "particularly in a teachers' training college two miles outside Chunchon."

His story of how that 'good headway' began is worth re-telling, for it is a revealing one. Mgr. Quinlan wanted a choir for his Cathedral. So he asked the professor of music at the training college, a pagan, if he would care to form one. He did. He got seventy of his students together, all pagans, and brought them along to the Cathedral. The Monsignor taught them how to pronounce the Church's Latin. They were soon practising the music for High Mass and Benediction and before long were providing all the vocal music for the church services. Koreans are very fond of singing and this expert choir, even though it was a pagan one, was much appreciated by the congregation. Then the professor began to enquire about Catholic doctrine.

There came the day when Bishop Byrne was to be consecrated in Seoul. The pagan professor went to the consecration, was enormously impressed by the Church's liturgy. It was, he said, the nearest thing to heaven he had ever experienced, and the Cistercian *Salve, Regina* was the most perfect piece of music he had ever heard. He came into the Church as a convert and before long the students in the choir, one after another, came in too.

"The conversion of the professor and his students was one of the grandest things that ever happened for us," Mgr. Quinlan told me. "I was sure hoping for big things because all those college boys and girls would have been trained teachers in due course."

More remarkable, exactly the same thing was also happening at Seoul Cathedral when the war came. There too the professor of music was converted along with the college students who formed a choir and learned Church music by singing it at Mass.

The Communists in his prefecture, Mgr. Quinlan said, were at that time one hundred per cent underground. When the North marched, all but some five hundred people fled from Chunchon. Those who came out to welcome the Communist forces were only a tiny minority. But Chunchon had a reputation for being the country's most peaceable district.

Eighteen months before the invasion, the Society's Superior had visited him and told him that it was the policy of the Society of St. Columban, and Rome's policy too, to 'stand and take it' if trouble should come. Even then he knew it was coming, although when it actually happened it came as a surprise.

He had, he said, often talked publicly against Communism. In sermons he had stressed why the Church was against Communism and had explained to his people that you could not reconcile the two. He had consciously sought to equip them with the Christian arguments against Marxism and to give them the Church's positive social teaching too, telling them of man's right to material security and that a Christian government had a responsibility to provide for its people. He recognised the threat of Communism to the Church and believed that in the last resort it was only the Church which had the answer to it.

I asked him if he intended going back to Korea. He seemed almost shocked at the implication that he might not want to return. He was, he said, going back at the earliest possible moment, to get among his people again and to his rebuilt Cathedral, which, he had learned, had been destroyed in the fighting.

"The Korean people are reaching out today for what we alone have got," he said. "When they become Christians they make marvellous ones, as this war has shown, and the converts spread their Faith wherever they go. There is a wonderful opportunity that we must seize at once. I want more priests, more nuns, new mission centres, a hostel for schoolgirls, hospitals, schools, orphanages."

There was no question of retreat here. No holding back. No counting the cost. No asking: "Dare we do it, " or "Is it safe?" Those were not the sort of questions you could expect from the big, kindly but forceful man from Tipperary.

Here was a front-line fighter who was consciously in the fight, not just against Communism—although he had recognised that the fight for truth involves one against falsehood, too—but for winning men's hearts and minds for God.

"The Catholic world holds the key to the Communist problem," he told me. "We must get down to the fight, but we must have the charity of Christ in dealing with it. It isn't the hydrogen bomb which will destroy Communism, it is we Christians. But we have to strip ourselves of wealth and privilege and practise the golden rule of doing unto others as we would have them do to us."

This man who for years had slept on the floor of his little house in Chunchon, who had lived in poverty like the people around him, who had given himself so utterly and completely in the nightmare days on the way to the Yalu and in the testing time that followed, had a right to say that. He had earned it as few men in our day have done. Coming from him there was no suggestion of cant about it. For he practised what he preached.

I had now met several Columbans and I wanted to see more of this body which, by an accident of history or by Divine Providence, had been in the thick of the trouble created by the Communists in the East ever since it began. So I went to Navan, in Ireland, where the Society has both its headquarters and its largest training college, the 'factory' which produces the men for the fight.

The Thomas Quinlans of this world are all too few. The Society of St. Columban has had more than its fair share of them, but, even so, they must be exceptional. Among the Church's élite Mgr. Quinlan stood out as one who had truly been made and moulded by his Faith. It was from that that he drew all that was good in him. Just as, at the other end of the scale, The Tiger was made and moulded by his Marxism, with all that was cruel and evil in him developed and strengthened by it. The new man in Christ and the new man in Marx stand at opposite poles. The one attracts, the other repels.

I did not expect to find a mass of Thomas Quinlans at Navan, but I was interested to see just who and what I would find there.

The River Boyne flowed noisily and picturesquely past my window when I stayed at 'St. Columban's', but it was almost the only reminder of battle which one was conscious of there. The 'High Command', the organisation's leaders, most certainly did not see themselves as some sort of generals in the fight. But from conversations over meals and in my room late at night I learned, almost incidentally, how almost all these men were 'old China hands' or had spent years in Korea, Burma and elsewhere in troubled Asia. Most had, as a consequence, seen the inside of a jail at some time or another. They had for the most part, I would say, gone to the missions much as Philip Crosbie had gone. Like him, they did not go in for heroics, they did not dramatise themselves or their work, past or present. They were doing a job for God and just getting on with it without any blare of trumpets.

I met there, too, four members of the Society home on leave from Korea, who came over to Navan to see me. From them I learned that there was still an unknown number of Communist guerillas holding out in the hills in the South. They lived by raiding the near-by towns and many operated in areas in which the Columbans worked. Some were North Koreans who had been left behind by the retreating Communist armies. Most were South Korean Communists who had fought as guerillas either before or during the war, and had taken to the hills when the North Koreans were driven back.

All four of the men from Korea were completely devoted to their work and to the country and its people. They took the view that Korea was today the most rewarding of all the mission fields in the Far East, and quoted evidence to support their point. They recalled how missionaries were poured by the hundreds into Japan at the end of World War II, in the belief that it was ripe for conversion, as compared with some fourteen sent to Korea. Yet Korea had five thousand more converts in one year than had the whole of Japan.

"And when a Korean gets the Faith, he has really got it," they said. The rarest thing was a Korean apostate. Not even the Communists had succeeded in making Korean Catholics apostatise. They stressed the Koreans' love of family, their sense of responsibility for their aged (something which we in the West are rapidly losing), their thirst for education, their interest in the things that really matter, their natural kindness.

What they did not talk about, however, was themselves. When I tried to draw them, they minimised the risks they had taken during the war and the importance of the part they were playing in determining the shape of things to come in the Far East. The idea that they might be front-line fighters in a battle the outcome of which might very well determine the world's pattern of life for generations ahead was clearly a novel one to them. They were just Columban Fathers, getting on with their job—shepherds of souls, whose flocks happened to be on the other side of the world.

I talked to the students, individually and collectively, in the seminary. They were youngsters in their early twenties for the most part. They showed some signs of being conscious that the job which lay ahead of them was of particular importance at this moment in history, but if any of them felt that some special heroism might be called for, they showed no sign of it to me.

There was, of course, an awareness that their Society had throughout its short life functioned in what were now recognised as some of the decisive parts of the world. Deep down they were proud of what the Society had done and what its members had suffered. The call of its martyrs was, no doubt, one which had influenced many of them to join it.

They could not be unaware of those martyrs, at any rate, for outside the door of the much-used chapel hung a list of the Columban Fathers who had died since the Society was established and for whose souls the seminarians were asked to pray.

"Very few died in their beds," said the priest who was with

me, with a rare touch of pride in his voice. Together we went down the list of names: "He died in a Communist jail in China," "He was killed by a shell in Burma," "He was executed by the Communists in Korea," "He was killed by the Communist Huks in the Philippines," "He died in a Japanese prison camp." And so it went on. Columbans, it seemed, had, despite their matter-of-fact approach to their work, tended to die with their boots on. In action.

IV

AERIAL SURVEY

"WHO wants the job ring night bell," said a note crudely written in blue pencil and pinned to the door of the Japanese Embassy in London's Belgrave Square. I did not want the job, whatever it might be. So I stepped under the decorator's step-ladder which almost filled the porch and rang the day bell instead. A porter or janitor came to the door. "I want a visa," I said. He looked at me pityingly, then told me that this was a Japanese national holiday and so the Embassy was not working today. It was clear from his tone of voice that he felt that I should have known already.

The afternoon was hot and I was tired. I had already called at the Burmese and Korean Legations, and in each case had been told that I would need to go back yet again. "So far as I am concerned they can keep the job," I told myself, "but somehow or another I must get that Japanese visa." For I had made up my mind that if I really wanted to see how the battle fared in the East in general and Korea in particular, the only thing to do was to go there.

In due course the Japanese visa was granted. It was only a transit visa. That was all that would be needed, as I would be treated as a passenger in transit, the courteous young Japanese man who issued it to me told me confidently. On that day I had at last got my Korean visa too, from a very helpful Mr. Kim. In due course I was to learn that there are only about twenty or so different Korean surnames and Kim is one of the most common of them. At that moment I was more interested in the two portraits which stood one at each end of Mr. Kim's mantel-piece. One was of the young Queen Elizabeth II. The other was of a very sublimated old Mr. Syngman Rhee, or at any rate he certainly looked a good deal more benevolent and handsome than the Western press usually made him out to be. 'They say the camera cannot lie,' I thought to myself, 'but whose, then, was telling the truth this time, theirs—or ours?'

I watched Mr. Kim's long, sensitive fingers painstakingly sketching in the curious Korean characters on my passport. He took a craftsman's pride in each one, it seemed, as he lingeringly surveyed his handiwork. Above it he stuck a one-thousand-eight-hundred-hwan stamp, which he carefully franked. He unhurriedly turned over the pages of the passport, taking a kindly interest in all my various journeyings around Europe, Africa, America, Canada and elsewhere. I realised as I watched him that this building in the heart of London was a little bit of Korea. Its atmosphere belonged to the Orient, with the East's entirely different approach to so many things. It was not just the picture of the bland Mr. Rhee on the mantelpiece which made it that. The atmosphere was Oriental, too. 'After all,' Mr. Kim seemed to be saying, 'if I find your passport interesting, why should I conceal the fact? Why should I suppress my curiosity, and briskly pass it back to you as though it was of no interest to me? And why hurry? You haven't a plane to catch—yet.'

As he handed it back to me I took a glance at it. I now had the Korean Government's permission to remain if I wished in the 'Forbidden Kingdom' from April 29, 1954, to October 29 of the same year. That was excellent. The formalities had been many and the wait had been a long one, for, after all, Korea was still technically in a state of war, but this was a good step on the way. As I left, the Korean typist in the outside office wished me a good journey. "I hope you like Korea," she said.

The last formalities for getting there, however, had still to be completed. British civilians cannot just enter unsettled Korea as they would France, Holland or Italy, for example. It was necessary to have United Nations Forces' approval. In practice that meant the American military authorities in Tokyo. This was required because, as they put it, civilians in Korea must be given logistical support and so their number must be strictly limited. Each and all must be accounted for. It was irritating

HONG KONG : REFUGEES

KOREAN PEASANT

Above : SHINTO FESTIVAL, TOKYO

Below right : A NUN SMUGGLED BY BANDITS THROUGH THE FRONT LINES

Below left : "THE LEPERS CROWDED AROUND OUR JEEP. AMONG THEM WAS A VERY ATTRACTIVE YOUNG GIRL OF PERHAPS EIGHTEEN OR NINETEEN."

but, one could see, necessary in the circumstances. After all, if civilians who wanted just to look around were killed by guerillas whilst they were doing so, someone, presumably the military, would be held responsible.

My application to enter as a war correspondent had now been passed to San Francisco, who had said that if the British War Office was willing to sponsor me, then that was all right so far as they were concerned. At this moment the War Office was, in fact, signalling the Public Relations Officers at British Headquarters in Tokyo and the British Commonwealth Division in Korea, to make sure that they were prepared to make themselves responsible for me.

In due course their 'O.K.' came back, along with an invitation to give some lectures to officers on the British sector of the Korean front whilst I was over there. So I was now an accredited war correspondent with the United Nations Forces, representing a number of the papers for which I work as freelance—the *O.F.N.S. agency*, the *Catholic Herald* and various Commonwealth and foreign papers—but 'travelling under my own steam'.

To my inoculations against smallpox, yellow fever, and typhoid, acquired for an earlier trip to East Africa, was now added one against cholera as well. I was ready to be off, to see for myself the way the fight was going on the Asian battle-front and in the land in which the two worlds had so recently clashed. Then it had been an armed fight which, like most modern wars, had, despite enormous suffering and sacrifice, left the issue still unresolved. Now the fight had shifted to the spheres to which it more properly belonged—the social, intellectual and spiritual ones. From my recent experiences it seemed likely that the men who were least conscious of their own vital rôle might prove to be the ones whose influence would in the end be decisive. At any rate, I was going to join them at the battlefront—see them in action.

Aircraft were queuing above Frankfurt-on-Main when our Tokyo-bound B.O.A.C. Argonaut arrived for its first refuelling stop. For nearly half an hour we circled the great

c

German city. As we were guided slowly down from one level to the next, a fire, which had at first been just a big red smudge among the twinkling city lights, gradually took shape and the outline of the burning building became clearer. That fire recalled to my mind how only a few years ago it looked as though the Communist flames might spread from the Eastern Zone to West Germany, bringing the frontiers of the Red Empire right up to those of a France already bled by two devastating wars and weakened from within by a powerful Communist Party.

Just before I left the Communists in 1948, the editor of the *Daily Worker* had told me: "It's all right, Berlin is in the bag— and after that the rest of Germany too." He had spoken confidently, for he had just come from meeting some of the East German Communist leaders in Berlin and had been talking to leading Soviet officials in London, too.

With that same confidence the Russian and German Communist leaders had set about trying to force the West out of Berlin. Rather than risk another war so soon after the last, Britain and America would forgive anything, they thought. They had had their own way ever since the end of the war. They saw no reason why they should not be able to continue to push further and further forward in Europe, so long as they continued to frighten a world longing for peace with their warlike noises. But instead, the West had at last decided that at some point a halt must be called. The process of open erosion ended in Berlin.

I was in Amsterdam when the Berlin air-lift began. No one quite knew what would happen now that the Communists' bluff was being called. "Do you think it will be war, and if so shall I be able to get out of here in time?" a nervous English writer who was staying in the city asked me.

"In a matter of only an hour or two, Red Army tanks could be in the Netherlands. They are nearer to you at this moment, than you are to London," a Dutch friend grimly intervened.

But it had not led to war. Instead, the stand made in Berlin showed the men in the Kremlin that the West meant business, that if they continued to attempt to gobble up all Europe, bit by bit, they must be prepared for war. There were going to be no more Czechoslovakias.

It took the Communists some time fully to digest the lessons of the Berlin air-lift. But Communists learn, which cannot always be said of their opponents. As Marxists and Leninists, they saw the fight for Communism in terms of warfare, sometimes armed, sometimes not; in one period conducted by military means, in another using political and economic weapons instead. The whole art of Leninism is to know when to advance and when to retreat. To recognise when the initiative is in your hands and when it has passed into those of your opponent. To push ahead when the going is easy, at the same time being careful not to get too far away from your base, and to consolidate as soon as that seems to be the danger. And always, under all circumstances, to keep on probing, probing, looking for any weak spots which may develop on the enemy's front and then, if any are found, to concentrate at once your main forces there with a view to a break through, whilst creating a diversion somewhere else.

I knew from experience how well that technique works. We had applied it to trade unions and to other political parties contending with us for the support of 'the workers'. At *Daily Worker* editorial conferences, members of the Political Bureau had explained Soviet policies against that background, reminding us that if we understood our Leninism sufficiently there would be no fear of our misinterpreting Soviet actions in the columns of our paper. I still saw and interpreted the pattern of Communist behaviour against the background of that earlier training.

Berlin had shown the international Communist leaders that the initiative had at last passed from their hands. When the lesson had been fully learned and they were convinced that there was no doubt about it, they began quietly to shift from offensive policies in Europe to defensive ones. You could see the process at work in the French and Italian Communist Parties' activities. Not long ago their leaders had been convinced that soon they would be the rulers of powerful Communist countries. Every European Communist had believed that too. Communism, we said, would thus be brought to the shores of the Mediterranean, the Atlantic and the English Channel.

After that, the rest would be easy. But gradually the leaders had to recognise that the initiative was no longer theirs. In step with Moscow, they switched to propaganda on behalf of the creation of 'national fronts', similar to the successful popular fronts of pre-war days, with the Communist Party and united workers' front as its vanguard, but reaching out to all the other 'progressive forces', liberals, peace-loving Christians, intellectuals and others. That was a defensive, not an offensive, policy. The Communist Party is interested in increasing the number of its allies only when they are needed for its own defence. The popular front tactic was used in the pre-war days when every Communist believed that Russia was in danger of attack and that a broad 'front' against war and Fascism alone could save her.

The switch to similar policies all over the West after the Berlin air-lift clearly indicated that the Russian and other Communist leaders had recognised that they had for the time being lost the initiative. That meant a period of consolidation behind the Iron Curtain, constant probing in the West and quiet waiting for the next round, throwing the main immediate emphasis on to Asia, where the initiative was still theirs, and searching, too, for new places for a break through, such as in Africa, Latin America and the Caribbean.

The disturbing thing was that the Communists knew quite well what they were going to do with the peace which the West had temporarily secured at Berlin. But did we? They would use it to consolidate their position and to prepare themselves for the next round. But what did we see ahead of us? Ever larger stock-piles of hydrogen bombs? Maintaining the crushing burden of armaments until at last the weak links in our own economic chain snapped, giving the Communists their chance once more to usher in what the Marxists called 'a new round of wars and revolutions'?

It was long past midnight when we circled Rome, preparatory

to making our next stop there. But the lights were still twinkling in the fashionable part of the city whose night-life contrasted so strongly with the grim struggle for existence in the near-by slums. I peered out of the window to see if I could catch a glimpse of St. Peter's and the Vatican, always such landmarks by day, but could see nothing of them.

In 1953 I had been privileged to have a private audience with Pope Pius XII, not in the Vatican but out at his summer residence at Castel Gandolfo, up in the hills.

"In England," he had said, "the Communist Party is small, is it not?"

I told him that it was, but added that it was a well organised and well-instructed one and so, as a consequence, had a considerable influence in the trade union movement, and was still able to use many intellectuals.

"Ah, yes, of course," the Holy Father replied. "The intellectuals are important. But here it is the poor. So many of the Italian people are so very poor."

And the poverty remains. Coming late at night out of the great Passionist monastery of Santo Paulo, last time I visited Rome, I had tripped over a homeless man asleep on the steps, and I saw many others on my way back to my *pension*. I had walked the narrow streets of the city's slum areas thinking to myself: 'If I were still a Communist leader, what a gift all this would seem! How easy it must be for the followers of Togliatti to do their propaganda in a land of such contrasts.'

On that visit, too, I had met Professor Gedda, President of the powerful Italian Catholic Action. He explained to me his organisation's rôle, which was the long-term one of providing its members with that spiritual formation which, as one of its by-products, as it were, would destroy Communism at its roots.

I had gone on from his headquarters to those of the Comitato Civico, the very lively organisation started by Prof. Gedda to meet the immediate Communist threat at, as it were, its own level. It was the Civic Committees with their well organised cadres, their tremendous propaganda campaign, their lively posters and films which, perhaps more than anything, prevented the victory of Communism in the elections of 1948 when Italy hovered on the very brink of Bolshevism.

But although a Red victory at the polls was prevented, the huge Communist vote still, to this day, remains stubbornly as high as ever. Propaganda and promises halted the Communist threat, but sweeping social reforms born of Christian charity and the spiritual re-birth of the Italian people are needed to destroy it. That positive job, the more difficult one, still remains to be done. Meanwhile, the politicians' continued failure to reduce the Communist vote leads to the fragmentation of Christian Democracy, with some people, who urge more drastic approaches, moving over to the Right, and others, demanding more 'progressive' policies, hardening off on the Left.

We flew all night down the Mediterranean, doing the long hop from Rome to Beirut. To the south of us lay the coast of North Africa, where Morocco, Algeria and Egypt were all in a state of profound unrest, with the Communists quietly probing around in the expectation that, sooner or later, the situation would play right into their hands.

Behind Mediterranean Africa lay the great continent where in the coming years, perhaps more directly than anywhere else on earth, the Christian and the Communist will confront each other in the fight for men's hearts and minds.

In London only a few weeks ago a conference had been held which received little attention from the general press but which was of considerable significance none the less. It bore the title of 'The Conference of Communist and Workers' Parties in Colonial Countries and Countries within the Sphere of Imperialism'. It might be a long-winded name but it was clear whom it was meant to include. Called by the British Communist Party, which for years has had a special responsibility to the Kremlin for aiding the spread of Communism in the colonies, it was organised on the initiative of the Moscow leaders. National Communist Parties do not organise international Communist gatherings without the highest authority and direction.

At Communist conferences the 'opening statement' is of supreme importance, for it lays down the party line for everything that follows. In the case of an international conference an enormous amount of work goes into its preparation and it is submitted to people in the highest levels of the international Communist organisation before it is finally passed on to the delegates in the form of a policy speech.

R. Palme Dutt, who directs British Communist policy and who for years has specialised in the formulation of Communist colonial policies, made the speech on this occasion. It got little publicity in the non-Communist press, although it was a clear pointer to the way Moscow was thinking.

"Today the colonial front is the principal active fighting front against Imperialism," Dutt said. "And," he added, "most significant of all in the present period is the upsurge in Africa."

The subtle shift of emphasis from Asia—which was regarded by the last such conference, held in 1947, as the area of greatest promise—over to Africa meant, as the subsequent discussions at the conferences revealed, that, although Moscow still took the view that the big fight at the moment was in Asia, Africa was tomorrow's battlefield. And the preliminary skirmishes had already begun.

In the Communist headquarters in London a special African department had recently been created, headed by a man with a life-time's experience of industrial and political agitation, riots, street fighting and militant class-war generally.

In Africa, Communist-directed organisations such as the World Federation of Trade Unions were sending potential African leaders on 'scholarships' to Eastern European capitals. There they were given the university education for which they craved. But they were also given training in Marxist leadership to ensure that on their return they would be able to step into positions of influence and responsibility. Equipped with that training and the prestige which comes from having had a European university education, they could quickly become leaders of the masses, turning them in the direction of Communism.

But in Africa I had seen that the Church, too, could be quick off the mark. Africa may be a continent of promise for the Communists but it is wide open for Christians, too. Inevitably, therefore, Christianity and Communism are, as it were, in direct competition, each conscious that the success of the one means the failure of the other.

In the present state of African development, the quality of leaders may be decisive. It is not only the Communists who are conscious of this. In Kisubi, Uganda, in 1953 I attended a conference of some two hundred young African Catholic laymen drawn from every country of Africa. We met under the leadership of Archbishop Kabana, a far-seeing White Father from French Canada, and in the company of a score of bishops and archbishops, some African, some European, and a large number of missionary priests and nuns. Together we and they hammered out how best they could carry their Faith into every sphere of activity, political, social, cultural and industrial, making a truly Christian and African contribution to the life of their own national organisations. They had discussed leadership techniques, too, and how best to achieve that spiritual formation without which their work as leaders would lose all meaning and significance and end only in self-glorification.

The conference did not stop at talk. For example, I heard, on my return, from the son of a Kikuyu chief in Mau-Mau-terrorised Kenya, how he and others of his tribe who had been to the Kisubi conference were now already busy establishing a Catholic Action organisation, with its own social programme, right in the very heart of the Kikuyu reserves. To do that at such a moment, when each Kikuyu Christian who refused to take the pagan Mau Mau oaths was regarded as a traitor, fit only to be foully butchered, required a true sense of leadership, and great courage too.

In Uganda I had met Bishop Graef, a Mill Hill missionary from Holland. When, twenty years ago, he first went to the diocese over which he now rules there were some five thousand Catholics there. Today there are more than a quarter of a million. Conversions on such a scale must have a profound effect upon the life and outlook of the whole people.

It was in Uganda, too, that I once went with the English-born

Bishop Billington, another Mill Hill man, out through miles of dense forest to a remote spot where two nuns, Sister Peter Mary, an American, and Sister Jude, an Irish woman, of the Franciscan Sisters of Africa, were running a camp for three hundred and twenty resident lepers and providing regular treatment for another six hundred out-patients who live around.

The lepers crowded about us as we went to see Bertha, whom we found sitting under a mango tree, where she had crawled from her hut. Bertha had neither hands nor feet, and was blind as well. But she recognised the voice of Bishop Billington, whom she knew and loved, and gave us a smiling welcome. The Bishop told me how for years this convert had crawled animal-fashion on her stumps to Mass in the camp chapel each day. He took a picture of us as we talked there, with the Dutch priest who lives with the lepers standing by. Before we left, one of the nuns told me of her happiness in her work, but added a little wistfully that she envied me my opportunities for participating directly in the mid-twentieth-century battle.

A week or so after my return to London a Communist Party member asked if he might meet me. Not long before he had led a much publicised strike which was aimed consciously and directly at Britain's defence and economic recovery. I found that he already had many doubts about his Communism. We talked in a Fleet Street café. After hours of discussion I suggested that we should review where it had led. He agreed that he no longer believed in the long-term aims of Communism, nor in its current policies; he had lost faith in its leaders and in the genuineness of its intentions.

"Logically, there is only one thing left for you to do," I said. "If you are going to be intellectually honest you must leave the Party."

He thought for a while, then, obviously deeply distressed, he said: "I know that that is the logical thing to do. But, you see, when I joined the Party I did so after a great deal of thought and a long struggle. For me it was a symbolic act by which I consciously identified myself with the scorned and rejected. I still think that that was the best thing I ever did.

"You were lucky. Your Communism was destroyed by

c*

Catholicism. By the time you ceased to be a Communist you were already a Catholic. For me there is nothing. If I leave the Party I turn my back on all that was best in myself, and I shall feel that I am deserting the people about whom no one else cares. I don't think I can do it."

I saw his point and, having been through a similar crisis myself, knew there was much in what he said. Yet if he remained in the Party he would in practice be hindering, not helping, the very people with whom he still wished to identify himself.

I remembered that Dr. Johnson had said that "that which is not of the reason cannot be defeated by reason."

This attitude of his, good and generous as it was, I reasoned, was not rational in its origin, it was emotional. It was at this level that it must be approached.

And then I remembered that I had just received from Bishop Billington a print of the picture of the Dutch chaplain and myself talking to Bertha the leper under the mango tree, with some of the other lepers standing around us.

"I understand how you feel and respect it," I said. "But there is one point on which I would like to take you up. You say that no one but the Party cares for the scorned and rejected. That is wrong, and I can give you proof of it."

I told him about the two nuns and the Dutch chaplain, way out in the remote forest clearing in Africa, spending their days among the lepers, tending their sores, dressing the wounds of the dying even when the stench of putrefying flesh on still living bodies had become too overwhelming for the other lepers to be prepared to face it.

"How many members of the British Communist Party are nursing lepers in Africa?" I asked him.

"None."

"Then don't say that no one else cares. Here is the evidence."

I took the picture from my wallet and passed it to him. He looked at it for a while, and the sightless face of Bertha the leper, a living picture of peace of mind and peace of soul—the very things he most lacked, looked back into his.

"All right, you win," he said. "I'll leave the Party."

That night I wrote to Bishop Billington to ask him to tell the nuns at the Nyenga leper camp that their work and example had been the means of bringing one man out of the Communist Party and to remind them that they were not outside the battle of our time. They were playing a bigger part in it than they knew.

That was it. No one was outside the battle: the leper in the camp in the forest clearing, the nuns who looked after her, the Bishop on safari, the disillusioned Communist trying desperately to cling to the tarnished thing he had made his ideal—all these were participants in one of those great struggles which occur from time to time in man's history and set the pattern of life for, maybe, centuries ahead. There was one battle and we were all in it, influencing its course, whether we realised it or not, either by our activities or by our indifference.

V

FLYING INTO TROUBLE

THEY turned us out, bleary-eyed and with crumpled clothes, to stretch our legs in Beirut next morning. It was fascinating to see how the cedars of Lebanon came down to meet the sand, which in turn crept into the outskirts of the city, just as the pathetic weedy little green patches still make their way into the suburbs of London and New York.

The Lebanon, with its large Christian population, is a little haven in a Moslem world. I recalled how a Lebanese Jesuit who had worked for years in Egypt told me not long ago that, when they made converts, as on rare occasions they did, they often, because of the strength of Moslem feeling, had to smuggle them out to the Lebanon, where they would start life all over again. And the Italian Bishop of Khartum, Mgr. Baroni, of the Verona Fathers, when I met him outside Khartum, had told me how the conversion of a Moslem girl there had once led to a general strike which lasted for days.

Yet all those missionaries with whom I have from time to time discussed the problem of work among Islamic peoples have emphasised that, fanatical as Mohammedans may be, Islam is today weakening as a religious force, whilst becoming more and more a political one. Recent experience has tended to show that, even though Islam is a greater barrier to Communism than some other religions, it is less reliable than it was at one time thought to be, precisely because it is losing something of its spiritual strength. For the peasant in the past to know that 'Allah is God and Mohammed is His Prophet' was enough. But that is not sufficient to hold the loyalty of the new intelligentsia or of the semi-educated, newly urbanised masses, who require something more than an eight-word formula. They become modern pagans, materialists, even though they still pay lip service to Islam. Something more than that is needed to provide an answer to what is at root an intellectual and spiritual problem. The Communists realise this, and today are paying increasing attention to the Moslem lands. Where persuasion is likely to work they keep up a barrage of propaganda to show that they are the friends of all believers. Where Islam is threatening to crack from within, as in Russia, they are moving over to direct assault.

For hours on end we flew across flat desert, broken here and there by mountain ranges which looked almost as barren as the desert itself. The sight of the thirsty lands of the Middle East from the air gives to all discussion of 'the development of the underdeveloped areas' and of 'man's ultimate conquest of Nature' a new meaning.

Some day, it is true, we may well make the desert blossom. Irrigation, combined with the cultivation of the right sort of grasses to restore the missing humus, may, at some time in the future, make what are today deserts support vast populations spilled there from the exhausted lands of Europe and America.

But meanwhile, what have people who try to scratch an existence from mere smears of green in crevices in the rocky hills to lose by any sort of change? Given skilful leadership by the frustrated intellectuals and the new proletariat of the towns, why should the land-hungry peasants not follow those who promise them a new life, with a full stomach and a plot of fertile land for each?

As we flew on and on over the seemingly endless desert the captain of the aircraft came to me and pointed out an oil pipeline which ran for mile after mile across its surface—witness of man's refusal to be defeated by the limitless sand.

"I once went in a motor-coach along the road that accompanies it to the Mediterranean coast. It took three days' continuous driving across the desert, with never a change in the scenery all the way," he said. "It's amazing what men can do today."

The Tigris and the Euphrates were in flood, as we came in from the vast expanse of Syrian Desert, so that the wretched people who live in a land impoverished by too little water were having to make their way to their homes by boat. Flying down the Persian Gulf to the island of Bahrein, I saw from a height of some nineteen thousand feet what I took for one absurd moment to be curiously ordered rows of huge starfish or sea anemones, floating on the surface of the water. But as we lost altitude in readiness for our landing on the island, I realised that these were the tops of tall and carefully tended palm trees which were now surrounded by water.

Stepping out of our air-conditioned aircraft into the humid atmosphere outside was like walking into an overheated laundry. The whole place, which is known to those who regularly call there as 'the worst place on earth', steamed in suffocating heat. A Greek shipping agent, who had come out from London and knew Bahrein well, expressed the view that the people who lived there were the most lethargic of any.

"They are depersonalised, devitalised and demoralised by the climate," he said. "I found when I worked there that it took twenty men to do the work that one would do in a temperate climate."

There is nothing temperate about Bahrein, as I realised when, with clothes soaked in sweat, I limply climbed back into the aircraft again. The plane had stood exposed on the open air-strip to the blazing afternoon sun whilst it was being refuelled. It was like an oven inside.

As the steward adjusted the air control above my head he said apologetically: "I'm afraid it's not cold, sir. Just hot air in a hurry."

He was right. As I switched it on it let loose a jet of something which more nearly resembled hot steam than cool air.

We flew out of Bahrein across the Arabian Sea, south of Persia. A couple of years ago it seemed that Mosadeq might, through his impatience to be rid of British influence, succeed in destroying the oil industry upon which the whole Persian economy rested. Certainly that is what the Communists hoped. That would have led to a classic collapse of capitalism according to the Marxist pattern—with Russia just over the border ready to exploit the situation if left free to do so. But the crisis proved to be insufficient to produce the necessary 'revolutionary situation' of its own accord, and the Communist Tudeh Party was too inept to create one. Or was it that Russia, fearing Western intervention, and having no desire to have a 'Korea' on her own borders, compelled her puppet party to hold its hand?

By nightfall we were in Karachi, where the hot night air wrapped itself around us like a blanket. But the heat did not appear to have 'depersonalised, devitalised and demoralised' the handsome Pakistanis who were there to greet us. Rather, one felt, it had got into their blood. These people most assuredly, were not too lethargic to make a revolution.

Communism has not so far directly threatened the new Pakistan State, but the membership of the Communist Party is known to be growing, more particularly in East Pakistan. The Government's readiness to associate with the Western Powers in defence plans against possible Communist aggression has reflected a consciousness of the danger just across its northern border, where lie both Russia and Red China. But that very association of the Government with the 'Western imperialists' gives the Communists a chance to make effective propaganda against it. For the common people of every Asian country increasingly tend to feel themselves to be Asian first and foremost and to believe that they have more in common with other Asian peoples, no matter what their politics, than with those of the West. And the people of Pakistan have blood brothers living in the U.S.S.R.—a fact of which Russian propaganda makes as much as possible.

The present bad blood between Pakistan and India serves the Communists well. They stand to gain everything by an armed clash between the two States, for it would give them an opportunity to arm on a large scale, have their own guerilla bands, allegedly fighting for their country but, like the Communists in World War II, in Malaya, China, the Philippines and, for that matter, in Europe, too, in reality fighting for Communism.

The future will not be easy for Pakistan. The Communist threat there is only in its beginnings as yet, and it has as its allies poverty, land-hunger and 'anti-imperialism'. They are a formidable trinity or a Moslem Government, ruling a country confronted with the impact of the West, to have to face.

As we crossed India on our way to Delhi and then on to Calcutta, I was reading Albert Nevett's *India Going Red?*, which the author, just before I left London, had sent me. Fr. Nevett works in the Social Institute in Poona, an organisation run by Indian Jesuits which is doing pioneer work in seeking Christian solutions for India's huge social problems. The book seemed suitable background reading. It confirmed much of what I knew from my own knowledge of the Communists' progress and intentions in India, although the author looked into the future with more confidence than I might be prepared to do. Fr. Nevett's answer to the question asked in the title of his book is this:

"The future of democracy in India is reasonably optimistic provided certain essential conditions are fulfilled. It must bring about a just and satisfactory economic and social order . . . it must be based on sound and tried values, especially spiritual ones, and not on empty slogans. . . .
"It follows that the future of Indian democracy is subject to a number of hypotheses which can be solved favourably provided that the proper means are taken. One thing, however, is absolutely sure, that no democracy can long survive which abandons the ultimate basis of all freedom and human rights, namely the spiritual values and man's essential relation to God. Where these fundamentals are given up there cannot possibly be any adequate answer to the Communist challenge."

Precisely. But where is that spiritual basis to come from to-day, in an India whose workers and intelligentsia are becoming increasingly materialist in outlook, except from the Christians?

The Communists have for years believed that India will before long be theirs. I still have notes of lectures on the subject which in my Communist days I gave to Marxist study classes and groups of party members. Among them are ones in which I drew a close parallel between pre-1917 Imperial Russia and present-day India.

In Russia there was a great mass of impoverished, land-hungry peasants. There was also a small proletarian class based upon pockets of highly-developed capitalist enterprise. Russia came late into the industrial scramble and so stepped straight into an advanced form of capitalism. The Putilov engineering works in St. Petersburg, for example, where the Bolshevik Party was strongest, were reputed to be the largest in Europe. They were also the most Communist.

And there were the frustrated intellectuals. The Communist-led proletarians were able to call upon, and use as allies, both the peasants and the intellectuals when the moment of opportunity came. Finally, the other great ally of the Communists was the nationalism of the subject peoples of the Imperial Empire.

In India today all those factors are present. The Bombay textile workers, with a long record of industrial and political action, correspond, in the Communists' opinion, to the Putilov workers. The new proletariat of the towns are the vanguard of the Revolution; the land-hungry peasants, the frustrated intellectuals and the deeply felt nationalism of the mass of the people, which takes the form today of suspicion of the Western Powers, are the allies they must use in the seizure of power.

That is how the Communists see it. That is why the leaders of world Communism are quietly confident that to the already enormous population of the Communist Empire will in due course be added India's four hundred million, thus giving them something approaching a majority of the world's population. And that is why both Russia and China are today taking a hand in fanning the flames of Indian Communism. Both send in growing quantities of cheap Marxist literature along with superbly produced propaganda films for India's literature-starved literates.

To both Russia and China go more and more delegations of Indian trade unionists, students, intellectuals, professional men, politicians. There they are fêted, fed on propaganda, then sent back, in the majority of cases, as enthusiastic and very effective missionaries for the Communist cause.

The Communists are playing for big stakes when they aim at India and they are prepared to risk a lot to get it.

But what spiritual force in India today is able to provide a counter-dynamic to Communism? For most Indians democracy is certainly not that. There is a minority of sincere democrats, but those with the degree of education and sophistication to be able to appreciate the value of democracy are already for the most part 'modern pagans'. Western democracy grew out of Christian soil and still draws deep on ideas as to the value of the individual which were Christian in their origin. A democracy backed only by materialism lacks an essential element. It cannot hope to counter the dynamism of the Communists. The materialist has no real argument against Marxism, least of all in a land of mass poverty, where millions long for revolutionary change in their own life-time.

Hinduism, left to itself, is no barrier to Communism. There are few Hindus who today appreciate the true nature of the Communist threat and many see it as no real danger at all. That is part of the background to India's present neutralism. There is no philosophical reason why the Hindu peasant or worker should not go over to Communism if that seems to be the winning side. Lacking any dogma, Hinduism has a tradition of tolerance based upon its ability in the past to absorb and assimilate other philosophies and religions, but has no tradition of resistance to them. There are some Hindus who believe that it will be able similarly to swallow and assimilate Communism. There is as much likelihood of that happening as there is that rabbits may take to swallowing stoats.

In one relatively small, though highly important, part of India today the only force which has shown itself in the last resort capable of standing up to Communism is challenging it directly. In Malabar the conditions are exceptional, calling for exceptional measures. There the Communist and the Christian openly challenge each other. Nowhere else in India would that be possible, for the Christian community is elsewhere too small.

But in Malabar (Travancore-Cochin) the Church is one thousand nine hundred years old, and its roots go deep into the life of the people. It is also invigorated by a steady stream of converts.

Malabar is the most densely-populated part of the sub-continent. Thirty per cent of the population are Christians, as compared with three per cent nationally. Because it is the most Christian part of India it is also the most literate—and the literates include, of course, the non-Christian majority. That makes it particularly attractive to the Communists, who for long have subjected it to an ever-increasing barrage of propaganda designed in particular for people with elementary education and with an unsatisfied hunger for cheap reading matter. They have exploited their frustrations and at the same time have sought the support of the numerous illiterate outcasts, too.

So today Travancore-Cochin is at one and the same time the most Communist and the most Catholic State in India. The Communists' present aim is to win it for the Party at the polls. At one time that seemed a possibility and it might easily be so again. The Communists would, if they won it, put everything they have got into making it a show-piece for Communism, a base from which to spread their influence wider and wider throughout the land.

The fight for Malabar is, therefore, much more than a struggle for just a single State. It is of great importance to India as a whole. Inevitably, the immediate fight is a political one and Catholics have been drawn directly into it.

The Communists' progress there was, until recently, spectacular. But it has recently been slowed down, largely through the activities of a Carmelite seminarian, Brother Vadakan, and the two-thousand-cell, anti-Communist front which he has organised. The tall, lean friar in his cassock of coarse homespun cloth is now a familiar figure all over the State and his influence is tremendous.

In the exceptional circumstances obtaining in Malabar, Brother Vadakan, a former Communist sympathiser, was temporarily released by his superiors to conduct something in the nature of a crusade against Communism. His remarkable oratorical skill draws hundreds of thousands to his meetings, where he quotes and refutes the Marxist-Leninist classics which he studied in his Communist days. But his fight against Communism is not a purely negative one. Brother Vadakan preaches social betterment, based not on the hatred and atheism of Communism, but on love of God and man.

One consequence of his campaign has been the election of Congress instead of Communist candidates at the polls. In view of the nature of the situation and the political character of the campaign which he has conducted to meet it, this is more or less inevitable. But where there is only one party strong enough to provide a serious opposition to the Communists there is the obvious danger—to which Brother Vadakan's superiors are said to be fully alive—of the Church becoming too closely identified in the public mind with that particular political party. For example, in parts of Malabar the votes for or against Congress have tended to take on a pro- or anti-Christian character.

Yet where the Church's supporters are a tiny minority, as is the case in India, there seems no escape from this when the fight is mainly at the party-political level. To create or associate with splinter parties would be to destroy the whole effectiveness of the crusade. The alternative would be for the Catholics, who are the ones who see the Communist threat most clearly, to abandon the fight, leaving the Communists an easy local victory. That might in time have nation-wide repercussions—not least upon the Church itself, and so would seem to most people, at this critical stage of the struggle, to be an abdication of responsibility.

The only long-term answer to that particular dilemma is the widespread acceptance of policies which are fundamentally, though not exclusively, Christian; but the conditions in which that would be possible will no longer exist if Communism is allowed to triumph.

In Calcutta a group of us sat talking as we drank cool drinks together. There were some European technicians, a Hindu and an urbane Pakistani, so Westernised in his speech and outlook that one entirely forgot that he was an Asian.

One of the technicians told how he had had to fly back to Europe to try and get parts for some sort of pressure boiler which he had installed in a factory in East Pakistan.

"The trouble," he complained, "is that the Pakistan Government insist upon the same safety standards out here as are enforced in Europe."

The Pakistani listened politely, making no comment.

"I had endless correspondence with them," the European technician went on, "and one visit after another from their wretched inspectors. In the end I had to go home and try and get something to satisfy them. Actually even then I didn't get what they are demanding. I expect as soon as I get back I shall have another of their inspectors on my tail and I shall have to try and get away with it."

Quietly and very courteously the Pakistani interrupted him. "You will," he said. "I'm the inspector. That's why I am flying to Dacca."

Out of consideration for the other man's feelings the rest of us suddenly found reasons for drifting away.

At Dacca airport life was going on as usual—but not in the city near-by. For the papers that morning told of a fight which had occurred in a jute mill right there in Dacca the previous evening, in which more than four hundred workers had died.

Human life may not, allegedly, count for much in the East, but even so four hundred people is a lot to die in a factory fight. As one looked at the clerks who stamped our passports and the porters who smilingly steered us through to the health and immigration authorities, it seemed incredible that such a thing could happen and that everything and everyone should still seem so quiet.

Once a massacre of that sort would have been attributed to sectarian hatreds, which the Communists would have said had been deliberately fanned by the British imperialists on the 'divide and rule' principle. Now India was partitioned, East Pakistan was Moslem, and British rule had ended. This time there was a good deal of evidence to show that the trouble, which had been building up for months, had been engineered by the Communists themselves to scare off foreign investors interested in the country's development.

It is not surprising that the Communists should be working hard in East Pakistan, which is so artificially separated and so remote from the administrative capital of Karachi. The situation there comes near to being ideal for them.

The jute industry of East Pakistan employs today some twenty thousand workers. None had any experience of industry until after the end of World War II. To many of them the wheel was unknown almost up to the moment when, quite suddenly, they were plunged into the life of a great mass-production factory. The revolution in their lives was as great as that of the African sitting at the conveyor belt in the tobacco factory in East Africa. They are fair game for Communists.

As in India and Burma, the Communists of East Pakistan store arms in readiness for the day when the revolution comes. And, as in most of Asia, there are Communist guerillas fighting in the hills whom the Government has so far failed to subue.

In 1950, in Mymensingh, there was a Communist-led insurrection. The Government put it down with a heavy hand, but its leaders took to the hills and there they have remained, building up guerilla bands and recalling to themselves, no doubt, that once, not so very long ago, Mao Tse Tung and Chou En Lai, who today rule nearly six hundred million people, were leaders of guerilla bands, too.

The fight for Communism in East Pakistan is on two levels, that of the ones who already fight with guns and those who penetrate the powerful United Front Party or lead the new proletariat in the jute mills. But, judging by the massacre of the night before I arrived in Dacca, that industrial activity of the Communists could hardly be described as non-violent either.

For such people Mao Tse Tung's oft-reiterated assertion, which all Asia is learning today, that "Communism comes from the barrel of a gun," is an intoxicating message. For such people Red China stands as living proof that a country with a poverty-stricken, restless peasantry, a new, small, rootless but Communist-led proletariat and a frustrated, semi-Westernised and equally rootless intelligentsia is ripe for Communism. It is impossible to over-estimate the probable influence of Chinese Communism upon such areas of the world in the years ahead.

In West Pakistan, where Communism is weak, one is told that this is because Islam provides an effective barrier against it. But East Pakistan is Islamic too. It is the local conditions that are different.

Airport buildings almost anywhere tend to look much the same. The new concrete edifices designed in the modern style which greet you in America, Holland, Iceland or India might equally well belong to any country, anywhere. Only the flags are different.

But Rangoon's is an exception. There the buildings which adjoin the airstrip are unmistakably Oriental and, what is more, distinctively, and refreshingly, Burmese. Bamboo takes the place of steel and concrete. The crowd which filled the small, low rooms, when we got there from Dacca, was very Burmese too.

Neat little Burmese women in colourful clothes greeted us smilingly at the airport, and one felt that same smiling friendliness everywhere. The people generally seemed a good deal less tense than their sub-continental neighbours.

When you get to Rangoon you feel you have really reached the Orient. Its crowded streets and bazaars have all the colour, smells and amazing confusion of the East. Houses built of bamboo and raised on legs line the roads to the city.

It was a great Buddhist feast day. Young Buddhist monks with shaven heads, dressed in their bright orange-coloured robes, which leave one brown shoulder bare, were everywhere.

Large men in delicately-shaded pink skirts with head-scarves to match came and went at the hotel where we had been accommodated. As I drank tea in the lounge, two Mongolian mandarins in long white gowns talked together at a neighbouring table. The hair of one, the elder of the two, was done into two plaits which were taken up over his head and met in the middle—I knew a Communist woman schoolteacher years ago who favoured exactly the same style. He had a scholarly face, long moustaches and American-style rimless glasses which, contrary to what one might have expected, far from looking incongruous, added to his general appearance of sensitive intelligence. He compared favourably, I felt, with many of our own intellectuals in appearance.

The Greek shipping agent from our party suggested that we should see the city together, and we decided to make the Shway Dagone, the largest pagoda in Burma, our target. As we went down to the waterfront he said that he would fix up transport, and I saw him haggling with a group of young Indians who were clearly enjoying it every bit as much as he was. In due course he turned up with a thin but very handsome boy of perhaps sixteen or seventeen years of age. His only garment was a long grey skirt, open at the side.

"You'll see more from his pedicar than you would ever see from a car window," said my companion, as he climbed into the front of the wooden, box-like side-car made for two.

I clambered up behind, so that we sat back to back, the boy mounted his bicycle and, with bare feet, went pedalling off as hard as he could go, ringing his cycle bell all the time along the crowded streets.

We made our way through a confused stream of ancient but wildly driven motor-cars, lorries, ox-carts and pedicars, with the boy enthusiastically directing our attention to the sights.

Flares were being lit over the market stalls. Quite suddenly, I realised, it had become dark. We had no lights on either the cycle or the side-car, and we spent as much time on the wrong side of the road as on the right. At cross-roads our boy rang his bell furiously and, without one look backward to see what might be coming, simply swung off across the road in the direction in which he wanted to go.

My companion seemed to be enjoying the ride immensely. I was not quite so sure. I loved the people, the sights, the noise and the colour. But I wasn't sure that I liked the idea of a human horse taking me there. He stood straining at his pedals as he propelled us along, smiling happily enough, whilst I felt bad about his bare feet. We went out through dark suburbs with ill-lit shops, and then came to a long hill, leading up to the Shway Dagone. I thought of myself attempting to cycle up it bare-footed and with two full-grown men as passengers in a swinging side-car.

"I think I'll get out and walk," I said, jumping off as we slowed down for a car to pass.

My companion did the same. The boy clearly thought we were mad as he rode his bicycle along beside us whilst we walked up the hill.

The huge pagoda was gay with the thousands of electric lamps which encircled it, tier upon tier to its topmost gold-plated turret, gleaming high up in the night sky. As we approached the entrance we made our way through the feast-day crowd who had come for their devotions. At the top of the steps outside, a rather excited little man told us that we must take off our shoes. I looked around for somewhere to put them. "You give them poor beggar woman," he said. "No steal here. At pagoda everyone very honest." I hoped he was right as a pathetic little creature disappeared with them into the gloom.

Whilst I mounted the steps I wondered what it would be like walking back miles through the filthy streets and bazaars to my hotel in stockinged feet. But soon the job of negotiating the filth on the steps themselves was taking all my attention.

Flight after flight of hundreds of steps went up and up. On either side were shops or stalls, selling paper flowers, joss-sticks and other things for use at the shrines towards which we were climbing. The shopkeepers shouted their wares, whilst mis-shapen, twisted and disfigured beggars thrust filthy palms into our faces as they pleaded for alms. Above our heads, mercilessly, bizarrely, illuminating the whole so essentially Oriental scene, was, of all things, modern fluorescent lighting. Oriental beggars and fluorescent lighting, I felt, do not mix well.

At the end of our long climb we came to the sixty-four shrines which encircle the giant statue of the Buddha, at the very top of the pagoda. Each one was the size of a small side chapel in a Western church. Each had its statue, and before each one men and women—with the latter very much in the majority—were engaged in their devotions. You may smoke as you worship in Burmese temples, and I watched fascinated as the little brown women bowed low before the Buddha muttering prayers between deep pulls at their cheroots.

When we got to the bottom of the stairs again, our excited little man produced the beggar woman out of the gloom, who in turn produced our shoes.

"You think beggar woman steal your shoes," he said accusingly. "She good Buddhist. No steal shoes at pagoda."

We travelled down the hill again sitting in the pedicar, but when we came to the city I opted to walk in order to be able to mingle with the people in the covered bazaars. The boy rode his cycle along at the side of the road, clearly expecting us soon to tire of such an eccentricity as walking when we might ride. We rejoined him earlier than I expected.

I was pushing my way happily through the noisy crowds which surrounded every stall, trying not to think too much about the smells, when I turned back and saw that my companion was looking distinctly green. "Let's get out of here quick," he said, "I'm going to be sick."

We rejoined our Indian boy, who greeted us with an 'I-told-you-so' look, and then took us triumphantly back to the Savoy Hotel again.

At dinner I told a Siamese business man who had flown with us from London about our visit to the Shway Dagone.

"Is it still open? Can I get there now?" he asked eagerly. "It is a great day for us."

I suggested that he should take a taxi and he dashed off at once to get one.

We had breakfast at five o'clock next morning, and half an hour later made straight for the airport. The monsoon had started and it had poured with rain all night. Already the shops were open, women were returning home with their purchases, and shopkeepers swept a mixture of garbage and flood water on to the streets.

At one point an already monstrously swollen dead dog, off which carrion crows were greedily feasting, lay at the roadside.

The stench was almost overwhelming. Corpses do not keep well in tropical heat.

I fell into conversation with the slim, dark little air hostess who had accompanied the passengers from the airport to the hotel on the previous afternoon, patiently answered all our questions, attended to our needs till late at night, and was now already in action, bright and smiling as she took us back to our aircraft again. Her voice was a soft, Oriental one, her English was perfect, but I felt that her slight trace of an accent was oddly familiar. For the purpose of later telling this story I asked her her name, hoping for something suitably picturesque.

"I was Miss McManus before I married," she said. "My father was from Northern Ireland and I went to school in India."

So that accounted for the accent.

"And what is your name now?" I asked, still hoping for the best.

"It's Mrs. Carpenter now. My husband had an English father."

A party of handsome Indian women, who, Mrs. Carpenter said, were flying back to Chittagong after visiting members of the Burmese Indian community, were waiting at the airport. They were resplendent in magnificent robes which, ample though they were, revealed brown mid-riffs, which tended in the case of the older women to take the form of bulging tyres of fat. But this was more than atoned for by the jewellery with which they were adorned and which included large gem-studded ear-rings and nose-rings. One had a safety chain of fine gold going from the wedding-ring-sized adornment on her nose to an even larger one in her ear. They had a pride of bearing, ease, grace and self-assurance which would have gladdened the heart of the most rabid Western feminist.

I liked Rangoon and I left the smiling Burmese people with regret.

It was difficult to imagine that here was a country torn by civil war, where armed Communist guerilla bands still hold considerable areas and some of whom quite recently made their way to the very edge of Rangoon itself. With China and Red

North Vietnam as near neighbours—and arms easily smuggled in from both quarters—the Communists are likely to continue to keep the country in an unsettled state for a long time ahead. All the time there will remain the possibility that they may take advantage of some new crisis in South-East Asia and complete the seizure of power.

From the air, as we left for Bangkok, I could see here and there groups of new white concrete factory buildings surrounded by the bamboo huts of their employees. Industrialisation, Western techniques, Western education, Western materialism, then the spread of Communism among workers and intellectuals. . . . That is the normal pattern of 'progress' in the East today.

Every little village and hamlet had its gold-turreted pagoda. Sitting with me was the business man from Thailand. I took the opportunity to ask him if he had got to the Shway Dagone before it closed. He said he had.

"It meant a great deal to me," he added simply.

He was an educated man and clearly at the same time also a devout Buddhist. He seemed an essentially good little man. I encouraged him to talk about his Buddhism. In Thailand, he said, the emphasis was on giant images of the Buddha, whereas in Burma they built pagodas. Their priests lived in monasteries; the Burmese monks lived in community in the pagodas.

"We do not permit selling in our shrines, we see it as a distraction from our devotions," he went on. "We erect the huge images to the glory of the Lord Buddha and to show our devotion to him." When he talked of "the Lord Buddha" he might almost, from his tone of voice, have been an evangelical Christian speaking of the Lord Jesus. I had noticed on the way out from London that he said his night and morning prayers.

"You are a devout Buddhist," I said. "It is obvious that your religion means a great deal to you and that you have gone to some pains to understand it. Are you typical in this?"

"I'm afraid I am not," he answered sadly. "Buddhism is coming to mean less and less to most of my people. The majority still observe some, at least, of its external practices, but it is losing its hold on their hearts. And even the educated ones do not trouble to understand it."

He saw the possibility that Communism might gain ground in his country in the future, and that this would be made easier by the people's growing indifference to their religion. As is the case all over South-East Asia, Thailand has a large Chinese population many of whom are Communists. The police force, he thought, was strong enough to keep an eye on all Communist activities at present and was determined not to let the Communists cause trouble. But he feared that, should Indo-China fall to the Communists, then armed struggle in Thailand might follow before long.

Looking down on the mile after mile of unbroken jungle-covered mountains below us, where Burma imperceptibly gave way to Thailand, I could imagine how difficult it would be to deal with guerillas in such country.

But after a time the jungle and the heavily-wooded unexplored mountains gave way to the fertile plain, we flew over Thailand's rice bowl, with the paddy-fields laid out like a draughts-board below, and came down at Bangkok's smart, Western-style airport, which was more like ones I had seen in America than what I would have expected to find in the heart of South-East Asia.

Dien Bien Phu had only recently fallen and fighting was still continuing as we crossed South Vietnam. Only a few weeks later the years-long war was to end at Geneva, with defeat for the French, and with the northern half of the country, along with most of its mineral deposits and some of the richest rice lands in all South-East Asia, in the hands of the Communists. That same area, incidentally, contained also the largest and most compact Catholic population, which was also the most solidly anti-Communist, on the whole of the Asian mainland. At Geneva they were officially brought under Communist rule and faced with the grim alternative of either fleeing to the South and forsaking the land to which, as peasants, they had been bound for generations, or remaining and facing pitiless persecution. The Catholics of North Vietnam were some of the staunchest allies the non-Communist world had got in Asia, yet at Geneva they and their future counted for little in discussions, nor did it in any way sway the decision to abandon their homeland to the Communists, who were known to be their mortal enemies.

Despite the truce which ended eight years of war, the total conquest of Indo-China, either by political and ideological means during the agreed two-year period of partition, or by force afterwards, remains a possibility. The threat of the spread of Communism to the whole South-Eastern Asian mainland and islands, which together comprise an area half the size of the United States, with a larger population than that of the whole of America, is enormously increased by the Viet-minh victory. The classic invasion route to South-East Asia is today already in Communist hands.

The Catholic community in Indo-China was an old and well established one, but that did not prevent it from being a very responsive mission territory, too. Some ninety thousand catechumens were under instruction in what is now the Communist half of the country at the moment when it was given to the Vietminh. The total number of Catholics there when the Geneva truce was concluded was one million, one hundred and fifty-eight thousand, and it is almost certain that the vast majority of these will now have to live under Communist rule. No more than a small minority could be expected to abandon the rice-fields which are the basis of their very existence. The evacuation of them all was never a possibility. The persecution of the Church, the execution of priests, the expulsion of missionaries and the 'brain-washing' of the faithful on the Chinese pattern had already started in the Vietminh areas long before they were officially passed over to the mercy of Ho Chi Minh.

The loss of North Vietnam was a major defeat in the battle of our time, not just because of the strategic importance of the territory which passed into Communist hands, nor because the threat to an immensely important part of the world was enormously increased. All these things were important, for we could afford none of them. But, taking the long view, we could afford still less to lose more than one and a half million allies whose opposition to Communism rested firmly where it properly belongs—on spiritual foundations.

VI

HOPE IN HONG KONG

WE looked out on to the mountains of Red China as we flew over the South China Sea to Hong Kong. Behind those high dark hills lived the six hundred million people who, if Mao Tse Tung succeeds in his plan to rush through his country's industrial revolution, may in our life time be world Communism's strongest and most decisive force.

There religious persecution has been brought to a fine art—an art which flows directly from the Marxist-Leninist philosophy of the Communist leaders. After only a few years almost the whole external edifice of the Church has been reduced to ruins and most of its leaders have been expelled or imprisoned. Yet every report tends to show that, after their first enormous reverses, the ordinary lay Catholics of China are beginning to grope their way towards ways and means of continuing in their Faith despite all that the Communists can do against them.

If you require evidence that it is the Catholics who are the last-ditch fighters in the battle of our time it is there in Red China today. The Catholics' influence is out of all proportion to their numbers. Around them, even though they are primarily concerned with the spiritual battle for their Faith rather than with the political struggle against Communism, are crystallising today the hopes and fears of increasing numbers of those who long for the ending of the Communist régime.

In a country which is almost ninety-nine per cent pagan, it is upon the one per cent of Catholics that the Communists direct their especial hatred. Upon them the Communists devote an entirely disproportionate amount of their time, their thought, their propaganda. For, although some Western Christians may be deceived into believing that Communism and Christianity are in some way compatible, the Communists know different.

Their aim is to remould the minds of men, to create the new Marxist man. They realise that they will never achieve that aim so long as the Church is on Her feet. So long as there are Catholics who cling to their Faith, even though it be in secret, the Communist rulers cannot feel that their regime is safe, they cannot claim total victory. For there is always the danger of the conversion of the Communists themselves, of that tiny Christian yeast leavening the whole. The preoccupation of the Chinese Communists with their tiny Catholic minority is one of the most eloquent tributes ever paid to the Church.

You fly into Hong Kong over—or near to—a chain of islands. Some are 'ours' some 'theirs'. From the air you cannot tell the difference; you can see that all are the heavily defended outposts of their respective worlds, and you sense how easily such an area, if it is patrolled by trigger-happy people of either side, could become the 'flash point' for World War III.

Indeed, only a few weeks after I flew over it, another British passenger aircraft, similarly making for Hong Kong, was shot down; then an American Forces' plane a few days later shot down some Chinese aircraft and for a few tense days the war clouds seemed to be gathering again. They cleared in due course. But you can have that sort of incident once too often.

The landing at Hong Kong is an exciting one—"the most exciting in the world," our steward told me as we came in between close-set hills which seemed almost to touch our wing-tips on either side. Then we dropped down suddenly on to the airstrip.

The little British colony itself is a place of extraordinary contrasts.

Fringed by the high mountains of Red China, the city is one of the most beautiful on earth. Yet within it there is concentrated a vast mass of appalling poverty. For from behind those dark mountains have come hundreds of thousands of pathetic refugees. Grand commercial houses stand side by side with tiny shacks which house large families from China. It is a place of contrasts, of huge despair, and yet also of tremendous hope. Standing on the very edge of the Communist world, it is

D

a bastion of freedom. But the first thing you notice when you arrive is the Red Flag of serfdom flying from tall buildings—banks and schools—which are the property of Mao Tse Tung's Government.

With Hong Kong situated in such a position, one might have thought that the West, in addition to using it as a listening post on Red China, would see it as a shop window for democracy too. For here is the only port in the free world where Chinese goods are officially available, and where people regularly and openly come and go between the two worlds.

The Hong Kong Administration understandably leans over backwards to be democratic—that is why the Red Flag is permitted to fly over the buildings owned by the Chinese Government—and a large Communist Party is able to continue to exist there. Yet such a state of affairs would only make sense if the people living under Communist totalitarianism across the border were daily reminded that this is what democracy is like.

The Administration has done wonderful things for the refugees who have trebled its population during the last few years and who have created enormous problems as a consequence. It has provided asylum for all who have come, it has rehoused thousands, it expends large sums on the care of the sick among them (although the tuberculosis rate still goes up by leaps and bounds). Yet again, it modestly keeps quiet about these things. This is surely one of those times and places in which modesty is not called for.

When again and again fire swept up the hillsides of Hong Kong, destroying the pathetic little homes of thousands of refugees, the Communist Government quickly made a small donation towards the relief of those concerned, and did an enormous amount of propaganda around it. The Hong Kong Administration spent vastly more, rehoused large numbers—and tells no one. If ever there was an occasion which justified the lusty blowing of trumpets across the border into the Red mainland and among the refugees themselves, that was it. But the colony's official trumpets were muted and continue so.

It is probably the most densely populated territory on earth, with up to as many as two thousand people to the acre, and as you push your way through its streets you are everywhere conscious of the refugees. They are, in the main, an industrious, thrifty lot. Their tiny shops open early and close late. Their little improvised workshops, erected at the roadsides, ring with the sound of industry until late into the night. Yet there is a limit to the number of things you can sell to each other and make for each other, if you are all in the depths of poverty. So the evidences of malnutrition are everywhere. Here is concentrated misery on the mass scale, a place of suicide and despair. Paradoxically, that has helped also to make it a place of hope.

For the effect of experiencing atheist-Communist rule, and of suffering so deeply as a consequence, has led to a great movement towards the Church. I had not realised just how great it was until I discussed it with a group of missionary priests in Hong Kong's big Catholic Centre. There I learned that, despite all the missionaries expelled from China who now live in the colony, enough people cannot be found to instruct the thousands of refugees who are coming and asking to be taught the Faith. What the missionaries told me there was confirmed by the Bishop of Hong Kong, Bishop Bianchi, when I met him in London shortly after my return to Britain.

"The number of converts is limited only by the number of people available to instruct them," he said.

He went on to say that he was at that moment in process of establishing a centre where lay people would be trained in the instruction of converts.

I talked in Hong Kong to many with great experience of the Chinese Missions, but none had seen any comparable movement towards the Faith among the Chinese people in the past.

Why do they come?

First, it seems that the heroic example inside Red China of the Catholics who, unlike members of other faiths, have refused to compromise with the régime has profoundly impressed them and earned their admiration.

Secondly, these people have suffered at the hands of atheistic Communism; they have seen it at work, know its methods, have experienced its disregard for the rights of the human person. They have seen it and disliked it. All their present sufferings are due to it. At the other pole to the Communist Party, with its Marxist dialectical materialism, stands the Catholic Church. It is natural that in rejecting the one they should think of examining the claims of the other. They know, moreover, that Communism is not just a military or political movement. They have witnessed and experienced its assault on hearts and minds. They have good reason to know that it is a spiritual problem, and that the lasting answer to it must be found at the spiritual level. It is significant that a majority of the refugees are, for understandable reasons, of middle-class origin, and that among those coming to the Church is a high proportion of intellectuals.

Thirdly, they have experienced great suffering and hardship, known deep sorrow. Many have recently lost loved ones. This has led to their thinking deeply on the things that really matter, the eternal verities, the things of lasting worth. Having lost almost everything in this world, they begin to think of the next. They turn to their own ancient religions, re-examine them in the light of bitter personal experience, judge them for their ability or inability to stand up to the Marxist philosophy, and discover their inadequacy.

Then, because the Catholic one per cent have stood firm and uncorrupted and their example is known to all, the refugees begin to think in terms of them and of their Faith. They are reminded of their heroism and of their refusal to yield, too, by the expelled missionary priests and nuns, the victims of Red jails, mob trials and persecution, who, emaciated but undefeated, come in a steady stream across the border which separates Communist China from the free world.

In other words, the present unparalleled movement towards the Church in Hong Kong is a direct consequence of practical personal experience of Communist rule. That is something to grasp, for its implications for the future go deep. It has a considerable bearing upon the point and purpose of this book.

What is the Church doing in this situation? For those who see Her as a highly organised, worldly and super-efficient body, astutely waiting, always ready to exploit any sort of situation, the answer is illuminating. The Church was largely unprepared for what has happened and is still not making the most of it. Despite all the priests and nuns who have come out of China in the last few years, there are even now too few in Hong Kong to meet the present need. And of those who are there, far too few are available for ordinary pastoral duties.

To the missionary societies who had put men and money into China in the past, seeing it as the Church's largest and most promising mission field, the victory of Communism was a terrific shock. One understandable reaction to that shock was a refusal to believe that the present disaster could last for any appreciable length of time. There was an orgy of wishful thinking. "It is only an agrarian revolution, not a real Communist one," said the old China hands. "The Chinese will never accept Communism, their whole temperament and traditions are against it. It will soon collapse." For that reason some missionary societies hesitated to commit to new mission fields even those young enough to make the change. Instead, they tended to bring their men back to the West and to find jobs for them there, or to put them on to work in Hong Kong which would leave them free to go back quickly when the expected collapse came.

It is true that evil régimes may in the end be brought down by their own wickedness. But history shows that the process is not necessarily a quick one. It may not be quick in China, either. Meanwhile, a new little Land of Promise unexpectedly opened up on China's doorstep, a by-product of the Communist revolution.

Few Catholics outside Hong Kong understood what was happening there. Even those missionaries who were already established in the colony were unprepared for the great new opportunity which came their way. Neither the cash nor the personnel which were suddenly required was available in sufficient quantities.

None the less, an outstanding job has been done. Hong Kong now has a big Catholic Centre, which includes club, library, a flourishing publishing house, religious art department, much-used meeting rooms and lecture hall. The Centre is the main-spring of a vast amount of activity.

With a hard-core Catholic population of only some fifty thousand when the first influx of refugees arrived, the Church did—and continues to do—an enormous amount of relief work which has aided people of every creed. It even sponsored a re-housing scheme. There has, however, been no attempt to make 'rice Christians', converts bought at the price of a bowl of rice, such as has been done by some Christian sects in the past in Asia. The converts coming to the Church today are definitely not the 'rice Christian' type. They do not crawl to the Church. They come because they are undefeated. Many of them are educated people who only make a first move when they are intellectually convinced of the truth of the Church's claims.

The Catholic Truth Society of Hong Kong has expended a great deal of time and money in producing literally thousands of different pamphlets and books in the vernacular, explaining the Church's doctrine, practices and liturgy. And the demand for them is insatiable. This appeal to the reason of the refugees has brought a rewarding response. So, too, have the opening of new schools and colleges and the expansion of existing ones.

Today there are thousands of Chinese refugees in Hong Kong going through courses of instruction preparatory to being received into the Church. Nothing is done to skimp or water down that instruction. Every precaution is taken to ensure that they know as much as possible about the Faith they are adopting. It would be easier to become almost anything other than a Catholic. Yet still they come.

To balance the picture, perhaps it should be added that I was told in Hong Kong that, at this moment of opportunity, one missionary society with a printing press found itself so short of cash that it had to put up for sale its invaluable and almost irreplaceable collection of Chinese type. It was sold in separate lots—many of them to non-Catholics—and so was dispersed, just when the demand for new publications is greater than ever before and is yielding an unprecedented harvest.

VII

HEART OF JAPAN

IN the course of one period of twelve months I calculate I flew at least fifty thousand miles. I found, as others have done, that air travel can be very dull, but that it has its exciting moments which compensate for a great deal of boredom.

Perhaps the best I ever had, or can hope to have, was on a flight home from Africa. In the evening I saw from the air the sun setting in a mixture of blood-red and the deepest purple, way out over the Sahara Desert and sinking slowly into the sand which had given to it its marvellous colours. Then, early next morning, as we flew over the Alps, I saw the first red rays of the rising sun pick out in striking silhouette the very topmost point of the Matterhorn. That is something that air travel alone has made possible.

My second most exciting flying experience came when I saw from across the ocean the incomparable Mount Fuji—Fuji San, the sacred mountain of the Japanese. We were flying up the coast to Tokyo, after a brief stop at Okinawa. The stewardess drew my attention to Fuji as it first came in view, miles away over the sea. I understood why it is that that twelve-thousand-feet snow-capped extinct volcano seems to appear in at least half the Japanese works of art, and why, too, it has been for long a place of pilgrimage. Its beauty is such as to make any man want to worship. Its peak, when first I saw it, was floating high in the sky, detached from its base and, it seemed, from this world altogether, by a circle of light clouds. And, to add to the effect, distance created the illusion, although Fuji is miles inland, of its rising sheer out of the sea itself.

On our way we had passed Formosa, around whose waters plied craft of both sides on errands potentially as dangerous as those of the aircraft which snoop suspiciously around each other in the South China Sea, back near Hong Kong.

In Hong Kong I had heard rumours of frequent raiding parties going from Formosa to the Red mainland. People spoke of them much as we in Britain talked in 1944 of the raids which were organised from time to time against the Nazi-occupied French coast, before the big assault on the Normandy beaches began. They were the prelude to the Second Front. But the difference was that here there was no sober, planned intention on the part of either America or Britain to create a front of any kind.

Seen from the air, as you drop down to its airport, Tokyo looks like some great Western city, with its big concrete factory buildings and warehouses packed close together near the waterfront. When later you get away from the works and the big stores of the Ginza and out to the suburbs, with their thousands of tiny home-workshops and their little shops full of strange foods, you realise how wrong it is to think that only the language on the neon signs and the shape of the people's faces distinguishes the Japanese capital from London or New York.

Tokyo's attractions are obvious. Most of the amenities which an American housewife takes for granted are to be had there, provided only that one has the dollars. There are American-type entertainments, eating-places, transport, and great shopping centres, all according to the familiar pattern. It is easy after a superficial glance to suggest that the Japanese capital is little more than an American tourist centre. But, although so many of the men in Tokyo's commercial centre may have their Anthony Eden hats, brief-cases and rolled umbrellas, many of the women, with their purely Japanese dress and hair styles, add a charming difference to the scene.

And there is another Tokyo, the Tokyo of the sweat shops in which hundreds of thousands of workers earn sufficient only to maintain a level of existence which bears no resemblance to that of the West. And there is the Tokyo of the great colleges where impecunious students study with desperate earnestness from early morning till late at night, keeping themselves awake by using drugs, and living on diminutive sums earned by doing the most menial jobs.

When the Pacific War ended in defeat for Japan no one knew what to expect. The state-created god of the Japanese people—the Emperor—was legislated out of existence. Almost the only religion with any virility left in it had been destroyed. The old way of life, it seemed, had gone, along with the nation's dreams of world conquest. Japanese cities had been devastated, human and material losses had been enormous. Everything, or so it seemed, was in the melting pot. Japan appeared to be wide open for anyone who could offer its people something which would satisfy them intellectually, since they are a serious race, emotionally, since they are an emotional one, too, and fill the vacuum created by the removal of the Emperor from his divine pedestal.

The Communists saw it as an obvious chance for themselves. Fortunately for them, although Russia had been on the winning side she had taken no part in the burning of Japanese cities; nor had she the atom bomb, and so no direct responsibility for Hiroshima and Nagasaki. The Communist Party made impressive headway; unstable political elements—youngsters who had been unsettled by the war, and people who were 'jumping on the bandwagon'—crowded into its ranks. The Party leaders talked and dreamed of a Communist Japan. There was much in the situation to help them towards the realisation of their dreams—material destruction, social chaos, political disillusionment and a spiritual vacuum.

Making the most of the prevailing trend, the Communists talked democracy and posed as a democratic party. Things went well with them for a time, but when other, genuinely democratic, parties began to make greater headway and the authorities began to tighten up on the Communists, they covertly changed their tactic. The new line was to foster 'revolutionary mass action' by campaigning for a country freed from 'American imperialism' and its agents, the ruling class of Japan.

But they misread the mood of the public, which had become more settled as the country began to get on its feet again. The

D*

Communists' 'boom years' were for the moment at an end. Their identification with the North Korean cause hit them particularly hard, for there is no love lost between the Koreans and Japanese.

By 1954 they were playing safe. Open activities likely to offend the susceptibilities of order-loving people were dropped, even though the Communists, as ever, continued behind the scenes to talk of and plan for revolution. As in Europe, the Party was on the defensive and so using the same tactic of 'fronts' of one sort and another, infiltrating non-Communist bodies and using any allies it could find.

This policy was not without its success. Its propaganda spread through other organisations which it used as its 'conveyor belts'. It filtered through to non-Communist Left-wing intellectual circles and was reflected in, for example, a softer attitude on the part of the press and newsreels to Red China and Communism generally, along with a marked growth in anti-Americanism.

During 1954 the Japanese Communists had two lucky breaks and they made the most of both. Their long campaign on the atom bomb had met with only indifferent success. The bomb, and all that, belonged to the past, to the days of national defeat which the public was trying hard to forget. Then the hydrogen bomb was dropped at Bikini and Japanese nationals were injured by radio-active dust. That was indeed a windfall in every sense of the word for the Communists.

It is impossible to guess how the public would have taken the tragic episode had there been no Communists to exploit it. But with the party using all its skill and all its allies to stimulate every sign of horror and anger, anti-Americanism spread and was given a new political content. The Communists appreciate perfectly well that in this mid-twentieth century, dominated as it is by the existence of the two ideological camps, political anti-Americanism amounts objectively to pro-Sovietism—no matter what the subjective feelings of the anti-Americans may be on the question.

When the Japanese fisherman, Kuboyama, died of the injuries he had received from the distant bomb explosion, the

Communists were presented with a gift indeed. They do not neglect such opportunities, nor are they restrained by any inhibitions as to the decency, or indecency, of exploiting such an event. The protest-front soon stretched from the Communist Party to the Y.M.C.A.

The other lucky break was the collapse of Western armed resistance in Indo-China and the Western Powers' impotence at the Geneva talks, where North Vietnam was officially passed to the Communists. Here, for the first time, there had been a straight, prolonged, national-liberation fight between an Asian people, led by Communists, and a Western one, which the Communists had won. The West in general, and America in particular, lost a tremendous amount of face when Ho Chi Minh collected his spoils from a defeated and discomfited West.

As Richard Deverall, head of the Asian Bureau of the American Federation of Labour's Free Trade Union Committee in Tokyo, put it, American-fashion, at the time to me: "H-bomb plus Indo-China means door open for little Red Riding Hood."

It seems evident that, although the membership of the Japanese Communist Party is considerably lower today than it was in the first post-war years, the number of students, intellectuals and workers who support campaigns which aid its cause is as great as, if not greater than, ever before.

And though the Party is smaller, it is undoubtedly stronger. Periods of declining popularity are used by the Communists as ones of natural 'purge'. The Japanese Communist Party is undoubtedly stronger for having sloughed off its hangers-on and unreliable members during the lean years of 1951, 1952 and 1953. Those who sympathise with it now do so from conviction. It has consolidated and strengthened its hard core. And that hard core is large enough to exploit the moment of opportunity and to lead the revolution if and when it comes.

Among Catholics in those first post-war years there were some who felt that the spiritual vacuum created by the official ending of the god-Emperor cult made Japan wide open for

conversion. It was an attractive idea. Japan, it was argued, was
as the most advanced Asian country, the key to Asia and the
natural leader of the Asian peoples. To convert Japan would
be to go a long way towards the conversion of Asia. It was an
idea which naturally caught the imagination of many people
abroad. The small minority of Japanese who over the years
have become Catholics have clung tenaciously and heroically to
their Faith. Nowhere on earth has the Church a prouder record
of martyrdom and fidelity in the face of savage and continued
persecution. When the Japanese become Christians they make
excellent ones. It is as though all those characteristics which
have been the undoing of modern Japan are sublimated in the
individual Japanese and become his strength and crowning
virtues when he receives the gift of Faith.

During the four hundred years since the early days of Zen
Buddhism, the religions of the Japanese—Buddhism and Shintoism—have been secularised and robbed of spirituality. They
have become increasingly materialistic, depriving their followers
of any spiritual ideal. It was this that made it possible for the
ruling clique in the 1930s to use Shintoist Emperor-worship for
their own imperialistic ends. The way the people of Japan
responded to this degraded Shintoist propaganda gives an
indication of the extent to which they had been starved of any
ideal and just how much they needed a faith. They had been
made by the last four centuries of their history perhaps the
most materialistic race on earth. That materialism goes deep.
It can be overcome, as the existence of thousands of good
Christians goes to prove, but the process will not be easy nor, so
far as one can see, a quick one either.

Today the god of the majority is material prosperity. Before
Christianity can conquer, devotion to that god must be over-
thrown. For Marxism to be victorious, however, that is not
necessary. The existing materialism has only to be given a new
twist and rationalised. There is no logical reason why the
materialistic Japanese worker or intellectual should not turn to
Marxism—particularly in the event of a profound economic
recession. He has no religion which is likely to be any sort of
answer to Communism, no philosophy which is any sort of

barrier to acceptance of the teachings of the Marxist dialecticians. In addition to being a materialist he is an idealist —the two often run together, particularly in sentimental or emotional people. The Communists will certainly know how to play on his emotions. They are old hands at the game.

The materialism of the Japanese people was a greater barrier to quick conversion of the masses to Christianity than was realised in the first heady post-war days. Here and there, it is true, there were mass conversions—in one case a whole village came to the Faith. But they were the exceptions. Old hands in Asia like Father Patrick O'Connor, a Columban Father, who has become Asia's foremost religious journalist and who earned the title amongst the troops during the Korean War of 'God's P.I.O.' (Public Intelligence Officer), for example, never suggested in any of his despatches that Japan was about to be converted.

Nor did the Jesuits who for years have run Sophia University in Tokyo think that Japan was on the verge of becoming Christian. They knew the Japanese people too well to suppose that the conversion of the nation could be accomplished over-night, no matter how many missionaries might be poured in there. But they also knew from experience that one Japanese convert is worth his weight in gold, and that for that reason the work there, though it may be slow, is wonderfully rewarding. Japan, they said, will indeed be converted, but it will have to be a very thorough job and when it is accomplished it will be of enormous importance to all Asia.

I was fortunate in that I was able to see both the Columban Fathers and the Jesuits at close quarters during my two stays in Tokyo—on the journey out to Korea and later on the way back —although in each case my visit was all too short.

I had made arrangements to stay at St. Columban's House in Tokyo for most of the time I was in Japan. So a group of Columban Fathers were at the airport to meet me. So, too, was Australian Colonel Staunton, the Public Relations Officer attached to the British Commonwealth Division of the United Nations forces in Japan. It was decided that I should first go to stay at the Ebisu British Commonwealth leave camp until I had been fully fixed up as an accredited United Nations war correspondent.

As we drove out there I learned from the Colonel that the Columban Fathers had several times been in touch with him before my arrival. Their habit of simply describing themselves as 'Columbans', it seemed, had led to a certain amount of confusion. "When they kept on telephoning about your arrival and saying that they were Columbans I wondered why the devil a lot of Latin Americans should suddenly be so interested in you," the Colonel told me.

I imagine that when he saw the group of smiling Irishmen waiting at the airport his fears were soon put at rest. Had he known that their names were Joseph O'Brien, John O'Donovan, Fred Hanson, Joseph Finnerty, Cyril Murphy, Bernard Gallagher, Dennis Curran and James McVeigh, he would have had still less cause for suspicion.

At the Ebisu camp I was put into the 'Leave Hotel', where officers on short leave from Korea were relaxing in a congenial atmosphere, and enjoying a fair degree of comfort. Just across the road was the big building in which 'other ranks' from Korea stayed in equal comfort, with 'Monty's' dream of a reading lamp by every soldier's bed come true.

"In Korea, especially up at the front, they have to do everything for themselves. Here everything is done for them," Colonel Staunton told me.

Every possible facility was laid on there for the men in the form of recreation and organised tours of the city. If too many of them preferred the less savoury facilities provided by the Japanese, whose questionable 'bar-stands' come right up to the camp gates, it was certainly not because there was nothing else for them to do.

At the quartermaster's store, on the day following my arrival, I was fitted up with officer's uniform. Since my period with the forces was only to be a limited one, I got it on loan. It came 'off the hanger'—and was ill-fitting as a consequence. But it was good enough for my purposes.

Meanwhile my U.S. Army-Airforce transport from Tokyo to

Seoul was being arranged. I was warned that it was likely to be 'grim'.

"You're probably going to fly by night, which is just as well," someone told me gloomily. "At least you can't see what is happening to you."

Whilst I was waiting for the formalities to be completed I moved into St. Columban's, which is the Japanese headquarters of the Society of St. Columban. There live the young men newly arrived from Navan, who, before they can be used in the parishes, must wrestle with the wildly unfamiliar Japanese words and characters, and so must go to language school. It is also a 'leave hotel' for the men who work for years on end in the mission parishes. Often these are in remote villages where the priest is the only Westerner for miles around, and the life of the simple people who live there has hardly as yet been touched by the Westernisation which has invaded and transformed the cities.

The Society has nearly ninety men in the field in Japan today, with the house in Tokyo functioning as their nerve centre. With the exception of two men, Fr. O'Connor, who merely uses Japan as the Asian base for his Catholic journalism, and Fr. Hanson, who edits the *Tosei* news service, and the administrative staff at St. Columban's itself, all are doing ordinary parochial work. They are shepherds of souls.

Having stayed at the Society's headquarters in Navan, I was interested to compare its atmosphere with that in Tokyo. The off-hand matter-of-factness of the men at Navan was equally characteristic of Columbans in action too, I discovered. If the men at home were reticent about their work, their achievements and their exploits, so, equally, were those on the missions. Men came for a few days from remote spots where their life is, perhaps, dominated by the building of a new village church or the running of catechumens' classes. They had temporarily left an all-Japanese existence, to stay among fellow Westerners, Irish, Americans, Australians and New Zealanders, members of the same organisation. They took off their boots and Roman collars to sit around together, pulling at their pipes and relaxing. But though there was much sharp-edged banter, there was an underlying if unexpressed sense of comradeship.

But there was no bragging, no attempt to outdo each other with romantic-sounding stories of their adventures, such as one expects of men who have travelled the world and lived eventful lives in out-of-the-way places. Yet if you somehow achieved the feat of getting them to talk you found that many of them had personal histories of jailings, escapes and dangers faced, sometimes alone, sometimes together. But there was nothing in their conversation together to remind you of this. They were just a group of men looking after parishes in remote spots in Japan, seemingly as unconscious of any drama or peculiar significance about their work as would be a similar group of priests meeting at a diocesan gathering at home.

It is an interesting thing that a Society which has existed for something less than forty years should so soon have produced such a marked type, even though the individuals who make up the Society are as unlike each other in interests and origin as are any other group of men taken from a cross-section of citizens of four or five different countries.

All the men who came to relax at St. Columban's could report recent progress. New churches being built here and there, new parishes established—these were the things which dominated their thoughts, set the pattern of their lives and formed the basis of their conversation when they got together. They talked of the 'ordinary' as opposed to the extraordinary, things. Their reports were of a constant trickle of converts coming in, sufficient to warrant continual expansion, and of steady congregations of solid, unshakeable Christians trying hard under the guidance of their pastors to achieve the difficult feat of living a Christian life in a non-Christian environment. This was all part of the battle, but the smell of gunpowder seemed deceptively far away.

Japanese morals are, to say the least of it, quite unlike those of the West—they owe nothing to Christianity, but are a sharp reminder of to what an extent the modern 'good pagan' of the West is still indebted to the religion he has rejected. On sexual matters it would perhaps be more accurate to say that the

Japanese are amoral rather than immoral—since immorality implies the rejection of an existing moral code. This amorality creates enormous problems for Japanese Christian girls and young women, who require more than the usual degree of heroism and resolution to continue to live a Christian life. One understandable by-product of this situation is an exceptionally high proportion of 'vocations' among girls. In other words, large numbers desire to become nuns. There may be an element of escapism revealed in this, but a stronger factor is their intense desire to be the best Christians possible.

So almost all the missionaries I met at St. Columban's and elsewhere in Japan told of having more women and girls wanting to be nuns than could possibly be taken at the moment.

It was my good fortune to be put in touch with Richard Deverall, the American Federation of Labour's Asian Representative, who has his headquarters in Tokyo.

Dick Deverall has travelled every country of Asia, knows almost every town and village of Japan, where he has lived since the end of the Pacific War. Dick is a 'character'. He has come to know the Japanese workers as few Westerners do by making himself one of them. He lives in Japanese lodgings, where he 'lives Japanese'. He genuinely enthuses over such delicacies as cooked seaweed and other local dishes against which Western palates normally tend to turn. He goes daily to the public baths (which really are public) like a good Japanese, and returns to his office happily sweating and steaming.

He took me one day on a tour of the city. We went first into suburban areas where every home is also a workshop. There men make metal and wooden components which are later assembled in large factories into completed products which they never see, and women stitch from morning to night, just as they did in Britain in the days of Thomas Hood's 'Song of the Shirt'.

A Japanese home is genuinely an 'open house', and so, with no introductions at all, we walked freely into middle-class apartments and small workshops alike. I felt embarrassed, conscious of the resentment that such an intrusion would create in

England. But Dick knew his Japanese people. No one objected and everywhere we were met with courtesy.

An international wrestling championship was being held in the city. In one area through which we passed we saw the Japanese wrestlers, with long black hair done up into a bun on the top of the head, streaming away from training bouts. These huge men, in a nation of small people, are put on a special diet almost from birth. They occupy a special place in Japanese society, for their wrestling is oddly linked with their Shinto religion. They walked, through streets thronged with admirers, with an enormous pride. Soon we were to see an even odder feature of Shintoism.

Dick had said that a visit to the city's Yoshiwara area of Asakusa, in which live ten thousand officially-approved prostitutes, was an essential part of any tour of the city by anyone interested in social phenomena. This was obviously so, and I accordingly agreed that we should take a look at it. Our driver was a priest and, not knowing what would be his reaction to even a quick trip through such a notorious district—even at such an innocent hour as midday—we decided that it would be better not to tell our destination. We were well into Yoshiwara before he guessed where he had, under our direction, taken us.

The entire district was nothing but street upon street of small, tidy brothels. At most road junctions there were police boxes, the police being there not in order to keep a suspicious eye on the prostitutes, but to protect them from any men who might try to cheat them of their lawful earnings.

When we were in the very heart of the district we heard a banging of drums, and came upon a curious semi-religious festival which was already in progress. It was, it seemed, the day for Yoshiwara's annual Shinto festival. A bamboo shrine had been set up, around which were gathered a crowd of small children in gay clothes, and huge young men in blue and white costumes, so cut as to show a considerable length of impressively large and muscular thigh. The children danced and banged the big drum which, crowned by a rooster, had been set up on a decorated wagon beside the shrine. The hefty young men meanwhile were competing with each other in drinking huge quantities of potent *saké*.

We stopped the car, and Dick and I proceeded, despite the rain, which was falling heavily at the time, to get some pictures. The area has an exclusively prostitute population. Behind and around us everywhere were brothels, with their front screens opened to air them, revealing the simple and shamelessly utilitarian furniture inside.

The sound of the drums was bringing the girls streaming out of their little houses. Some were carrying umbrellas, but others, only just rising although it was midday, were in their underwear. When we tried to get pictures of the 'priests' and their 'acolytes' we quickly became the centre of a gaily chattering but entirely circumspect circle of 'bad girls'. But our driver by this time, in something of a panic, was desperately revving his engine as hard as he could, the rain was getting worse, and so we dashed back to our car again.

Each district, even Yoshiwara, it seems, still has its festival day. Once the festival had a strongly religious character. To-day little of that side of the occasion remains, and most of the cash for the *saké* and the festivities which are provided for all the inhabitants comes from local traders. They support it for commercial reasons, much as in England the village seedsman, ironmonger and general storekeeper will provide the prizes for a flower show, or in America commercial interests will exploit a Hallow E'en, which has now lost most, if not all, of its religious significance for the majority of those who make it an occasion for fun and feasting.

The little world of Yoshiwara, so remote from our own, gave me an insight into the peculiarly difficult job which faces the missionary in amoral Japan. So much in Japan is like the West, yet so much is different—particularly in the moral sphere, which is the one which most closely touches the Christian missionary in his work.

Outside Lisbon in 1952 I visited a mission art exhibition at which some superb examples of Japanese Christian art were on view. Now that I was in Tokyo I was anxious to take back to

Britain with me some such picture or statue which would be a permanent reminder of Japan.

I discovered a Catholic art and book shop and, full of hope, asked if they had any examples of Japanese Catholic art.

"Not here," I was told by an assistant, who was surrounded by plaster casts from Italy. "Our customers are mainly Japanese people, so all our things are Western. If you want something that is genuinely Japanese you had better go down the road to the shop that caters for foreigners."

On the Saturday, three opportunities came my way to see and meet quite different sections of the Japanese people.

In the morning I went to Sophia University to give a lecture. I had visited the Jesuit-run University two or three times already to meet Fr. Roggendorf, the learned Dean of Studies, and such prominent members of the staff as P. V. Kobayasin, the prominent Christian author, and others.

Mr. Kobayasin, who is famous for his translations of Western Catholic books into his native Japanese, is a scholarly, cultured convert. The Church has attracted a significant number of such types to Her ranks, a group of whom I was fortunate enough to meet later that day.

When I went along to give my lecture, I found the University assembly hall packed with hundreds of students. They filled every chair and stood row upon row at the back and sides, ready and eager, it seemed, to hear a forty-five-minute lecture in English. I never had a more attentive audience.

As soon as I climbed down from the rostrum again, one of the Japanese professors went to the microphone and proceeded to give a word-for-word translation of the entire lecture, backed up with a wealth of gestures and asides of his own, which made it entertaining even for me, who understood hardly a word of it. Only once did he break off. That was when, translating a reference of mine to a man having gone to jail in London, he stopped and asked: "Was it Brixton?"

I nodded.

"I know Brixton jail, too," he said gaily. "I was sent there during the war as an enemy alien. I was working in the Embassy in London at the time." The students roared with laughter. Neither the translator nor the students showed any sign of bitterness.

It takes much longer, I learned, to say anything in Japanese than it does in English, and, by the time we broke up, the students had had almost a solid two hours of lectures, throughout which many of them had been standing all the time.

The students, I was told, although all present had some knowledge of English, had been glad to have the lecture repeated in their own language, so that they could check how accurate— or inaccurate—was their own interpretation of what I had said. The Japanese student takes his education seriously.

Under Fr. Roggendorf's direction, Sophia University is doing a magnificent job in Japan in the best Jesuit tradition. It is influencing a small but potentially decisive section of the community in the direction of Christianity without in any way mixing 'Catholic propaganda' with its educational work.

It was founded as a college some forty years ago, receiving university status twenty years later. It has two faculties, one of economics and the other a liberal arts school. There is a total of one thousand two hundred students, another hundred do postgraduate studies, and hundreds attend its evening classes. In addition there are two-year courses in theology for the laity. Though small and situated in a city which abounds in colleges, it has made its own mark on Tokyo's academic life. Its newly started evening courses in social studies may well have wide repercussions. One of these, a diploma course, taken in the main by trade unionists and workers, covers such subjects as the economic problems of Japan and parliamentary debating.

Such courses, based as they are on Christian values applied to the world of industry and politics, are bound in time to have their influence, even though the number of those taking them is not large.

A relatively high proportion—perhaps as much as a third— of Sophia's graduates sooner or later become Christians. The Church in Japan has, indeed, been notably successful in the way in which it has attracted intellectuals and members of the privileged classes. The fact that the number of ordinary folk coming to the Faith is small by comparison tends, of course, to create special difficulties, not the least of which is that there is a real danger of Catholicism coming to be seen as something which is not of the common people, the great mass of poor and less well-educated who make up the vast mass of the country's population. That is why the work of the Jesuits, whose greatest influence is upon the highly-educated, on the one hand, and that of the Columban Fathers, for example, who concentrate upon ordinary parish work and the care of souls in towns and villages, on the other, is equally important in the fight for the soul of the Japanese nation.

At lunch with Sophia's very international Jesuit community (it was at first entirely German, but now draws men from many nations), I learned of the resignation of Louis Taruc, the Communist leader of the Hukbalahap guerillas in the Philippines. I expressed the view that the resignation of the man whom the Communists had called 'the symbol of the national liberation movement' and who for years had been seen as the Mao Tse Tung of the Philippines might indicate that international Communism—in this case headed by China—was not at this moment giving full backing to causes which were unlikely to meet with victory in the near future. It had for some time seemed clear to me that the Chinese might, for example, have given much greater support to the Communist guerillas in Malaya but had instead let them suffer one defeat after another, content that they maintained their nuisance value and continued as a potentially revolutionary force.

In the Philippines much the same situation had obtained and this led to Taruc throwing in his hand.

Louis Taruc joined the Communist Party in the crisis years of the mid-thirties. Between 1937 and 1941 he was imprisoned in connection with various strikes which he led. When the Hukbalahap, or People's Anti-Japanese Army, was formed in March 1942, he became its leader. Like the Communists who led the Malayan People's Anti-Fascist Army, he saw the fight against the Japanese as providing an opportunity to learn the art of guerilla warfare and to arm a Communist-led movement which would have to do the more important job—that of establishing Communism—when the Japanese had been defeated.

So the 'Huks' obtained arms from the Allies and took them from the Japanese as well, and within their ranks the Communists established themselves as their leaders. Gradually the anti-Japanese movement was turned first into a national liberation movement and then into an openly Communist-cum-Nationalist one.

The Philippines were given their independence by America in 1946. But Taruc and his fellow Communists, like their Indian comrades, said that the new independence was largely a sham. The Philippines, he claimed, were still tied to American imperialism. Thus a national liberation movement, which could be used to carry through a Communist-led revolution, was still needed. So within three years of the end of the war the 'anti-Japanese army' had become a 'national liberation movement' still under the leadership of the Communists.

Taruc, like other Oriental Communist leaders, learned lessons from Mao Tse Tung. He stressed that his aim was not just an agrarian revolution but one like that of China. The agrarian revolution was but the first stage on the road to Communism.

The Huks were outlawed in 1948 and took to the hills. Taruc, their Commander-in-Chief, lived for years with his armed bands in the mountains of Luzon, in hiding by day and going to the people for food by night. Their position has become increasingly difficult as the Government has built up its campaign against them. Taruc's autobiography, *Born of the People*, which he wrote whilst he was in hiding in 1949, reveals him as the bright boy of a peasant family whose father sacrificed to send him to school so that he might escape from the toil and grinding poverty which had been the main features of his own life.

But when Louis graduated from high school in 1932 there was unemployment in the towns and economic crisis everywhere. In Manila there were strikes and hunger marches, into which the disillusioned young peasant-intellectual who had dreamed of becoming a doctor was soon drawn. The things which drove him into Communism were those which have sent so many there: personal disillusionment and a desire to escape from the conditions he had known as a child, idealism, an only half formulated dream of a better world, hatred of the landlords who had kept his father poor and the capitalists who had exploited him in his youth, desire for retribution and revenge. The usual mixture of good and bad which Communism can take and use for its own evil purposes.

Now the forty-one-year-old Communist leader, leaving behind his ragged, barefooted army of outlaws, had, it was reported, given himself up, disillusioned and defeated.

Everywhere in Japan, and throughout the Orient, people were discussing the implications of the news. It had upon them something of the effect that a report of the defection of Thorez or Togliatti might be expected to have in Europe.

I discussed the Philippines with the Columban Fathers. With some one hundred and fifty men in the field, they are the third largest Catholic missionary society there. They regarded the Philippines, they said, as the brightest spot in the Orient from the Church's point of view.

Once large areas of the Philippines were Catholic. Seven priests accompanied Magellan's expedition when it sailed from Spain in 1519. A year and a half later, in March, 1521, the explorers discovered the Philippines. The Cross and the Mass arrived with the expedition. Less than a century later almost the whole of the Philippines had been evangelised and civilised —an enormous missionary achievement.

Spanish Catholicism and Spanish colonial government, in close association, shaped the pattern of life of the Filipinos for over three hundred years. They were the only Christian nation in Asia. But in Filipino minds the Catholic Church was identified with Spanish colonial rule.

So, when that rule ended with the defeat of Spain by America in 1898, the people of the Philippines rose up in revolt against the Spaniards and most of the Spanish missionaries were forced to leave along with the colonists.

With the narrow political vision of their day, they had failed to build up a strong native clergy. The result was that when America took over the Philippines, some seven hundred parishes were left without priests. Two hundred and fifty Spanish and a mere handful of Filipino priests were faced with the impossible task of caring for some five million Catholics. There followed a long and tragic period of priestless parishes, in which churches crumbled into ruins and the work of three centuries of missionary activity went into decay.

A new undenominational school system on the American public school model grew up. The majority of the teachers, almost inevitably, since Catholics were still weak in America at that time, were Protestants. Some, as was to be expected, proceeded, perhaps almost unconsciously, to proselytise.

Thus to decay was added schism. The almost priestless Church took blow after blow, whilst education became secularised and the people, still with Catholic names and much of their Catholic culture, came near to forgetting the practice of the Faith of their fathers.

The population grew by leaps and bounds. Today there are twenty million people in the Philippines, fifteen and a half million of whom are, nominally at least, Catholics. To cope with them another fifteen thousand priests are needed immediately.

Despite that enormous shortage of personnel, the situation in the Philippines is a bright one for the Church today. There has been a tremendous change since the end of the war, much of which is due to a great drive to bring Catholic education and instruction back to the people. In the Columbans' area, for example, eighty-one per cent of the children, one hundred and twenty thousand of them, are receiving instruction in the Faith. The Legion of Mary, the lay organisation which has proved to be such a tower of strength in China, and other lay bodies are providing catechists by the hundred, who teach the Faith to both adults and children. I have talked to missionaries who have gone back to the Philippines after only five years' absence in the post-war years, and who say that the change in the whole outlook of the people is phenomenal.

In 1945 or 1946, when the Huks were at the peak of their

power, the possibility of a Communist Philippines was in everybody's mind. Today it is of a new and reconverted Catholic Philippines that they talk. But whether that will quickly become a reality hinges on the speed and thoroughness with which native clergy can be provided, and the number of missionaries, priests and nuns who come from America and Europe to aid them.

After lunch with the Jesuits at Sophia, I went on to meet members of the Council of Catholic Men, a group of influential professional and business men which is headed by Lord Chief Justice Tanaka Kotaro, a member of one of Japan's leading families. This organisation is evidence of the success which Catholicism has had among some of the country's most educated and influential people.

Present were some of Japan's best known surgeons, diplomats and business men. We sat around a kidney-shaped table drinking tea from paper-thin cups which were a delight to see and handle. As these quiet-voiced men asked their questions and received my answers with exquisite courtesy, I got a glimpse of a gracious mode of life of which I was to be reminded many times as I went into what had once been Japanese homes in the weeks that followed in Korea.

They asked me my views on the spiritual background to the spread of Communism in our day and questioned me about the strength of Communism in Britain, British trade with China, my impressions of Catholicism in Japan, the influence of Chinese Communist thought and practice upon Communists elsewhere, and, of course, about Louis Taruc's surrender.

In Tokyo's Communist bookshop a day or two earlier I had bought English translations of the theoretical works of Mao Tse Tung, Lui Shao Chi and other Chinese Communist leaders. I had, incidentally, also seen a new consignment of such books arrive, whilst I was there, from Peking—via Hong Kong! The shop was filled with workers and impecunious students. As happens in every Japanese bookshop, many of them stood around reading the books they could not afford to buy. But these Marxist-revolutionary books which bore

Peking and Moscow imprints were dynamite in their hands.

So I had to admit, under polite questioning from these members of the Council of Catholic Men, that British trade with China could have strange, and dangerous, consequences.

From meeting the employers, I went to a reception, which someone had been good enough to throw for me, at which were present more than a score of the country's most responsible trade union leaders. Their questions came thick and fast, on the strength of the Communists in British trade unions, British colonial policy, our industrial conciliation machinery, trade with China, Bevanism and a host of similar subjects. And, of course, on the defection of Louis Taruc.

They were, on the average, younger, slimmer and, one felt, nearer to their own rank and file in their standard of life than would be a comparable group of European trade union bosses. They seemed moderate and responsible without having lost their fire. For a couple of hours we questioned each other as we nibbled at a mixture of American and Japanese delicacies. Most of the Japanese drank drinks which had reached Tokyo via the United States but had had their origins in the distilleries of Scotland, whilst the Westerners drank Japanese beer.

These Japanese labour leaders were strongly anti-imperialist. They condemned their own country's imperialist past and viewed with suspicion, born of the principles they held, Britain's present colonial policies too. They wanted to know more about Mau Mau in Kenya, and asked, was the recent trouble in British Guiana and British Honduras really Communist-inspired, as the British Government had alleged? I gave a qualified 'yes' to the former and a qualified 'no' to the latter, whilst stressing the anxiety of international Communism to get its foot inside the Caribbean.

Knowing that a Labour Party delegation led by Clement Attlee was due to call on their country whilst on its trip to Red China, they wanted to know more about the men and women who were coming. But they were far more interested in Aneurin Bevan than in Mr. Attlee. They had read that Bevan was a miners' M.P. and that he had gone to Parliament with the financial backing of the National Union of Mineworkers, and wanted in particular to know how far he could be regarded as representing his union's policies. They seemed relieved when I told them of his clashes with the union's leaders, that he was often out of step with his own union and that his main backing came from the political rather than the industrial wing of his party. If that was so, they said, he was a type with which they were already familiar in Japan, and it would be helpful to let their members know the situation, since many trade unionists in Japan had been looking forward to his visit primarily as that of a fellow trade unionist. That sense of identity of interest with other non-Communist trade unionists in the West was, I found, very strong among them. It springs in part, of course, quite naturally, from their trade union philosophy. But I felt that a good share of the credit for this very encouraging aspect of the Japanese labour leaders' approach to the international scene must go to the Labour Division of the American Embassy in Tokyo, who have done a very worthwhile job among them.

Precisely because the whole field of ordinary democratic labour relations is new in Japan, where a great deal of feudalism lingers on in the countryside and a surprising amount also still intrudes into the industrial life of the cities, they had a freshness of approach which was stimulating. In the West one gets all too accustomed to the rather tired, somewhat superior and sophisticated approach of the trade union leader to whom there is no such thing as a new situation and who has all the answers even before a problem arises. Their approach to Communism seemed thoroughly realistic without being in any way hysterical.

An indication of the way in which Oriental minds, because of their very different background, may find it difficult to grasp a point which is easily taken in the West came during a discussion about the London *Daily Worker*, of which for some years I was the News Editor. I mentioned the financial sacrifice made by both readers and staff to keep the paper going—a necessary point to grasp if one is to have any understanding at all of the psychology of Communism. There followed some twenty minutes of questions, which came from all sides.

What particularly puzzled them was my reference to the fact that there are factory workers in Britain who donate to the

'Worker's' fighting fund without being Communist Party members, and whilst still continuing to vote for the Labour Party at election time. I like to think that their bewilderment at this piece of intelligence shows that perhaps the Japanese mind is more logical than ours after all.

On the following morning I went to Mass in an ordinary parish church run by the Columban Fathers in one of the city's outer suburbs. There I met for the first time the Eastern practice of going into church in bare or stockinged feet. The congregation passed their shoes to a young priest, who put them on a rack in the porch. He was still learning the language and so was making himself useful in such ways as he could.

This practice of taking off the shoes is, of course, the one which is followed in the home as well and no Japanese or Korean would dream of showing less respect for the house of God than he would for that of his friend or neighbour. It is a major factor in maintaining the spotless cleanliness of the highly-polished floors of the Orient.

In appearance the congregation was an ordinary cross-section of the people of a Tokyo suburb. There were schoolchildren, students, intellectuals, a preponderance of 'white collar' workers, and ordinary housewives and mothers with small babies on their backs. Some were dressed in Western style, some in the colourful, traditional manner, the proportions being much what one would expect to see in any other gathering of Japanese people of their class. The adoption of Christianity, in other words, had not resulted in their making themselves more 'Western' than their fellows.

When the time came for the sermon, a French Canadian priest, who had been conducting a special mission in the parish that week, came from the sacristy and preached with obvious eloquence. But one did not need to be told the subject of his sermon. He belonged to an Order known among Catholics for its determination never to permit the faithful, and still less the not-so-faithful, to forget that the fires of hell burn eternally for those who backslide. No knowledge of the Japanese language was required to get the general drift of his message. Brimstone smells much the same in any language.

The church was dedicated to St. Patrick. Recalling all I had said and written in the past about the need for the international Church to make Herself as truly national as possible wherever she goes, I wished that it had been called, say, the Church of the Japanese Martyrs.

But my recent experience in the sacred art shop had shown me that the action of the Columban Fathers at Toshima-Ku, when they made such a very Western saint as St. Patrick the patron of their church, was completely in accord with the Japanese outlook.

Ever since I left Rangoon I had been suffering from a mild attack of dysentery which had kept me awake for the larger part of each night, but I had been too busy to do anything about getting it treated. It was by now, however, beginning to weaken me and, with a five-hour flight that night to Korea before me, I decided that it was time that something should be done about it.

Along with Father Hanson I called at the great International Catholic Hospital of Seibo Byoin, run by the Franciscan Missionaries of Mary. As we went through its cool corridors it might well have been one of the many hospitals run by nuns which I have visited at home. The illusion was increased when I was attended to by Mother Mary, a white-robed, briskly efficient doctor-nun from Newport, Monmouthshire.

For Catholics, 1954 was a 'Marian' year, especially dedicated to Mary. The Tokyo Archdiocese was to have its biggest Marian rally that afternoon. Already as we drove back across the city to St. Columban's, in Azabu, three hours before it was due to begin, parties of students, schoolchildren, Japanese priests and nuns were making their way there on foot, walking many miles, in some cases, to get there.

At the rally there were some five thousand people present, including large numbers of Japanese nuns, looking very attractive in their familiar habits. Here the crowd was more Japanese-looking in its dress than the congregation at St. Patrick's had been that morning. It was an 'occasion', and the majority of the women and quite a lot of the men had got out their best clothes in its honour. The hundreds of students were, of course, in the inevitable regulation uniform—white tunic blouse and black skirt for the girls, black, high-necked, unlined jacket and black trousers for the boys, making them look like crowds of Jesuit Seminarians.

A Catholic is equally at home anywhere in the universal Church. The ceremony and Latin words of the service, with the Archbishop of Tokyo giving Benediction, were, of course, identical to those used at home. Some of the hymns were sung in the vernacular, to Oriental-type tunes. But when the crowd broke into the Lourdes hymn, with its *Ave* chorus, I remembered that the last time I had sung those same words was when I was taking part in a great procession of African Catholics to the Church of the Martyrs at Namugongo, in the heart of Uganda. The time before that, I had been with a well-dressed crowd at a Marian shrine outside a fashionable church in New York.

The rally was held on a long, narrow, weed-covered, bomb-site, with buildings on either side. There was a tall, rocky grotto at one end, before which an open-air altar had been set up. The front rows of the great crowd, which stretched back, long and narrow, down the funnel-shaped site, were composed entirely of young girls. Right along one side ran a roughly-made path of large stones, down which members of the crowd had to pass to get to their places.

When the ceremony had been going on for some time, and the people had packed themselves closer and closer towards the front, one of the young girls was brought back down the path in a fainting condition by two of the boy scouts who were acting as stewards. Soon another was brought back and another and another. Before long there was an almost unbroken traffic of boy scouts, transparently conscious of their male superiority, filing down to the front singly and coming back supporting fainting adolescent girls between them or actually carrying their prostrate forms.

Then the inevitable happened—one of the boy scouts fainted and had to be carried off, rigid as a log. After that their male superiority was not made quite so obvious.

.   .   .   .   .   .

"Notice. The bearer of this card is a civilian noncombatant serving with the armed forces of the United States, whose signature, photograph and finger-prints appear hereon. If the bearer of this card shall fall into the hands of the enemies of the United States he shall at once show this card to the detaining authorities to assist in his identification. If the bearer is detained he is entitled to be given the same treatment and afforded the same privileges as an inividual in the grade, rate or rank of the military service of the United States indicated below, with any and all rights to which such personnel are entitled under all applicable treaties, agreements and the established practice of nations."

So said the two certificates of identification now safely in my pocket as I set out for the military airport outside Tokyo on my last hop to Korea. The rank given on the cards was 'Major Thru Colonel, U.S. Army'. At United Nations Army Headquarters in Tokyo, when I went for my credentials and orders, the man who handed me the two cards told me: "There are still guerillas over there. If you are taken prisoner you give one up to the Reds and keep the other yourself." But someone standing by added: "I guess if *he* gets taken by Reds those cards won't help him much."

Anyway, I was off—dressed in British uniform and with the rank of a U.S. colonel, a very phoney military man indeed. A Columban Father drove me out to Tachikawa Air Base in the evening, after the rally, and it was hard going all the way. It was, it seemed, Japan's 'Derby Day'. The race-course was not far from the airport, and we were just in time to meet the return from the races in full flood.

The Japanese make the taxi-drivers of Paris, and even the army truck-drivers of Korea, appear sober, careful people by comparison. There were so many lanes of oncoming traffic, with none of the drivers thinking of giving way for anyone, that we had to hug the roadside all the way.

From time to time we would pass 'honey carts' going out from the city and would then have to force our way into the nearest lane of traffic heading towards us. The 'honey carts', I should explain, are made necessary by the fact that Tokyo, with its vast population, has no sewers. This is presumably in part because of the rapid growth of the city and also because the frequent earth tremors might break the pipes, with the consequent threat of epidemics. The sewage from the whole eight million population has therefore to be taken regularly out of the city.

Once, as we rounded a blind bend, we found the entire road filled from hedge to hedge with cars charging towards us. There was a screeching of brakes that went back down the line until it was out of earshot. The driver of a three-wheeled truck, the nose of which almost touched our radiator, swung into his near-side traffic lane, whilst his passengers roared with a merriment which we found it difficult to share.

Army-fashion, I had to report at the passenger terminal at 18.30 hours for an aircraft which was not due to leave for at least two hours. Just before the waiting period ended, a plane arrived from Seoul and among its passengers was my colleague, Patrick O'Donovan, of the London *Observer*. He had just come from covering the Korean elections, and was depressed about the growth—or what he considered the absence of any growth—of democracy there.

We were standing on the tarmac talking together in the dark when the order came to board the aircraft. As I walked out with the straggling crowd of officers and men—all Americans apart from myself—a friendly G.I. paired up with me and made conversation. It went like this:

"I heard you two talking over there. Say, what language were you guys speaking?"

"We call it English where I come from."

"Gee, where's that?"

"England."

"It sure is different to the way we talk it where I come from."

"It certainly is."

Back at the camp in Tokyo I had been told that I was lucky to be flying at night because I would not see what was happening. But we were told what to expect as soon as we boarded the plane.

E

It was an army transport: a bucket-shaped affair, in which there were no seats, but a large quantity of freight, mails and luggage. We were told to put on our Mae Wests. To each Mae West was attached what seemed to be an enormous weight which we strapped to our posteriors. Then we attached ourselves by hooks and buckles direct on to the fuselage and the 'weights' proved to be seats, to which we were thus securely fastened. A helpful U.S. officer, obviously an old hand at the operation, seeing me fumbling hopelessly with all the many gadgets, gave me some expert advice.

Meanwhile, as the aircraft prepared to leave, a young lieutenant, who had been lecturing the 'other ranks', now came and addressed us.

"The journey to Seoul will take just over five hours," he said, "so you should be there by half-past one tomorrow morning. This type of aircraft, as you know already, has a reputation for losing engines, but there is no cause for any panic. You will not be more than forty miles from the coast for most of the trip.

"If, however, we should lose an engine, the freight will be thrown out first, then the mail and only after all ballast has gone will you be expected to jump. Human life comes first.

"Should this be necessary you will file in orderly formation and jump in turn. Don't rush the doors or you'll be crushed to death, and don't linger either. He who lingers is lost. Last week, when one of these aircraft lost an engine on this same trip a man died unnecessarily because he lingered."

Then he described how we should use our parachutes and how, just before we reached the sea, after jumping, we should operate an attachment which hung down by our feet and which would open out into a small raft.

Keeping up the 'rugged' line right to the bitter end, he concluded: "There is a bucket at each end of the aircraft. The crossing is likely to be turbulent. If you want to vomit make for the nearest bucket. If you fail to reach it in time, officer or man, you will clear it up yourself. We're busy."

I was to see plenty more of the American soldier's cult of 'ruggedness' in Korea. It is, I imagine, a defence mechanism

evolved by men who, in the conditions of the recently-finished
Korean War, were face to face with death for much of their
time.

The airport at Seoul was almost deserted when we arrived in
the early hours of the morning. A British jeep and driver were
waiting for me, and I was taken direct to the United Nations
press billets. As we went through the city streets we had to
follow a snake-like course, which my driver explained was made
necessary by the deep pot-holes and shell-holes which were
everywhere. If you charged straight at them you would
certainly break a spring and might possibly turn right over.

The night was cold, but, passing through the city centre, we
saw in the moonlight the figures of large numbers of people
huddled together at the roadside, in the public squares and
elsewhere.

"They're homeless. There are thousands of them, poor
devils," shouted my driver, a young conscript, sympathetically,
as we bumped along with my bags noisily jumping up and down
behind us.

At the press billets, which in Tokyo had been described to
me as 'pretty grim', I was told my room number and made my
way to bed. The floors were bare, there was a minimum of
furniture, and quite clearly someone had spilt a bottle of brandy
there not long before. At least, I hoped that the brandy, whose
smell seemed all-pervading, was still unconsumed when it made
that big stain on the floor. However, the important thing was
that there was a bed on which to sleep—and that this was
Korea.

VIII

KOREAN GUINEA–PIG

IN June, 1950, Korea was made a guinea-pig for war. International Communism, testing how far the democracies would go in their resistance to aggression, launched its most flagrant armed attack of the post-war years there. And the United Nations for the first time collectively used armed sanctions against aggression in Korea.

But if Korea was made a guinea-pig for war she must also be seen as the guinea-pig for peace. No country was ever more devastated by war, its human and material resources destroyed on a more extravagant scale. The long-drawn out fight against Communist aggression was conducted in the name of, and on behalf of, us all. By virtue of our membership of the United Nations we were all equally responsible for the fact that what might have been a brief and all too successful military campaign by the Communists became a full-scale international war in miniature, with the actual needs and welfare of the Korean people themselves coming to count for less and less as time went on.

If so many of Korea's cities today lie flattened, and such huge numbers of her people are either dead or maimed by fire or bomb, it is because in June, 1950, a point had been reached in international affairs when the free world was prepared to say to those whose aim was and is a Communist world: "Thus far, and no further."

Yet there never was a war which began so well and ended so badly. Never in modern times had men and Governments more self-consciously gone into a fight against evil. And never did that crusading spirit more quickly evaporate. What began in 1950 as a crusade against Communism rapidly degenerated into one of the most squalid affairs of all time.

It is true that it was not just an altruistic hatred of evil which led the United States Government to react so quickly and so forcefully to the North Korean aggression, committing herself to war there when she had only so recently brought home the men required for the job. Fear and self-interest, no doubt, played—as they have done in most of mankind's crusades—their part, too. That is not in any way to underrate the high-minded generosity which contributed to the making of that historic decision. The threat of Soviet aggression and Communist penetration had only recently, suddenly and somewhat belatedly been recognised. And, precisely because it was both sudden and belated, the American reaction to it was all the sharper and more violent. The North Korean attack came just when the mood of America was least likely to tolerate Communist aggression anywhere. America, carrying the United Nations with her, decided to meet Communist force with force.

For the European members of the United Nations who went along with the U.S. the issues were not so stark and clear. At home they had lived much closer to the Communist danger for years and were more familiar with it, possibly dangerously so. For years already they had been conscious of the fact that Red Army tanks were only an hour or two—or even less—away, and Red bombers could reach their capital cities in a matter of minutes. They were more preoccupied with Europe than with Asia—excepting those parts of Asia, like Malaya, Indo-China and Indonesia, where they were already involved in armed struggle with Communism because of their own links with those countries.

For them Korea was especially significant as a symbol of united democratic resistance. But for all, for one reason or another, the crusading character of the campaign in its early days was more than just something engineered by the propagandists. They wanted to clear away the clouds of World War III, which were already darkening the lives of a generation weary of war. They believed that their cause warranted risking a long war among the homes and fields of the Korean people. They fought for Korean freedom, but they fought for themselves and their own future peace as well.

With some such ideas as that the men (or boys as most of them were) of the United Nations Forces first went into battle. But the very nature of the country and of the war itself made short work of the idealism of the troops in the field and of the people at home as well. The crusade was soon forgotten. Ask the average non-Communist European what he has learned about Korea in these last years and you will probably be told that the fields reek with the smell of the human excrement the peasants use as dung; that the Korean winter is apparently much more severe than it was understood to be in the West; that although the Communists' claim that the South attacked first is probably phoney, it wouldn't be surprising if history showed that Syngman Rhee, a proven double-crosser, was preparing some sort of provocation at the time anyway; that the Americans used napalm there as an anti-personnel weapon as well as against military objectives and that this can result in a human being, roasted alive, running around with skin like the crackling on roast pork; that the armistice talks must have been the longest and most half-hearted of all time, and that the war went on much too long and had, long before the end, become quite senseless anyway. Ask the average politically-minded Korean what he thinks of the war and he will probably reply that everything he fought for was betrayed at the armistice talks.

That is a sorry end, indeed, to what was at first fondly believed to be a noble and inspiring thing. Left at that, it represents a moral victory for the Communists.

We cannot now in decency just walk out and leave the Koreans to start life all over again, alone and unaided. The shape of the future Korea is our responsibility too. For the first time the democracies have a collective responsibility for rebuilding, almost from the ground up, the pattern of life of a country devastated by Communist aggression and Western resistance to that aggression. For the first time we should be sharing the burden with men who are starting a new life after experiencing Communist rule. That is why Korea must be seen not only as the guinea-pig of war, but of the peace as well.

For all over the world today there are exiles from the lands where Communism has triumphed who dream of life in a post-Communist régime. All too many think only in terms of going back to the old life, to régimes like those they knew in the past —even to the old positions of power and privilege. But it just cannot be. Nor will those who live behind the Iron Curtain be strengthened in their desire for freedom, and their willingness to sacrifice for it by the belief that the only alternative to Communism is a return to the old ways. "Life cannot just be the same again," men who have suffered at the hands of the North Korean Communists have told me. Yet one has a haunting fear that that could happen, that, far from any brave new Korea arising from the ashes of the old one, that war-wrecked land may just be allowed to drift back to the old corrupt and squalid ways whilst men enslaved by Communism watch the process with growing disillusionment and the Communists watch with glee. We owe it to ourselves, as well as to the Koreans, to see that that does not happen. If the war was worth fighting, if it was worth the lives of scores of thousands of Americans and Europeans and hundreds of thousands of Koreans, if it was worth all the cost in money and human misery, then the peace is worth a great deal too.

But although a lot has been written about the war, very little has been written about the peace. To defeat Communism, or to fight it to a standstill, is not enough. There must be a positive aim too. A free Korea must be one to which, in particular, those Asian peoples who are threatened by Communism can look for inspiration.

A land ruled either by corrupt dictators or weak puppets, or in which the people's level of existence is even lower than before, will be a priceless propaganda weapon for the Communists, not an asset to the free world. Mothers will have wept over messages bringing news of the loss of sons, and wives will have lived through years of suspense, waiting for a word from their captive husbands, in order that Communism throughout Asia shall be strengthened by the failure of the West. That would be unthinkable. But the unthinkable can and does happen—precisely because men will not face up to it.

The Korean War, like all wars, produced its heroes, men who suffered, sacrificed and died either because of their natural courage or for love of their fellows or because of a deep belief in the rightness of their cause and devotion to the Faith that was theirs. They included ordinary soldiers and airmen of all nations. Some day their story—or part of it—will be told.

They included also that devoted band of Christian missionaries who found themselves overtaken by the war even before news of it had reached them. Among these were the Columban Fathers, priests from Ireland, America, Australia and New Zealand against whose forces the North Korean and Chinese armies were making war. They were known to the Communists for the fact that their Church was absolutely uncompromising in its hostility to the Communist creed and way of life. Theirs is a tale of sacrifice, heroism and martyrdom. But these were things with which its members were already familiar, for their missions had taken them to almost every trouble spot in Asia. From the start, their Society has been in the front line. And of nowhere is this more true than of Korea.

Theirs is an essential part of the story of Korea's hour of trial, but it is an essential part of Korea's future too. For around them and others like them is a minority of the faithful, implacable in its hostility to Communism, essentially Korean and of the people, yet sharing its Christian Faith with the West and free from the suspicion of corruption and double-dealing with which so many of its country's prominent leaders are tainted. Had that Catholic minority been larger, and had it numbered in its ranks more people equipped with higher education, trained to mould and lead public opinion, the story of the country as a whole might today be a different one. But even so, here is something upon which the West can build. Here is hope in a land and situation which at times seem hopeless. I am not for one moment suggesting that this minority should be viewed as just a convenient political asset for the West. But I do suggest that it should not be forgotten in the search for alternatives to those doubtful elements upon whom the West has had in recent years to depend.

Just as in any evaluation of the European scene it is unwise to forget that there is at least one organisation besides the Cominform which cuts across the frontiers—the ancient Faith of Christendom—so it is equally wise to remember that throughout Asia, too, today there are Catholic communities similarly linked by their religion with each other and with all the civilised free world. That is just a fact of history and of our times.

This is putting their importance at its lowest, political, level. The battle of our time is fundamentally a spiritual one. And in that battle they are bases for the spread of Christianity. Some day, in the perhaps not very distant future, if their homelands are not overrun by Communism, they will be colouring and enriching the thought of the once-Christian West, making their own mark upon Christendom just as did ancient Greece and Rome.

These are not necessarily the ideas and wide perspectives which fill the mind of the missionaries who work among the Asian peoples, as I soon realised when I saw them at their work in Hong Kong, Ceylon and Japan, as well as in Korea. For them it is sufficient that twenty centuries ago Christians were told to 'feed My sheep' and to go into all the world and preach the Gospel. They heard that same voice echoing down the ages, commanding them to make that their work. In moments of human exhaustion and depression these soldiers of Christ may sometimes have felt that they would like to see the whole of Korea disappear down the nearest rat-hole. Then, after a period on their knees, they declare that, given the chance, they will gladly go back to the scene of their suffering and carry on their work. They recall the past, review the present and ask: "What more must we do in the future?"

Their views, their hopes and fears are of importance. They are men who know more, perhaps, about the country and its real problems than anyone. They are men whose records are bright and untarnished. Some have already won the admiration of the whole Christian world; their names, because of their courage, are known to everyone who follows the

E*

news. But they are humble men, who do not tell their stories readily, they minimise what they have endured and give their views on what should be done next only with reluctance. They are witnesses of integrity who should be heard.

IX

THE CUTTING END

"THE Koreans are the laziest, dirtiest people on earth. Look at all these men and women standing around in broad daylight doing nothing whilst the road is still full of shell-holes that are absolute death-traps. The Korean Government is just as bad. It doesn't do a damned thing to the roads. And the country is the most awful bloody country on earth. It stinks."

So said the brash young man who was driving me across Seoul on the morning following my arrival. It was what returned prisoners of war and National Service men had told me in England, before I left for the Orient. It was pretty much what some of the war correspondents had written too. But it did not add up right, so far as I was concerned.

I might have asked the self-confident young sergeant in how many countries he had previously travelled and to what extent he was able to make any comparisons with other peasant peoples. I might also have pointed out that the men he referred to were standing idle because they were unemployed and that that type of idleness, far from being reprehensible, is tragic. Possibly his own father may have experienced it in the depression years of the 'thirties.

I could also have added that it was hardly surprising that a Government which could not afford to pay its police force with any regularity—with all that that means in terms of the possibilities of corruption—could hardly be expected to be able to pay for repairing every road, or even just the main roads, in a huge city like Seoul. To all that I could have added that people who live in holes in the ground, sleep on public squares or in the gutters, or spend their days and nights in shacks smaller and more primitive than the shed in which I keep my garden tools, could hardly be expected to be particularly clean.

But the jeep was noisily pursuing its bumpy way, going from side to side of the road as it zig-zagged around the pot-holes, and so I merely asked: "Do you really think it is their fault?" and left it at that. Before long, however, I was to be marvelling not at the dirtiness and laziness of the Korean people, but at their cleanliness and industry; and I was to be impressed, not by the ugliness of their country but by its grandeur and its beauty.

I understood, however, his—and the others'—purely subjective approach to these things. Had I come from the other side of the world to fight and possibly to die whilst others lived in peace I might have felt the same. And had I been put to spend a winter in a trench on a bleak mountain side in the heart of say, lovely Snowdonia, I would have to be unusually detached not to hate Wales, its climate, its countryside, the Welsh people and everything to do with them. Equally one could understand the feelings of the British or American soldier or war correspondent who reacted similarly to Korea.

I knew before I came out to Korea that it could not possibly be as bad as it had been painted by those who had seen it only under such unfavourable conditions. My hobby is growing ornamental shrubs, and I was aware that some of the loveliest in my own collection came originally from Korea. This hardly suggested that the country had no redeeming features. And I knew enough about the proud history of the Christian community in Korea to know also that its people must have some exceptionally good qualities.

Before the next month was out I was to love both the Korean people and their 'Land of Morning Calm'. It is a love which I shall keep throughout my days.

I was the only British journalist staying at press billets; the majority of the other war correspondents there were Americans. Some of them loved to put up a great show of being 'rugged', hard-drinking types, but an entirely endearing characteristic was revealed when a small boy in checked lumber-jacket and jeans came bouncing into the bare dining-room in the morning. His clothes were American, his talk was American, even his walk and his mannerisms were American, yet he was un-mistakably Korean. I got his story from a friendly U.S. news agency man. He had, it seemed, been brought to these all-male billets by an American correspondent when he was five years of age. He was an orphan who lived on the streets, keeping himself alive by earning a few hwan blacking shoes. When he was found he was completely black all over, ragged, lousy, wild and uncared for.

The correspondent brought him back with him, cleaned and fed him. Then he arranged with his wife back home to adopt him. The correspondent had been recalled to America by his paper and the small boy continued to live at the billets, cared for by the hard-drinking, 'rugged' pressmen whilst he waited for the adoption formalities to be completed. Then he would proceed to the U.S. to join his new foster-parents. Meanwhile he was the club mascot, spoiled by everyone, and lording it over a Korean staff who had to wait on him hand and foot. A difficult job awaited those foster-parents 'back home'. There were other waifs also around the billets whom the pressmen between them supported.

The U.N. Army Public Information Officers kept a steady flow of reports coming off the mimeograph machines, most of them about the work of rehabilitation conducted by the various U.N. and American agencies created for that purpose. That day's 'rehabilitation' news included a number of projects visited by a U.S. 'Governors' mission' which had just arrived in Seoul. The four governors had been to lay the corner-stone at the Buk Han San orphanage, third of three buildings being constructed under the sponsorship of the 314th Ordnance Group. It was a twenty-thousand-dollars project, which included the construction of three stone buildings and would provide living and school facilities for over a hundred orphaned children.

There had the previous night been a fire at Chunchon which had made homeless three thousand people who had only recently come back to the newly-reconstructed town, up near the 38th Parallel. The Army had already taken tents from the quartermaster's depot in Seoul by truck to Chun Chon as temporary shelter for the homeless. R.O.K. ('Republic of Korea', i.e. 'South Korean') Army units had erected the tents and additional homeless were being housed in a large warehouse. Food and blankets were being provided by the local Korean Civil Assistance Command team. Food was being augmented by army rations and "elements of the 24th Infantry Division and the Chunchon Area Command," said the report, "are being held in reserve in case needed to assist the K.C.A.C. team."

It all sounded very efficient and humane. I was later to hear the criticism that the nearer one got to the 'front', the more impressive were the rehabilitation and humanitarian activities, and the further one got away from it, the more was one likely to be conscious of the size of the bureaucracy rather than of the speed and effectiveness with which it worked. But even the sharpest of critics would still concede that there were many honourable exceptions to that wide generalisation.

I called at 'St. Columban's', the administrative centre of the Society of St. Columban in Korea, in Don Am Dong, a road leading out of the city to the north. I left some of my bags there, telling the Fathers that I hoped to be able to call again within the week. My immediate job was to get up to the British Commonwealth Division's sector of the front as soon as the necessary transport was available.

At St. Columban's that morning I met for the first time Fr. Brian Geraghty, Director of the work in the Korean Mission. My driver was waiting outside and Fr. Geraghty was busy preparing for a retreat for U.S. chaplains, and so we had time for no more than a few words together, but we were to see a lot of each other in due course.

No transport to the front would be available, I learned from the British public relations office, until next morning, and so, with time to kill, and knowing that the opportunity was not likely to be repeated, I spent the afternoon at the Chang Duk Palace, which had been the home—or rather homes, for there are in fact many palaces clustered together there—of the former imperial family.

The palaces and their huge grounds are right in the city itself, providing an enormous contrast to the thousands of close-packed houses which surround them.

The Chang Duk Imperial Palace was built by Tai Jong, third king of the Yi dynasty, in 1404. It became the main royal palace early in the seventeenth century, and between 1615 and 1910 (the year of the annexation of Korea by Japan) it was used by thirteen Korean kings.

Around the main palace, and in its grounds and gardens, were built over the years some one dozen lesser palaces and pavilions for other members of the royal family, or for the use of the emperors themselves. A hint of the life which is now gone, and which must always have been remote from that of the common people, is given by the uses to which some of the pavilions were put. For example, the Jon Duk Jong palace, built in 1644, was used by ladies of the court who, disguised as barmaids, sold drinks to the king and his courtiers. Another, Bum Woo Sa, which is on the way to the Jon Duk Jong, was built so that the king might rest as he went to and fro between his main palace and the 'bar'.

And in the magnificent gardens, the trees of which house the nests of hundreds of storks, is the Oak Ryu Chun, 'the artificial crystal stream' where the playboy King Yun San Kum in the sixteenth century played the game of 'Satyr pursuing the nymphs' through the woods.

All the buildings are wonderfully well preserved. They are built almost entirely of wood, every square inch of which is painted. Ceilings are heavily carved, and fascinating Eastern-type gargoyles chase each other over the brightly-coloured roofing tiles above.

To go, as I did, straight from the quiet, spacious palace gardens to some of the worst of the city's slums was to go from one world to another. I wandered for hours on my own through streets where the houses were piled up against each other on either side of narrow lanes along which ran open drains. Everywhere there were women washing clothes in little bowls outside their homes, beating them and pounding them to remove the dirt. The area was out of bounds to the troops, the war correspondents normally jeeped everywhere, and so my British uniform, with its United Nations 'flash', attracted more than usual attention. Over the markets hung the pervasive smell of the pickled turnips, onions, garlic and raw dried fish which form so large a part of the Korean diet They were smells with which I was soon to grow familiar enough, but they give one a feeling almost of nausea when first encountered at close quarters.

There was something curiously unreal about the jeep journey to the front. I had been warned that the dust was something exceptional, the road rough and the traffic fantastic. But I was still not prepared for what we got.

Before we set off, my driver covered my bits of baggage with huge army capes, which he tucked under and over each piece with great care. "The dust gets into everything—including your lungs," he said, "but you can't wrap them up in capes, unfortunately, so you just have to swallow the ruddy stuff instead."

We bumped along out of Seoul, taking the inevitable zig-zag course around the pot-holes, and then, as soon as we began to reach the country we met the dust, super-bumps and traffic all at once.

We ran into what appeared to be something a good deal worse than a London fog and found that it was created by a convoy of perhaps a score or so of huge army trucks on their way to the 'cutting end'—as the former front was still called. Slowly we began to overtake them, one by one, nosing our way blindly through the great white cloud that stretched across the road and out over the rice-fields on either side. But soon we found ourselves face to face with an even larger convoy of enormous lorries carrying anything from broken-down trucks to derelict tanks. We had neither heard nor seen them, for the noise of the convoy we were overtaking had drowned the sound, and the dust had hidden them from our view. With a quick turn of the wheel our driver brought our jeep sharply between two great trucks, leaving me feeling like a man riding a Shetland pony in the middle of a herd of elephants careering through the night.

So it went on for forty miles, passing one convoy after another, with dust clouds everywhere.

Our jeep jolted along over the rough roads until my back ached and I thought I would never again sit in comfort. The sharp grey dust swept out over peasants as they worked in the paddy-fields. It invaded the little newly-erected shops and homes which had replaced their burned or bombed-out villages, penetrating the high wooden screens the people had erected in a vain attempt to keep it out, in front of them. It lodged itself in throat and eyes, into every seam and stitch of my uniform.

Every few miles we passed trucks and jeeps stuck in the ditches at the roadside, with drivers waiting for the 'wrecker' gangs to come and drag their vehicles out again. Others were smashed beyond repair. Gloomily, my driver whiled away the time by telling me of all the men he had seen killed or injured— British and Americans—on this same road in recent months.

In the paddy-fields the peasants worked knee-deep in mud and water transplanting rice from the nursery beds or wading behind ox-drawn wooden ploughs. In those same fields were to be seen also the rusting remains of wrecked tanks and trucks, reminders of the battles which had so recently been fought there.

In the little village of Ui Jongbu (pronounced 'Wee John Boo' by the troops) through which we passed, there was the new Church of the Immaculate Heart of Mary, built very largely, I was told, by money subscribed by Catholic forces men. Then the road forked and we lost the American traffic which had constituted the bulk of what we had so far encountered.

With the consequent diminution of dust I was better able to see, and to appreciate, the countryside through which we were passing. It was, in any case, clearly improving scenically, for we were running into a more mountainous region. Villages became less frequent, the signs of military in residence more obvious, and soon we were in the fully militarised zone, almost entirely cleared of Korean civilians. By the time we reached Press Camp, where I was to stay, I knew that this was even better than the Korea I had hoped for. My tent was on a hill which looked down on to the Imjin River and across it to Red North Korea.

But as we unloaded our jeep, I found also that the dust was

even more penetrating than I could have believed possible, for it had got under the capes, despite all my driver's care, into every seam and stitch of my bags and even inside the case of my portable typewriter, and so into its mechanism.

Press Camp was as unlike the press billets in Seoul as anything could be. The billets were in the heart of the grim, wartorn capital. They were depressing both in themselves and in their surroundings. Up at the front the mountain scenery was superb, the spirit of the men serving under General Horatius Murray was magnificent.

"This place is a challenge to us," the General told me a few days later. We were sitting outside his tent looking out across the Red-occupied hills. Around him were his officers, to whom he frequently referred as he answered the questions I was putting to him.

"There is no civilian population here," he said, "and there were no amenities of any sort when we arrived, so we had to do everything for ourselves. We had to make our own light and power, lay on our water, make all our recreation and amusement."

He and his men had certainly measured up to the challenge. It was an unmistakable fact that in sharp contrast to what one found at the base, the spirit of the troops stationed on the edge of the six-thousand-yards demilitarised zone which separated the free world from the Communist one was superb.

Every possible facility for education, recreation and amusement had been provided for them. A man could learn anything from accountancy to Russian, photography to woodcarving, right there where only a few months earlier men of the same regiments had been fighting and dying.

At night I lay in my tent listening to guns being tried out on both sides of the corridor. The whole sky was lit by gunfire and, with the front winding about as it did, it was impossible to tell which was from the Communists' guns and which from ours.

In the morning I would wake and lie looking out through the open tent-flap, watching magnificent golden pheasants strutting unhurriedly among the camellias which covered the hillsides and which grew between the very tents themselves.

In the British Commonwealth Division were Australian, Canadian, New Zealand and United Kingdom troops, each with their own sector, but all under General Murray's command. As soon as one group finished a military exercise another would begin, so that there was constant activity around us all the time.

For the men concerned those exercises had an atmosphere of reality which no 'Blue versus Red' battle staged in Europe could possibly provide. For there, so recently, in those same hills, the battle had been hot and hard and cruel. The men who had fought in the famous battles of the Korean War had only a few months earlier been living in those same bunkers, hauling their guns and gear through the same passes, throwing bridges over the same rivers, dying in hundreds in that famous 'Gloucester Valley' so near at hand. The enemy they had fought then could still be seen and heard, not much more than a mere three miles away.

I was flown one day all over the front in a tiny two-seater Auster aircraft. "It's as near to being a bird as you can get," Colonel Derek Hogg, who was in charge of Press Camp, told me. The young pilot who took me up seemed as much at home with his tiny aircraft as any bird with its wings. The tiny open plane flew with roaring engine, twisting up and down the narrow valleys, actually turning round within them so that we skimmed the mountain sides closely enough to be able to shout to troops as we passed. Travelling up to the 'cutting end' from Seoul I had been conscious of how mountainous the country was, but it was only now that I saw the way in which one range of hills joins the next right across the face of the land.

I visited every part of the Division's area and many other sectors, too. I found plenty of evidence to support the view which General Murray had expressed to me that the Communists, knowing as they must do the strength of the defences which they would have to break through, would not be likely to invade again unless they had overwhelming air superiority. And if they had that, they would be ready for World War III— in which case Korea's plight would be no worse than that of the rest of the world.

The General was confident that there was nothing to show that any attack from the North was being prepared. All the military activity 'on the other side' was 'clearly defensive, not offensive'. This supported my own view, based upon political rather than military analysis, that the Communists, having unsuccessfully invaded once, when the Southern defences were relatively 'soft', and the South Korean Army almost non-existent and untrained, were not likely to try again, now that the opposition would be so much greater. Communists do not usually make the same mistake twice—and South Korea, strategically important to them as it may be, is hardly worth two major wars.

In fact, at that moment South Korea was the only place in Asia which was in direct juxtaposition to the Communist Empire, which was protected by a powerful defence system, manned by a highly-trained and mechanised army. General Murray, like the Americans, had been deeply impressed by the speed and success with which the 'Roks' (soldiers of the Republic of Korea) had learned the art of modern war.

At our meeting I naturally questioned the General and his officers about the possibility of a new war being started, this time by the South against the North. The consensus of opinion was that, although the Korean President had many times called for an attack upon the Communist North, he would need the aid of America and, to a lesser extent, of the other Allied Powers and that this would not be forthcoming. Indeed, the general view, I found, was that the Americans were deliberately keeping the R.O.K. Army on a short rein so far as cash and petrol were concerned in order to prevent him from taking any precipitate action. The one danger lay in his thinking that he could launch an attack which, although he knew he could not sustain it for more than forty-eight hours, might none the less lead to counter-attacks from the North in which American personnel might become involved and so the U.S. would be brought in too. The withdrawal of U.S. forces from South Korea, which had already started (and was subsequently to be stepped up later in the year), would possibly reduce this latter risk.

I had been lecturing to officers of the Australian Forces one day and was lunching with Father George Smith, one of the two keen young chaplains who between them were responsible for all the British Catholics at the front, in Seoul and right down to Pusan, in the extreme south, as well. With Father Smith was an Australian chaplain. For some days I had had an idea which I had been turning over and over in my mind and which I now put before them.

It was one of those hunches which are based upon intuition rather than upon any evidence, but which seemed sufficiently promising to be worth following through.

It was that this was a 'Catholic potters' area. That meant that it was, if my idea was right, one of the mountain areas into which the early Catholics were driven by persecution years ago, and where they have since remained as self-contained Catholic communities. I suggested that we should take a jeep and an interpreter and set off to see if I was right. The two chaplains only vaguely knew the extraordinary story of the 'Catholic potters' and so over lunch I was able to tell it to them, much as Korean missionaries had earlier told it to me. It is a fascinating tale of fidelity on the part of ordinary Koreans.

The Christian Faith penetrated Korea years before a single missionary had set foot upon its soil. It was propagated by Korean laymen and, by the time the first Mass was said there, Korea had four thousand baptised Catholics and could already claim two martyrs.

It was brought to Korea by Korean envoys at the court of Peking, where for years some learned Jesuits resided. These Jesuits were accepted at the court, where they occupied positions as lecturers in the physical sciences, and, of course, exerted an influence there. The envoys met both Fr. Ricci, an Italian of noble birth, and Fr. Verbiest, a Belgian, were impressed by them, and absorbed, and later passed on, some of their ideas. After the two Jesuit missionaries had died, later Korean envoys took home with them some of the books on Christian doctrine which the Manchu Emperor had permitted them to publish.

In the year 1777 a group of Korean savants decided to go into solitude for the purpose of contemplation and the study of philosophy. Among the Chinese books they took with them were some of those which the envoys had brought back from the Chinese court. They discussed at great length the doctrines expounded there, and found them so attractive that in the end they decided to apply the Christian precepts to their own lives.

From those curious beginnings there grew up a fervent Christian community. Only partly instructed, they convened a council at which they elected their own bishops and priests. For two years these men administered the sacraments, said Mass and continued to make converts. Then, in 1789, they examined their books more closely, and began to have doubts about the validity of their appointments. They submitted their case to a bishop in China, which led to the end of the clergy as such, but they still continued to teach, preach and baptise. When, in 1795, a Chinese priest at last managed to enter Korea, he found some four thousand Christians eagerly waiting for him. Thus, from the start, Korean Catholic laymen were accustomed to carrying on alone, and the persecutions which followed strengthened this tradition.

In 1801 the Government launched a terror campaign against them, cut many of them to pieces and for years tried to exterminate the Faith, for which hundreds willingly died. Those concerned were mainly members of the ruling class, but, to avoid the persecution, they were forced to flee to the hills and there, propertyless and landless, they became potters—the lowest of the low in Korean society. For eighty years, on and off, the persecution continued. The Korean Christians died for the Faith in their hundreds, their villages were razed to the ground, whole communities were wiped out. But Christianity lived on.

For fifty of those eighty years, members of the Paris Foreign Missions tried one after the other to get into the 'Forbidden Kingdom'. Each left the seminary in France expecting and ready for martyrdom. And one after the other they were caught and cruelly put to death. Their story is one of almost incredible pertinacity and heroism. Even before one missionary disguised as a Korean had entered, made first contacts and then been caught and executed—all usually within a matter of weeks—the next would be on his way, ready consecrated as a bishop in order to be able to ordain native clergy should he survive long enough to do so.

The first Korean priest, Andrew Kim, was ordained in 1884. One year after his ordination he was caught in dramatic circumstances and, at the age of twenty-six, beheaded. He is now Blessed Andrew Kim, whose statue may be seen in many a Korean home. In the last great persecution of 1866 two French bishops and seven priests of the Paris Missions were executed. Many of those Korean Christians who survived took to the hills and added to the number of 'Catholic potters' already there.

The Communists who now rule North Korea have already spent years trying once again to exterminate the Faith and already the ordinary Catholics have proved that their tradition of withstanding persecution and carrying on without either pastors or aid from outside is still a living thing. During the Korean War and in the period of disruption of ordinary life which has followed it, it is a tradition which is proving tremendously useful in South Korea too.

We set off together after lunch with a New Zealander driving our jeep and a Korean Army interpreter, a Catholic, to accompany us. The Korean had already told us that he knew that a Catholic village did, in fact, exist some twenty miles or so away, and he had a rough idea of its whereabouts.

We scoured the mountainous area just behind the front, passing through the Greek and Turkish sectors and making enquiries of the few Korean civilians who were just beginning to come back to re-start life in what had been the scene of years of bloody warfare. We found it at last, lying back off a road in a secluded valley. One could see how isolated it must have been before the days of motor vehicles, and why the persecuted Christians had chosen it as their hide-out.

As our jeep bumped along a rough ox-track we came in sight of the newly rebuilt village. At once the population came streaming out to see who we were. Our interpreter told them that there were two priests in our party and, as he did so, every face lit up, the word spread and from every house around us whole families came pouring out. Someone who had heard the news dashed straight for the church, rang the bell and soon the entire population was gathered around us, talking excitedly together.

Little children and men and women too came and dropped on their knees before us, asking a blessing. As all three of us were dressed more or less alike, in officers' uniforms, I found I was getting just as many requests for blessings as were the two priests. The scene was one of tremendous, happy excitement, but I saw the interpreter's face fall.

"It is Ascension Thursday," he said, "and they are not working today. Although they have no priest to remind them, they are keeping it as a holiday—as they were taught to do years ago when they had a priest of their own. They prayed this morning in the new church which they have built, asking that they might have the Mass. When I told them we had two priests with us they thought it was an answer to their prayers. Now we shall have to disappoint them."

He spoke to the crowd for a moment, telling them that the priests had not brought the Mass with them this time but would come again now that they had discovered their whereabouts. There was bitter disappointment on every face, women's eyes filled with tears and some of the men turned sharply on their heels and went back to their homes again, followed by the women and children.

We had a quick conference and decided that the jeep driver should dash back to camp, collect Fr. Smith's Mass kit, and then return as quickly as possible. The driver was a Catholic, and was the first to volunteer to do the long, rough trip. The interpreter told those of the crowd who had remained what we proposed doing. They clapped their hands with excitement at the news.

I asked them to show me their church and we all went in together. There I sat on one of the few chairs, which they insisted I should take, whilst the Koreans sat around me on the

floor answering my questions. It was my first real contact with
the Korean people in their own surroundings. There were
bright young women who sat quite unselfconsciously with their
babies at the breast. Some women gave the breast even to
children of three or four years of age who stood feeding whilst
their mothers sat on the floor. There were young men and
girls wearing a mixture of Korean and Western clothing, and
old men and women with the sort of deeply-lined faces, full of
character, which one finds in such abundance among peasant
peoples everywhere.

They had, they told me, lived in this same village of Hwang
In Sun before the war. When the war first began the men hid in
the mountains, hoping to be able to re-emerge when things
became more settled. Then, when they found that the Communists were driving all before them and looked as though they
might have come to stay, some came back and tried to carry on,
living their lives as Catholics as best they could. But the North
Koreans found some of the men in the hills and shot them, and
life became increasingly difficult. Having no priest, they had no
Mass, but, despite the presence of Communist troops in their
midst, still regularly met in their church for prayers.

So far my questions had been answered, in the main, by two
or three bright-faced, intelligent young fellows who acted as
spokesmen for the rest. Having been away fighting with the
R.O.K. Army for much of the war, they had constantly to refer
to the others before giving their replies. I noted with interest
that the women came into the conversation at least as much as
did the men. It was clear that there was no custom here of
women remaining silent in the presence of their men.

Then an elderly man came into the church and joined the
others. From his bearing, his intelligent face and his ease of
manner in my company it was obvious that he was a leader.
He was introduced as the 'headman', but my questions soon
revealed that in this village, where for generations Catholic lay
folk had had to depend on their own resources, the headman
was also the lay catechist—in other words his responsibilities
were both civic and religious.

The grandparents and great-grandparents of most of those

now living in the village, he said, had arrived there some seventy years ago, fleeing the persecution. They had become potters as so many of the early Catholics had been obliged to do, and to this day some half of the inhabitants still followed that same craft. The other half, having acquired a little land, were now peasant farmers. From the day of the arrival of the first refugees from the persecution they had remained solidly Catholic. Of the two hundred people now living there every single one practised the Faith.

The attempt to remain under Communist rule in the village, he said, had to be given up when it became part of the active fighting front, and all but a handful of the old and the sick who could not make the journey set out on the road south, taking as many of their possessions as possible with them. They were driven further and further down, along with hundreds of thousands of others, until they finally arrived in Pusan, in the southernmost tip of the country. After six months there the first ones began to make their way back, and by the end of the first year most had started on the north-ward journey home. But some thirty had died in exile, and others had been wounded, and a number of children had become separated from their parents on the roads choked with refugees and had never been found.

When the villagers got back they found that all but nine of the houses in their village had been totally destroyed along with the church. So they all set to, building new houses and a new church, together. One day an American chaplain discovered them, collected some money from his troops and returned with a gift with which they were able to acquire some materials and proper fitments for the church.

With immense pride the headman, with others joining in, told me that only two weeks ago a boy from this village, which throughout its history had had for most of the time to do without priests, had been ordained a priest in Seoul.

Each morning and evening they met in the church for prayers, led by the headman, and on Sundays, again under his leadership, the whole village gathered to sing the prayers from the Mass and to say the Rosary.

As the headman talked to me the bell began suddenly to ring excitedly and the church quickly filled with people. In answer to my question he told me that the people had posted watchers in the hills to look out for our jeep driver returning with the Mass kit, and they had sent a messenger to say that he had now been spotted.

It was more than five minutes after the ringing of the bell that he actually drove into the village. Their watchers, it seemed, had sharp eyes. By the time he arrived one hundred and ninety-seven of the two hundred people in the village were in the church. The remaining three were too ill to get there.

As Fr. Smith prepared the altar, the Australian chaplain told the people, through the interpreter, that Mass would now be celebrated and asked that those who intended taking Communion should raise their hands. At once half a dozen, speaking together, said that they had all eaten that day and so could not communicate.

"We'll give you a dispensation, just as we do for the troops," the Australian chaplain answered. With neither priest knowing a word of Korean, confessions were out of the question, but the overwhelming majority none the less went to Communion.

Throughout the larger part of the Mass the people, still sitting on the floor, repeated prayers aloud, led by the headman, then melodiously sang hymns together as the Mass ended.

It was a scene I was to see repeated scores of times in every part of the country during the weeks which followed, but there was something peculiarly impressive about these simple Christian folk, observing the holidays of the Church on their own and continuing their worship with no priest to lead them, just as their forefathers had done in the early days of the Faith in Korea centuries ago.

Before we left, the two priests promised to come regularly with the Mass in future.

At this first direct contact with Koreans I felt an immediate liking for these simple, shrewd people, with their ready smiles and quick, intelligent response to questions. And as

Catholics they impressed me enormously with their restrained fervour and their great loyalty to the Faith. Those first impressions were immensely strengthened when I later came to see more of them as I went around the country.

**In Pious Memory
of the deceased**

Father Adelard Thuente, O.S.B.

Born in Festina, Iowa, June 6, 1910; professed July 11, 1932; ordained priest June 6, 1938; died April 15, 1962.

Absolve, we beseech Thee, O Lord, the soul of Thy servant Adelard from every bond of sin, that, in the glory of the resurrection, he may rise to a new and better life with Thy saints and elect. Through Christ, our Lord. Amen.

Eternal rest grant unto him, O Lord. And let perpetual light shine upon him. May he rest in peace. Amen.

Father Adelard Thuente, O.S.B.

X

PROFIT AND LOSS IN PUSAN

IN the summer of 1954, when I visited Pusan, there was, perhaps, nowhere on earth where there was more concentrated misery to be found. Yet a year or two earlier the hardship and suffering had been on an even greater scale.

Pusan is the city into which vast masses of the civilians of South Korea were driven as refugees by the North Korean Army in the first days of the war. When the Chinese came into the war even more were driven down, until the numbers involved ran into millions.

The refugees came from every part of the Republic. Peasants who had left their land and the place where their families had for generations had their roots, and workers from Seoul and other urban areas, alike, left home and went further and further south, with the guns and tanks of the enemy behind to hurry them on. They went till they could go no further. So they reached Pusan, beyond which was the sea.

Pusan was the port into which the United Nations forces streamed when U.N. came into the war. For this reason it was seen as a place of refuge—and there was no end, it seemed, to the number of refugees who streamed into it. Its population doubled, trebled, quadrupled and went on growing and growing until no one could even guess how many suffering human beings had crowded into it.

The city's natural setting is quite delightful—a much lovelier version of Dover or Folkestone. The city is much like any other Oriental port. Dockworkers' homes huddle together near the waterfront, there is street after street of small shops and then comes a commercial centre behind them. It was already a crowded city even by Eastern standards and a vastly overcrowded one by those of the West, so when the refugees arrived they had to build any sort of shelter they could throw together, on any few spare feet of space which they could find. Row upon row of dreadful little shacks, made from cardboard packing-cases, scraps of wood, sacking and old oil drums, sprang up everywhere, with often no more than two feet or so between one row and the next. It goes without saying that there was complete absence of any sanitary arrangements, water or other amenities.

The refugees showed enormous ingenuity, as Koreans always do, even making roofs, and in some cases whole houses, from one-pint beer-cans, which they flattened out, then riveted together into sheets. But all the inventiveness on earth would not have prevented Pusan from becoming the most appalling slum.

Those shacks were still there, just as overcrowded and older and shabbier than before, when I arrived one morning early in June, 1954. The largest was, perhaps, the size of the garden shed in which I keep my tools; even the best among them was not in such good condition or as solidly made. The average size was, perhaps, four feet by six feet. In these cold, draughty, leaking, ramshackle constructions lived whole families.

I had said my good-byes to Colonel Derek Hogg, in his Press Camp on the camellia-covered hillsides of the front, and then, teaming up with Fr. George Smith, had jeeped to Seoul and caught the night train down.

Like him, I travelled on my army orders, on the special train which is reserved for U.N. personnel.

The United Nations trains had formerly been American hospital trains. Now the coaches were fitted with reasonably comfortable bunks, which stood three tiers high on either side. Guards with revolvers at their hips patrolled the train from end to end all night in case of a possible ambush as we went through what was still guerilla country.

This, of course, was what officials had meant when they told me that I should stay, and travel, only where logistical support could be provided. The people in charge had no desire to have a civilian-turned-soldier who was temporarily their responsibility shot by Communist guerillas.

But one journey on the comfortable U.N. train was enough to tell me that if I wanted to get to know Korea and the Koreans this was no way to do it. Going only where logistical support could be provided meant that you met only Westerners and Korean camp followers and stayed only in places dominated by Western personnel.

And that, of course, is as much of the Korean land and people many a war correspondent and military man saw at any time.

However, for the moment I was still making the most of the facilities offered me as a war correspondent and I travelled in relative comfort.

It was just before seven in the morning when we got to Pusan. An army jeep was there to meet us, which took us the length of the waterfront on our way to the camp where we were to stay.

Already the refugees were busy outside their shacks. Women, sitting on their heels in the mud, which came right up to their doors, valiantly wrestled with clothes in tiny bowls of thick water and contrived, in some way which I never could explain, to produce finished laundry of astonishing whiteness. Men blew at fires lit in the open, from which came huge clouds of the most foul-smelling smoke I have ever encountered.

Small fish lay spread in rows on roofs, or were impaled on the railings surrounding military buildings and other establishments on the dockside, drying in the sun and wind. The smoke, the fish, the piles of green onions which were being carried to and from the shops, the lack of sanitation, the filthy mud and the mass of human beings living in too close proximity to each other combined to produce a heavy, stifling smell which almost took one's breath away.

I had marvelled in the past when I had seen Dublin slum children setting off to Mass on Sunday morning in snow-white boots and shoes; negro girls emerging from shockingly dilapidated houses in Chicago, resplendent in well-pressed and gay clothes which outshone the sun itself. I had marvelled, too, as I had watched Indian women in Delhi come up from the holes in the ground in which they lived, to greet the morning in sarongs of the most beautiful colours. But nothing mystified me more than to see teen-aged girls in Pusan setting off from those dreadful stinking shacks for school, dressed in snow-white blouses with not a crease nor a spot of dirt on them anywhere. They are the answer to those who have said and written that the Koreans are a lazy, dirty race.

That first drive to the camp outside Pusan gave me some idea of the depths of squalor to which hundreds of thousands of peaceful people had been driven by the Communist attack. Later I was to see something of the suffering they endured, too.

I had gone with Fr. Smith to the station, in the city centre, to enquire about ways of getting to Mokpo, over on the country's south-western tip, to which I proposed moving on when I had finished at Pusan. Mokpo was not a military centre, there were no U.N. personnel there (and therefore no 'logistical support' either). The R.T.O. did not even know of its existence. After consulting Korean rail clerks and guide books and making various phone calls he finally discovered a train which, he understood, ran from time to time. He would give me more details next day. But he went on to suggest that probably the best thing would be to go back to Seoul by U.N. train and let the military authorities there fix transport for me. I had no desire to continue under Western control any longer than was necessary and so said I would call back again. I was as keen to be free of that 'logistical support' as he was that I should have it. Meeting the real Koreans in Hwang In Sun had whetted my appetite for more.

As we came out from the station a boy in his early teens threaded his way through the traffic which careered past him. He walked horizontally, on all fours, like an animal, stiff-backed from some war injury, holding a wooden block in each hand to save the palms of his hands, and lifting his head from time to time to see where he was going.

Then a legless boy of eight or nine years of age propelled himself past us, pushing himself along the pavement on his behind, again by means of a block of wood held in either hand.

Around the station the shoe-shine boys—homeless war-waifs ranging from four or five to fifteen or sixteen years of age, black as the polish they used and dressed in incredibly torn and filthy rags—clamoured for business. The majority suffered from ringworm and other scalp and skin diseases.

We climbed a near-by hill together, through yet another shanty district. As on the waterfront, the tiny, improvised huts were massed together on every available inch of space, reeking of pitifully overcrowded humanity. And again there were the inevitable women conscientiously washing clothes in tiny drops of precious water; pounding and rubbing and beating them to get them clean. There were dirt and squalor in plenty, but it was not because they were not resisted by the people condemned to endure such things. It was because when bad conditions are on such a scale they must at some point defeat those who live in them.

I peeped into some of the shacks as I passed. Typically, the Koreans did not resent my curiosity. The more permanent-looking 'houses', constructed of wood and roofed with corrugated iron, had well-scrubbed wooden floors. They were the homes of the richer refugees. Others, made of cardboard and bits of old rice-straw matting and sacking, had mud floors wet from the rain which came in through their leaking roofs and trodden in from outside.

Lacking any fireplace in such improvised dwellings, the people cooked on fires which they lit on the ground outside their front doors. The rainy season had started (it had come early) and that made things bad enough. What life was like in winter for these wretched people just did not bear thinking about.

That night I was taken to a club where members of the various United Nations rehabilitation bodies congregated—almost within sight, sound and smell of some of the refugee areas. People sat in groups or stood at the bar in an atmosphere which was one of relative comfort and good living. The conversation was sophisticated, urbane and, in the main, trivial—much as it is in any club, anywhere.

The men told 'blue' stories in quiet voices over their drinks.

F

Rather frighteningly efficient-looking women laid down the law to anyone who would listen. Others, wives of officials, talked local gossip—the gossip, that is, of the little world which they had built for themselves within that hungry, squalid, over-crowded, larger world about them, where women cooked their food in rusty tins thrown away by improvident Westerners, over fires made of refuse, or washed from morning till night to defeat the lice and diseases which come with dirt. The world where sick children lay on wet mud floors and rain drove through holes in soggy cardboard walls.

The atmosphere, refreshingly sweet after the stench I had endured earlier in the day, was none the less disturbing and unreal. Such relative comfort seemed almost indecent in such a setting.

People were pointed out to me by name. "He gets £1,500 a year for his work on such and such a project." Or, "That one gets £1,500—never earned a penny more than £600 before he got in on this racket." The stench of the shanty towns began to seem almost attractive.

I talked also to men trying hard to win a battle against bureaucracy so that they could make rehabilitation a reality. They were fighting against one of the besetting sins of people in all such organisations—to see the compilation of impressive-sounding reports as an end in itself. To see their work, not in terms of human beings rescued from degradation, but in terms of statistics. In the main they tended in fairness to blame the nature of the organisations, which, having grown out of war conditions, were almost inevitably imperfect affairs, rather than individuals. One felt, too, that the sheer immensity of the job and the sense that no matter what they did they could as yet do little more than scratch the surface, weighed heavily upon those who worked in them.

"We were told that the rehabilitation of Korea was going to be carried through like a military operation," one intelligent, conscientious official told me. "So far I cannot claim that we have yet started making the serious attack. We're still preparing for it, and we're hoping that the funds don't run out before we are ready to go over the top."

Remembering what I had already seen of the size and urgency of the problem, I hoped so too.

He talked wistfully of plans for building power plants and bridges; huge schemes for putting the country's economy on some sort of a sound basis, but again he voiced the fear that, despite all the preparations, many of these larger schemes would not materialise because of a shortage of cash arising from a loss of interest on the part of the people of the West.

Of the achievements of the less ambitious projects there was clearly more to tell—attempts at rehousing refugees and the victims of the fires which had robbed so many of even the pitiful little homes they had, distribution of food, clothes, blankets. But still only the fringe of the need seemed to be met. The great mass of hungry, homeless people remained. And so did the basic causes of their hunger and homelessness.

I set out next morning for the clinic run by the Maryknoll Sisters. I had already been given glowing accounts of the work of these nuns by officers at the R.A.S.C. camp where I was staying.

"That's where you will really see things being done," they told me.

We left at ten o'clock in the morning, planning to do the five or six miles by jeep, meet the nuns, see their work and be back at camp for lunch. In fact, we did not get there at all, thanks to a typically Korean situation.

We had just got into the commercial part of the city when we met a traffic diversion which took us down streets completely unknown to our driver. Soon we realised that we had become part of an enormous traffic jam. At first we moved slowly forward, along with a wonderful assortment of Western and Oriental vehicles. Then we proceeded in short spurts, broken by long intervals when we remained stationary. Finally we came to a stop in a shopping street in which the jam was absolute. Traffic pointed in both directions and spilled over on to the sidewalks on either side of the road. Motorists blew continuously at their horns, not with any hope of achieving any movement of traffic as a consequence, but to relieve their own feelings. Then came a cloud-burst to add to the general inconvenience.

The jam was at least a democratic one. Behind us was a huge six-wheeled open truck on which was an American Army band. The men sat on folding stools, instruments in hand, with the rain pouring down over them. In front of us was a Korean with a handcart. Beside us on our right was a weirdly home-made-looking van driven by a young Korean. On our left a British Army brass-hat sat in a jeep, very straight and stiff, never flicking so much as an eyelid as the rain battered in through the open sides of the vehicle.

And there we stuck for an hour and a quarter, never moving an inch. In London or New York it is fairly safe to say that those involved would have been thoroughly irritated. Most of the Koreans, however, seemed either to regard it philosophically, with impassive faces, or to treat it as a huge joke.

The jam was caused, we were informed, by a Government-organised demonstration of students, all of whom had been ordered to march in support of some demand which the Rhee Government was making on the Americans or the United Nations, no one seemed sure which.

We talked with Korean pedestrians who threaded their way through the mass of vehicles, here and there finding one who knew enough English to grumble at the waste of their time and, in particular, of the wasted time of the students.

At last straggling groups of teen-age girls and boys, soaked to the skin, began to pass us. The girls' white blouses clung to them like wet rags, rain ran down from the fringes of black hair over their foreheads and into their eyes. In their hands they held limp little flags. They looked thoroughly miserable, but when they saw us grinning they grinned back, for Koreans rarely miss a chance of smiling at their own or each other's misfortunes.

Then the traffic began to move and we passed large orderly processions making their way back to schools and colleges in various parts of the city.

"If Syggy Rhee would cut out all the compulsory parades for students the school hours could be cut by twenty-five per cent," someone said as we set off, not to the Maryknoll nuns' clinic, but to camp again. For the entire morning had gone in trying to travel the few miles across the city and now it was already lunchtime.

The one thing I had got out of it was an insight into the contrast between the reactions of a Western crowd, obsessed with speed, and those of an Oriental one, to whom time means so much less. On the whole the reactions of the Orient seemed to be the more sane and much less likely to lead to stomach ulcers and psychopathic states.

We tried again in the afternoon and this time did the journey to the convent clinic in some twenty minutes. Outside the gates sat women and children who had climbed the hill and were resting, too exhausted by illness or hunger to go the few steps further until they had had a rest.

Inside we met a great throng of people, mainly woman and children, who filled the courtyard and spilled over into a long queue. There were sick women sitting on the ground, leaning limply against walls or trying to feed babies at the breast. Others sat with sick and, in all too many cases, dying children lying across their knees. Passively, with amazing patience, they just waited their turn.

A nun in a white, starched habit showed us into a cool, clean waiting-room. Then we were taken down a passage smelling of the usual hospital mixture of antiseptics and medicines and into a dispensary, where we met the smilingly efficient Sister Rose of Lima.

Sister Rose, like the other Maryknoll Sisters there, was very American. That is to say, she was justifiably conscious of the value of statistics and of publicity. She had most of the facts and figures concerning the clinic at her finger-tips, and where this was not the case she had them readily available in a large card index. She had drive, enthusiasm, and a great love of God and of suffering mankind.

There were, she said, eighteen of the Sisters in all, fourteen of whom had had full medical training. They were aided by a group of Korean nuns and nurses and a Korean doctor. Ten men and women were employed full-time as catechists. In all they had eighty-five Koreans on their pay-roll in various capacities. The work this team was doing was tremendous.

The past four weeks, she said, had been their record month. In that period they had treated in the clinic forty-three thousand three hundred and twenty-four patients, mainly women and children, and had made thirteen thousand and eleven home visits, taking with them gifts of food or attending the sick. More than half of those treated had tuberculosis, regardless of what else they might be suffering from. The overwhelming majority also suffered from malnutritional diseases and illnesses arising from bad social conditions—skin diseases, worms and flukes of every sort.

The sicknesses treated ranged through leprosy, cholera and other highly infectious fevers and on through almost the whole catalogue of lesser human ailments. At that moment they had more than eight hundred children with tuberculous bones who were in plaster casts and ninety-three with the dreaded tuberculous meningitis.

All were 'out-patients', since this was only a clinic. The one redeeming aspect of this situation, where even the worst cases got no hospitalisation, was, said Sister Rose, that the sense of family among Koreans was so strong that the child lying desperately ill on the mud floor of a refugee's shack was probably happier than he would be in the cleanest and best of hospital wards. To that extent, and that only, there was sometimes a greater probability of recovery in those wholly unideal conditions than would be present in hospital. Otherwise, of course, the situation was in every way deplorable from the medical and social point of view, particularly when it came to infectious and contagious diseases.

Other information she produced concerning the Sisters' work for suffering human bodies included the fact that the nuns were supporting an average of three hundred and ten families on full food relief, they were distributing five hundred lbs. of free milk-powder daily, they were giving employment to forty war widows whom they had taught to paint on textiles and another fourteen who made women's garments in the traditional Korean style, out of men's shirts sent from America.

The drugs, clothes, milk-powder, food and cash were almost all coming free of charge from American Catholic War Relief Services.

The statistics for the spiritual side of their work, which the Sisters kept with equal care, were equally impressive.

In the past four weeks they had had two hundred and forty-nine baptisms, one hundred and sixty-six of whom were infants. In the preceding three years and two months, since the nuns had re-established themselves after the end of the first phase of the war, they had had seven thousand three hundred baptisms. Four hundred and twenty-two adults had that week, at the clinic or through the home visitors, heard of Christianity and the Church for the first time. Each month more than five hundred people heard of God for the first time. Over seven hundred children attended catechism classes every Sunday morning, under the guidance of nuns or their catechists. In addition, they were making themselves responsible for the education of one hundred and forty young children whose parents could not afford to send them to school. All education is normally paid for directly by the parents and the average Korean will make every possible sacrifice in order to send his children to school.

Behind the statistics were of course the human stories. Sister Rose, for example, told me of the woman whom they had recently nursed and who for over twenty years had been a devil-worshipper. She died in the Faith after two Sisters had taken it in turns to sit with her for the whole of each night for two weeks.

She told me, too, how she sat up at night with the dying, reading to them translations she had done from Gerald Vann's book, *The Divine Pity*—and making converts by it.

"You should see this place on Sunday," said the tall, white-robed nun, with her eyes sparkling. "The whole hillside is ablaze with groups of people on every little rocky gap between the refugees' houses. In the centre of each group is a nun or catechist instructing them in the Faith they are clamouring to have. The number of converts here is limited only by the number of people available to instruct them. If we had the missionaries and priests we'd make the country."

Over and over again I was to hear almost those same words, wherever I travelled, among Catholic missionaries in North, South, East and West of the Republic of Korea.

Then I went to see the work in practice, mingling with the patients who sat in the corridors, crowded the waiting-rooms, queued outside, and filled the courtyard like some great crowd waiting to attend a football match. It was a great mass of patient, suffering, afflicted and deprived humanity.

A mother carried in a boy of perhaps eight or nine years of age in her arms and laid him on the floor. The nun who was in attendance pulled up his clothes to examine him. His arms and legs were those of a skeleton, his face was just a skull with still barely living yellow flesh stretched over it. His eyes were already dead. His abdomen was enormously extended and hard as a football.

"He is beyond hope," said the Sister to us over her shoulder. "We get so many of these cases of sheer starvation."

As Sister Rose of Lima took us among the crowd, mothers tugged at her habit begging her to do something for their dying children. They begged urgently yet quietly, in broken voices, knowing that before them in the queue were hundreds of others, equally in need of urgent attention. They knew, too, that soon night would come, the gates would close and hundreds would have to be told that they must come back tomorrow. But tomorrow for many would be too late.

Inside the building were the handful of nuns, the doctor, and their life-saving drugs. But there were so many sick, so few to attend them, and only twenty-four hours to the day.

That situation had made the Sisters lose nights of sleep. What *does* one do when the stream of suffering never dries up? When you work from daybreak till dark and still the queue is just as big?

At first you are magnificently, recklessly heroic. You toil on literally night and day. But the queue stays just as big. And the team of helpers grows smaller as one after another the over-heroic ones break down. Soon the daily total number of cases treated grows less as a consequence and you realise that in the long run you will achieve more, not less, by limiting the hours of work to allow yourself at least some little sleep. But that means closing the gates, telling people to come back on a tomorrow which they will never know on this earth. It means going to bed aware that there may still be hundreds waiting, just as patiently as ever, refusing to go away, so that they may be among the first in the morning. You hear them in the night and go out and try to do something for the most urgent cases, losing the strength which comes from sleep and which you will need tomorrow and the next day and the next and the next.

That is the life of the nursing nun in Pusan. And it is just one aspect of what the war which the Communists launched upon the Korean people means to the women and children who have broken under the strain of living the lives of refugees in an Eastern land which lacks all those facilities we take for granted.

We went through the dispensary, saw the war widows working in the 'Nazareth Workshop' from which they sent abroad hand-painted head-scarves and other painted textiles to raise much-needed cash to help carry on the work. As we left the clinic, drugs and medicines were being passed through a hatch in the outside wall to a queue of men who were getting what they could for wives or children too sick to come themselves.

Sister Rose of Lima led us down to the gates, telling us as she went of the one-hundred-and-sixty-bed hospital they hoped soon to have, with a nurses' training school which would be in many respects the most important part of the establishment, since from it would go a stream of trained Korean nurses to spread healing far and wide.

It was, she said, to be an Armed Forces Memorial Hospital, and already promises of handsome gifts from American Forces men were coming in. The evidence of the G.I.s' magnificent generosity are everywhere in Korea.

As she let us out through the gates we saw lying on the pavement a woman sprawled in a faint, with a child still tugging at the breast. And as our jeep took us away I saw Sister Rose lifting the baby as she stooped over the mother's prostrate form.

The jeep hurried off down the hill, but as it slowed down behind another vehicle I just had time to see a woman sitting

F*

anxiously looking down on her man as he lay stretched on the sidewalk with his head in her lap.

In London or New York in such circumstances you phone for a doctor, an ambulance quickly arrives on the scene, the patient is taken to hospital and soon he is getting every possible care.

But what do you do in a city where there are thousands of such cases and where, moreover, there are no public telephones, and where there are no ambulances available and no doctors or hospitals either? What, indeed, but hope that Sister Rose of Lima or someone like her may get there in time?

Was Sister Rose's estimate of the prospects for conversions in Korea a too optimistic one, based upon an exceptional response to an exceptional effort? I went next day to see Father Connors, an American Maryknoll missionary in another part of the town, to see what he had to report.

Fr. Connors knew his Korea well. Before coming to Pusan in 1951 he had spent ten years up in Pyongyang, above the 38th Parallel, in what is now Communist North Korea.

He had worked there until the Japanese war began, had six months in jail, then was sent back to the United States. By the time he returned North Korea was Communist-ruled and the South was a battlefield. He set up a little parish in Pusan with just forty-five people who met in a small room. Catholics among the refugees helped to swell their numbers, but to them he had added eight hundred converts whom he had baptised, and the number was going up and up.

His house had been the home of a Japanese official in the days when Pusan was a Japanese city, and the grille he used for confessions was made from a typically Japanese door-screen which still bore a traditional-type painting. As we talked, a Korean house-boy slowly emptied bags of rice on to sacks laid out on the ground, letting the wind blow away the chaff as he did so.

"We've just had a big new consignment in for distribution to the hungry," Fr. Connors told me. "By tomorrow it will all be gone."

He had, he said, been able, as the result of gifts from America, to give rice, fish and flour, received from the National Catholic Welfare Conference, to more than five thousand families.

"We give it out to the neediest first-comers," he went on, "regardless of whether they are Pagans, Protestants, or Catholics, and regardless, too, of whether we can hope ever to see them again. We don't want 'rice Christians' and we don't need to try to make them. Genuine would-be converts are coming more quickly than we can handle them in any case. It is very sad that there are so few priests here at this moment of opportunity. The French and German missionaries worked hard for generations with no hope of ever seeing anything like the present opportunities."

He estimated that at that moment there were some ten thousand Catholics in Pusan as compared with five hundred before the war. From Pusan were now going out to every part of South Korea converts who had found the Faith whilst they were refugees. His own progress, for local reasons, he said, had been comparatively slow. A near-by priest who was using a former Buddhist temple as his church had had twice the number of converts.

"Put a man in any place anywhere in South Korea today," he said, echoing Sister Rose of Lima's sentiments of the previous day, "and you will get a stream of converts at once."

I asked him why he thought this sudden opportunity had come. His answers were ones I was to get in one form or another all over Korea in the following weeks:

"The Koreans have a deep religious sense—and a very inadequate religion. Since their recent troubles, and as a result of all their suffering and their experience of atheistic Communism in practice, they are asking: 'Is there a God? Is there a soul?' They don't shy away from religious discussion."

They had, he went on, seen the extent of Catholic generosity as revealed by the aid which had come from the American Catholic community. Equally important, they had seen that, unlike some Christian sects, the Catholics had distributed that aid regardless of the religion of the recipients. There were seventy free milk distribution centres, in all parts of South

Korea, run by Catholic organisations and maintained by the generosity of U.S. Catholics. "Here in Pusan nearly five thousand children are regularly getting free warm milk," he said.

He had a tremendous respect for Koreans generally and the Korean Catholics in particular. On the previous day Sister Rose had told me that Koreans made "the loyalest Catholics on earth." Fr. Connors now made that same point.

"Koreans are great at taking trials and tribulations, in accepting adversity without too much complaint. I never heard any cry-baby stuff right through all the worst days we ever had even here in Pusan, with all its misery. And our Catholics were superb. Their faith was a tremendous help to them and they took everything that came magnificently.

"The Koreans are always willing to work and greedy for education, for jobs and for any opportunity. They would far rather have a job than charity. The women are great with the needle and wonderful at contriving ways of earning cash. You can see them any time selling apples, home-made drinks, and ice-cream on the streets."

But he was gravely concerned about the effect of the war and the impact of Western troops and Western ideas upon Korean morals.

"There has been a terrible change," he said. "In the old days I never dreamed of having locks on my doors, but I have now. I'd lose everything if I didn't."

I asked him what he thought was the direct cause of this decline in honesty and morals generally.

The Koreans, he answered, had always been thrifty. They had very little, so what they had they valued. There was no waste and practically no pilfering. They were pagans, but their ideas regarding honesty were based upon their value of every smallest thing capable in any way of being put to human use. And, of course, the Japanese by their strictness had helped to keep any pilfering in check.

Now, for the first time, they had large numbers of people living among them who had an entirely different approach. They observed the way in which Americans wasted things they would have valued and could still use—empty bottles, beer and food cans, cigarette stumps, timber. They found in army dustbins food for want of which Koreans were dying, discarded socks and other clothes which a Korean would use for years.

It was an easy step from picking up the quarter-smoked cigarette which the G.I. had stubbed out and thrown away—which was regarded by the American as legitimate—to taking the cigarette lighter he left for a moment on the beer counter—which was regarded as quite different by the American but not by the Korean.

As I later went around Korea I was to hear many stories of that decline in honesty: of tyres, carburettors and even engines, whipped off cars and trucks which had been left unattended in the streets, stolen jeeps and a host of other things, appearing on the black market. In some cases the thefts had clearly been made with the connivance of Western troops. How else explain the bulldozer, of all things, which in one town I visited was changing from one hand to the next on the black market? Or the book I saw offered for public sale in a Pusan second-hand book shop, giving details of a wide variety of arms and ammunition, supported by pictures, and marked 'Restricted security information'?

Any old Korea hand will tell you that prior to 1945 the Korean people as a whole were more than usually honest, and that the new reputation for dishonesty—and the grounds for it —which they have acquired came with the arrival of Western troops. It is, therefore, rather hard on the Koreans that one of the things some of those same troops now hold against them is their constant pilfering.

In fairness to the Korean people, one must also add that it is still probably only a minority which has been demoralised in this way—principally those who are directly in touch with Western personnel or living in centres where their influence is strong. But those, of course, are usually the only ones the people from the West ever get to know.

In Pusan, too, I first saw at close range another consequence of the impact of the West upon Korean morals. There were many troops and employees of the various rehabilitation projects in the city. There were also a lot of Korean prostitutes, some unofficial brothels and a good many Korean girls who were obviously being kept by someone in a position to get supplies of Western clothes, cosmetics and cheap jewelry.

Korean girls can be very lovely, with their straight dark hair, their ready smiles, good teeth, magnificently upright carriage and pride of bearing, naturally good figures and general lack of sophistication. The national costume, worn by practically all those women who have not been Westernised in the wrong way, suits them superbly. It is simple, but just right, with the short coatee and long, loosely hanging skirt and Oriental shoes with turned-up toes. Sometimes the outfit is all white—usually so with the peasant women—at other times, colourful and extremely tasteful.

But there is something pathetic, and almost indecent, about the girl who has been changed from that natural beauty into something which belongs neither to East or West.

She has permed hair, sometimes even peroxided, clothes bought for her from a mail-order firm on the other side of the world, high-heeled, sling-back shoes and cosmetics intended for a complexion quite unlike hers. She walks in a different way from other Korean girls, has a different, bolder manner and a great air of sophistication. She would not look a good type in Britain or America. She looks revolting—and pathetic—in Korea.

She, too, is a new phenomenon in Korea. Koreans have more than their share of natural goodness. That is a view held by every missionary I met, and I had many evidences of it myself, as I travelled around the country.

In the past, among the signs of that natural goodness were not only their honesty but their strict moral code in relation to sexual matters.

There was polygamy, but prostitution was rare, it had little part in Korean life. Big cities like Seoul or Pusan might have their 'bad girls', but outside that there was remarkably little promiscuity, either amateur or professional, of any kind. The 'camp follower' type, now all too common, was unknown. The girl who was no longer a virgin stood little chance of marriage.

She was made an outcast by a pagan peasant community which had its own stern code and its own stern way of dealing with those who defied it.

When, after the arrival of the Western troops in 1945, the first seductions, and some cases of rape, occurred, fierce reprisals were taken by the Koreans themselves. Some of those thought to be responsible are said to have been killed, others were mutilated in such a way as to ensure that they would never again repeat that particular offence. Depriving an innocent girl of her virginity was something which was seen as the worst of outrages, deserving the worst of punishments.

Today there are probably some thousands of prostitutes and a far larger number of kept women. The Westerner has an extraordinary ability to make something known to be reprehensible seem almost respectable by finding a new label for it. The label in this case is 'shacking up with a moose'.

'Moose', or 'moosey-may' is taken from the Japanese word *musume*, a girl. 'Shacking up with a moose', means quite simply keeping a Korean as your mistress. Only a minority of American and Commonwealth troops 'shacked up with a moose' and the British boys could not afford it. (Those so inclined, therefore, tended to go for the prostitutes, which was much more dangerous, resulting in a higher incidence of V.D.) But enough have done so over a period of years to leave behind a large number of these girls, who have been spoiled in every way. No decent Korean man will have them. They are outcasts among Korean women. Their outlook, their standards, their mode of life are all alien and cannot, in any case, be supported once the troops have gone. And most are still teen-agers.

Here and there a bad example has been set of a type which undermines a great deal of the good that has been done in other directions. In some American Army circles, when a Servicemen's club planned a dance or event at which the men wanted to let themselves go, there would be a ruling that no Western women were to be present. Instead, army trucks scoured the area for 'mooses', who were checked against venereal disease, then transported to the club. This was known as a 'moose-call'. It sounds much better than just 'rounding up Korean prostitutes for an evening's illicit entertainment'. It cannot, of course, be too strongly emphasised that in all this only a minority of troops are involved.

But the result of these activities is that today, as soon as the Koreans are allowed back into an area which used to be the front, the first to come in are the 'mooses'. And of course they crowd into each town where troops are stationed, and hang around every camp.

Within a stone's throw of the camp in which I was quartered in Pusan—and this is what first brought the situation to my attention—was an unofficial brothel. In and out through its doors each night went a stream of Service men, among whom were a large number of Negroes. It is a curious paradox that the coming of the West to defend Korea has given the country its first half-black babies.

War, of course, normally brings such things as these. It is part of the price and problem of war. But in this case the problem goes deeper, for it strikes right at the foundations of the moral code which has kept a pagan society relatively decent. The breakdown of that code, unless it is replaced by Christianity, will lead to the ultimate demoralisation of the nation. There is no reason for restraint in a pagan society whose moral defence system has been destroyed.

I stress the rôle of the West in this collapse of ancient moral codes because, although we have brought much that is good to Korea, we have brought some bad, too, and it makes it all the more necessary that we should do the right thing by its people in the future. Many factors have quite obviously contributed to the present situation. There has been the total disruption by invasion and civil war of a nation's life, the uprooting of a peasant people from the soil which gives stability to their whole existence, the impact of an attractively successful though materialistic way of life and a quite different culture upon one which has changed little in four thousand years, the impact, too, of a quite different sense of values. And there has been the corrupting influence of association with troops who are immensely rich by comparison with Koreans, and the bad example of a minority.

The Christian charity, the kindliness, and the willingness to sacrifice shown by the American nation in particular towards a people remote from them in distance and in culture is one of the most encouraging and heartening things I have ever seen, and was something for which I was quite unprepared. But this would only make it all the more tragic if the net result of our defence of South Korea against the Communist attack should be the demoralisation of the very people we went to defend and whom so many of the visiting troops befriended.

To come back to Fr. Connors in his Japanese house on the hill in Pusan. The old Maryknoller told me one story, in particular, which brought home to me an aspect of the sufferings of the people of Korea which had until then not registered with me.

It concerned a woman who came to Pusan as a refugee. On the way down, a great mass of people were crossing a river whilst being strafed from the air. In the panic and confusion she lost her two small boys.

She reached Pusan alone, not knowing whether they were dead or merely lost. But as time went on she knew that there was a growing danger that even though they were still alive, they might not recognise her and, even worse, since they would be growing and changing, she might not know them either, even though they might some day meet.

One day someone told her that lists of children who had become separated from their parents and who were now in orphanages were regularly displayed in the Pusan Town Hall. She went there, searched the lists and to her joy found the names of both boys. She eventually ran them to earth in an orphanage in the city.

Another woman of Fr. Connors's acquaintance had been walking down a Pusan street one morning when she thought she recognised the twelve-year-old son who had disappeared in the panic rush. She approached him, and as she did so he recognised her too.

"But they're the lucky ones," said Fr. Connors. "Enormous numbers of very small children who became separated from their parents will never now be recognised, particularly those who at the time when they were first lost were too young to be able to say their own names and have since grown and developed out of all recognition. Many of them are among the ones who now roam the streets looking for food, live on their wits or earn a few hwan shining shoes."

He told me another story, which cast a curious light on the Chinese Communist leaders.

During the truce talks which preceded the end of hostilities, Mgr. Carrol, a Maryknoll missioner, who was in charge of war relief, took the opportunity to go up to Pyongyang. His billet was a dug-out which had at one time been used by a top-level Chinese Communist leader. He found the walls lined with bookshelves and an excellent library. When he began to browse through them he discovered that some had belonged to his friend, Fr. Connors, whose parish and presbytery had formerly been in Pyongyang, and others came from the library of the German Benedictines at Wonsan, a high proportion of the books being theological ones.

His story conjured up a curious picture of the literature-hungry Chinese Communist chief sitting up late at night studying Christian moral theology, then going off next day to try to outwit the representatives of the Christian nations at the conference table.

Pusan is on Korea's most south-easterly tip. Mokpo occupies a similar position on the south-west—perhaps one hundred and thirty miles away as the crow flies. They are the two largest cities in the extreme south of the country and my map clearly showed a railway which seemed to connect the two. For days I tried to make the journey, alternating it with attempts to get a courier aircraft to Kwangju, so that I could then travel by road from there to Mokpo. But I was frustrated on both counts.

Just one aircraft in theory went to Kwangju each day. Day after day I enquired about its expected arrival and departure time for the following day, since they were never the same on two days running, and time after time I was disappointed.

One morning I went optimistically to the military airfield at soon after five, conscientiously following the instructions I had been given on the previous day. I waited for seven hours, reading over and over again the caption to a poster on the waiting-room wall, which portrayed a skeleton holding an hour-glass in its bony fingers. "Time is short for narcotic users," it said. But time did not seem to matter a thing to the ground staff on the airstrip. The young Negro behind the counter, with little to do for hours on end, seemed to think I was mad when I asked him every couple of hours whether any news of the plane had yet been received.

At twelve-twenty-five p.m. precisely it arrived. A big Negro who seemed to be mechanic and porter combined told me to put my bags inside.

"We'll be off in half an hour," he said.

Half an hour later I climbed up inside to join my bags. The big Negro strolled up some fifteen minutes later. "Flight's off," he said, "we've since had a report that weather conditions are unsuitable, so we're not going today."

Wearily I took my bags out of the aircraft, phoned my R.A.S.C. camp and asked them to send out the jeep again. In due course the driver who had brought me down more than six hours earlier took me back again.

Trying to travel by the train was just as bad. Because of alleged guerilla activities along the line the train was not running. It was, in any case, a Korean train, on which neither U.N. personnel nor troops were expected to travel, and so the usual degree of helpfulness was not forthcoming from the R.T.O.'s office.

Finally I had to admit defeat and booked a berth on the United Nations' night express to Seoul. Waiting at the station that evening I got another glimpse of the disintegration of public morals. This time it concerned the police. Four young men stood in an out-of-the-way corner, tied together by their wrists to form a square, with a guard keeping watch over them. They may have been young criminals or possibly army deserters. A rather prosperous-looking man came along, had a brief word with the police guard, then passed him a wad of notes. He walked away, the guard took a quick look round, saw no one in sight, and quickly slashed the cord and walked away.

The next minute the four, still tied together but no longer in square formation, ran across the tracks as quickly as they could and jumped on a train which was already slowly rattling out of the station. The timing was perfect. The whole thing was over in a matter of minutes.

The corruption of the police was an open scandal all over Korea. It was, in fact, one of the worst features of the situation there and could lead to great hardship for the common people. For example, many people living under dreadful conditions in Pusan are longing to get back to the little bits of land which they left years before as refugees. Once back, they would grow their own food and live a comparatively decent and healthy life. Instead, they contributed nothing to the country's economy and rotted away with tuberculosis in Pusan.

The reason why many of them did not go home was that the police were 'squeezing' returning peasants, charging them fantastic unofficial taxes before they were allowed to return to their own fields.

The corruption of the police, too, made it possible for equally corrupt politicians to pay them and use them to terrorise supporters of other parties and compel the populace to support them instead.

In this case the root of the problem was economic. The Government simply had not the cash to pay its police. Often they would go unpaid for weeks or months on end and were expected to get what 'squeeze' they could, wherever they could get it and by any means they cared to use.

Back in Seoul I made for the headquarters of the Columban Fathers. I was determined to break free as soon as I could from the military machine so that I might see the Koreans more closely. The Columbans, as the foremost Catholic missionary body in Korea, with men in towns and remote rural areas of both the North and South of the Republic, were likely to know far more about Korean conditions than anyone else from the West.

They had known Korea and its people in the past, stuck with them through the Pacific War and the Korean War, shared their sufferings, knew their language and were completely accepted wherever they went. Moreover that curious Columban characteristic which I had noted back in England, and at their headquarters at Navan, of refusing to overstate or dramatise any situation or any action of their own, was a valuable one, now that I wanted all the first-hand information possible about a people whose language I did not know.

The inevitable jeep, driven this time by a young Columban, Fr. Dave Richers, who was newly out from the States, met me at seven in the morning at Seoul Station. As I waited, the filthy, ragged little bootblack waifs crowded around me clamouring for trade.

Fr. Richers, I learned as we crossed Seoul, came from Altoona, in Pennsylvania. I told him I had been there only a few months before.

"I know," he replied. "You were giving a lecture there and my mother and father were in your audience. Your host was my closest friend when we were at school together."

Korea, America and Britain, for both of us, came very close together as he said it.

St. Columban's, in Don Am Dong, was formerly a Japanese house. It is situated in a part of the town which before 1945 was mainly inhabited by Japanese officials. Behind its high gates is an attractive garden, all shrubs and rocks, designed by some gardener who is now, presumably, back in Japan, but whose work lives on in a little masterpiece of planning. Within the small compass of a city garden, by the careful selection of ornamental shrubs and conifers of various heights, he succeeded in creating the illusion of space. So when today you look out from the windows of what has become the Columbans' headquarters, you have the impression that all around it is some great estate. In fact, the blue-tiled houses with upturned eaves, housing a large Korean population, crowd on top of each other right up to within a matter of a few yards of its walls.

Beside it, within the compound, stands a fine, new, two-tier building. Its upstairs is a tasteful chapel, below is a priests' hostel. It was built as a memorial to the little band of American Catholic chaplains who died during the Korean War "and all those who lost their lives in the cause of peace and justice." The entire cost was covered by collections among American troops.

Standing as it did on the road from Seoul to the front, St. Columban's became a haven of peace for many a weary chaplain who would come back from the firing line for a short leave, exhausted and with nerves frayed, spend a day or two in its homely, informal atmosphere, in the company of his fellow priests, then return to the bloody battle restored in body, mind and spirit. For it was in those days, and still is, always 'open house' for Catholic priests and laymen at St. Columban's.

All over America today there are men who spent a period as chaplains in Korea and who must remember with gratitude St. Columban's, and Fr. Brian Geraghty, who runs it.

Fr. Geraghty is Director of his Society's work in Korea. For several weeks I was in Brian Geraghty's company for most of the time and I came to have a tremendous regard for the big quiet-voiced Irishman with the disturbing deep-set, grey-blue eyes. As I got to know him and his story, I realised that their peculiar quality was no figment of my imagination, nor were they any mystery either. They had seen more of the evidences of man's inhumanity to man than have most in this troubled age, but they had seen some wonderful things, too.

It was he who took me into the city to see Bishop Ro, the Korean Bishop of Seoul. For years the Seoul diocese had been in the hands of the Paris Foreign Missions, who, as in so many parts of Asia, did most of the original pioneer work in Korea. In the 1930s, however, when Japanese nationalism was growing, the Japanese authorities who ruled Korea urged that native bishops should be appointed—as they also did in Japan. It is the Church's policy to pass responsibility to the native clergy wherever possible and in response to this demand various French missionary bishops stood down, making way for Koreans. This was the case in Seoul.

I was interested to meet the Korean clergy, since it is upon them, in the long run, that the future of the Christian cause will depend. In Asia, as in Africa, the missionary paves the way in readiness for others to take over.

The Bishop, a slight, scholarly man in early middle age, spoke English. Like all his generation of educated Korean Catholics, he also spoke French fluently. In such company, where there was a Korean-speaking Irish missionary present, the conversation was liable to be conducted in a mixture of Korean, English, French and Latin, with the occasional bits of classical Chinese thrown in—a combination with which I could not hope to keep up.

Bishop Ro was, like all the priests and nuns I had met, also conscious of the big opportunity of the moment and was racking his brains—and scraping the bottom of his coffers—to do as much as possible to seize it and use it.

There had been, he said, some fourteen thousand adult baptisms the previous year, and he expected the number in the current year to be far in excess of that. More young men were coming forward for training as priests than he could take. In the previous twelve months ninety had applied. Lacking both cash and accommodation, he had been able to take only forty-five.

He was planning to increase the number of Catholic hospitals, orphanages and schools. Although the Catholic missionaries had been the first, at tremendous cost, to get to Korea, and though the first orphanage in the land had been a Catholic one, other Christian bodies in the past had gone in for such activities in a far bigger way than could the Catholics, who had always lacked funds. Now, with so much need all around them and such undreamed of opportunities for the Church, it became imperative that somehow the means should be found. For the moment he had plans, no money, but a lot of faith that somehow it would be raised.

Six new building projects were being worked on, plans for four more had been approved, and the plans had been submitted for another thirty, including churches, schools, orphanages and other establishments.

"As a result of the war," he told me, "the minds of our people have been opened up. They are re-thinking out their position, and they are more sympathetic to us than they have ever been. More and more are coming to us. Whilst it is true that we are still a small minority and we are still outnumbered among the governing class and the intelligentsia, our influence is considerable and all the community hold us in high regard."

From the Bishop's house we went to see Dr. John Chan, Korea's most prominent Catholic layman, and an outstanding man judged by any standards.

Dr. Chan has an alert, intelligent face. He speaks perfect English, and is a man of great culture and breadth of outlook. Still in middle age, he is exceptional in every way, and comes from an extraordinarily talented family.

His sister was Mother Agneta of the Korean Sisterhood of Our Mother of Perpetual Help, who was arrested by the Communists in October, 1950, and is believed to have met her death in prison. His brother is Professor Louis Chan, dean of the faculty of Fine Arts in the National University, Seoul.

Dr. John Chan was brought back from America, where he was his country's first Ambassador during the Korean War, to become Prime Minister. He ran for the presidency, but, as the only serious rival to Dr. Syngman Rhee, political life was made impossible for him and, after spending a period in hiding in a hospital, he dropped out of party politics.

We found him in his newspaper office. The daily paper which he edits is politically independent, criticising, when necessary, both Government and Opposition from a Catholic standpoint. Although the majority of its readers are pagans it is publicly known to be Catholic-controlled. Bishop Ro is associated with it, but it is not the voice of the Church as such.

Editing such a paper under Korean conditions must be a more than usually difficult job. As with Japanese papers, those of Korea carry enormous editorial staffs. Dr. Chan had a reporting staff of forty. Of these only two were Catholics.

The building in which it is now edited and printed was from 1945-1947 the Communist Party headquarters, and the Communist paper was published there. On its presses, too, the Communists printed counterfeit money with which to finance

their activities. They were caught and jailed. The proprietors
of the Catholic paper (which had appeared first in 1896, but was
suppressed for forty years by the Japanese) applied for the
building and got it.

But many of the print workers were still Communists when
they moved in. The result was that the four priests who were
then on the staff would write up news and comment from the
Christian angle, but the Communist print workers would take
it out at the last moment and replace it with items written with a
Communist slant instead. As a consequence there was the
danger that at any time the paper might discredit the Church,
and for this reason the priests were withdrawn.

During the war the building was destroyed and the paper had
to start up all over again. Now, in the new post-war conditions,
there were, so far as he knew, no Communists on the staff,
although the majority of those writing and printing the paper
were still non-Christians. The paper was seen as one of the
country's 'big four', probably ranking as second in influence in
the land. Since the leading one is Government-subsidised, it
might fairly be called the foremost independent paper. In 1947
its sales were one hundred and twenty thousand daily. During
the chaos of the first post-war period they slumped heavily.
Now they were building up again and had got back to fifty
thousand daily.

Dr. Chan took me round the works. In the composing room
we watched compositors setting the type for the next day's
paper. They worked with incredible speed, setting the matter
by hand as quickly as would any skilled compositors in the
West—with the difference that they worked with five thousand
basic characters instead of our twenty-six letters of the
alphabet.

A weakness in his position, which Dr. Chan himself
recognises, is that he is remote from the overwhelming majority
of his fellow-Catholics in education and training. Because the
Church in Korea has always been poor it was in no position in
the past to compete in the field of education with the highly
efficient Japanese-run State schools. The consequence was that
the number of Catholic intellectuals remained small.

He was eager to see the gap closed. What was needed, he told me, were more scholarships made available in the West to young Koreans. He dreamed of young Koreans going to European and American Universities, and others to agricultural colleges in Denmark, for example, until such time as the Korean Catholics had their own.

Incidentally, since my return to England a first step, at least, has been taken, with the arrival in Korea of one of Tokyo's German Jesuits, from Sophia University, charged with the job of starting a teachers' training college, and with the probability of a group following soon after, charged with the task of establishing a University. A university like Sophia, right up to the same standard, somewhere in Korea, will have an enormous influence and should transform in time the whole weight of the Christian impact upon Korean thought.

Until there are more John Chans in the country's public life such a man, if he goes into the political fight, must be very isolated and, therefore, vulnerable too.

I was to meet Dr. Chan several times later and my regard for him grew with every meeting. The last occasion was just before I left Korea, when he translated a lecture I gave to the junior and senior students—priests-to-be in Bishop Ro's seminary.

With Fr. Brian Geraghty, too, I went later that day to Inchon, the port on the Yellow Sea made famous by the United Nations landings there during the war.

Inchon had been in the battle area. It had not therefore had a refugee problem. But it had had the experience of being for some time under Communist rule and of being in the front line. Much of the town had been destroyed and was being rebuilt.

We went to a clinic, school and orphanage run by the Sisters of St. Paul of Chartres, whose name I had first heard when Philip Crosbie told me his story of the Death March to the Yalu River. Sister Eugenie, it will be recalled, who was the unsung heroine of the march, belonged to this order of nuns. The Sisters had been in Inchon since 1888, since just after the persecution.

Living in an otherwise exclusively French community was

Sister Philomena, who had been born in Northern Ireland, then taken as a child to America. She was the only English-speaking woman among the thirty nuns in the Inchon convent. She would be the last to call herself—or even to want to be—an intellectual. She is a woman of tremendous drive and tenacity, the sort who, having set her mind to a thing, will obstinately stick at it until she gets her way. For four years during the Pacific War she had been confined by the Japanese, and then, only five years or so later, found herself in the thick of the new and even more vicious war. Now she was requiring all her drive and resourcefulness to get the things she wanted in order to meet some of the needs of the unfortunates of Inchon.

Her convent had been destroyed when it became part of a battlefield, but American troops had rebuilt it for her in 1952. She was trying at that moment to 'scrounge' some furniture for it. Meanwhile, the good nuns were managing with an absolute minimum of comfort of any sort.

I went with her to her clinic. As we crossed the courtyard two young Korean nuns and two senior girls from the orphanage sat crosslegged on the ground rhythmically beating clean white sheets with long polished wooden batons. This process is the Korean equivalent of ironing, and the results are every bit as good as any obtained by the most expert Western housewife using the most up to date of electric irons.

The nuns ran a crêche, a kindergarten, a school attended by one thousand six hundred children and the large orphanage. In addition they have their 'Star of the Sea' clinic and hospital, similar in purpose to the Maryknoll Sisters' clinic in Pusan. But they clearly have not the same funds available.

In the previous month they had treated five thousand six hundred cases there. Skin diseases and tuberculosis—both 'social' in origin—were most prevalent.

The children in the orphanage crowded around us, hanging on to our legs and hands as Korean children everywhere do. Among them were one or two half-Negro toddlers. Inchon, of course, has no refugees, but it has its 'occupation babies', whom the nuns often find on their doorstep in the morning.

Life was beginning to get back to something approaching

normal in the villages on the Seoul-to-Inchon road. Entirely new villages had been built of wooden shops and houses, the timber for which had as usual been provided in most cases by U.N. rehabilitation agencies or by the U.S. Army.

As we drove back to the capital, I managed to get Father Brian to tell a little of his own story. As with almost all Columbans, it was the most difficult of jobs to get him to talk about himself; yet no man in Korea has more to tell. He can most certainly, with no shadow of exaggeration, be described as a front-line fighter.

Brian Geraghty, I found, was no more than a year or two older than myself, although I had thought of him as being a good many years my senior. His home was in County Galway. He went to Korea in 1933, fresh from college. The Society of St. Columban had only recently been asked to take over missions there and he was therefore one of those with the longest service in the land. Of that generation of Columbans who went either to China or Korea, there were few who had not been in jail. He was no exception.

Almost from the moment the Columbans took over their first vicariates and prefectures ('mission dioceses') things had not been normal. The consequence was that whenever they had begun to show signs of progress something had come to put them back. They had been in Korea just four years when the Japanese war with China began. Korea, as a part of 'greater Japan' was put on an emergency basis and all foreigners were suspect. The Columbans were watched by spies wherever they went and faced with every sort of restriction.

Four years later came World War II. Then five years after its end the Korean War began. That was the background to Brian Geraghty's whole life—and that of his Society—in Korea. Always in danger of arrest, imprisonment or violent death, yet forever trying to build up a hard core of Christians who would themselves some day take over entirely the running of their own Church. And, of course, always dreaming of, and working for, the conversion of the nation.

Yet, in spite of everything, the number of Catholics had steadily risen and now, all over Korea, the converts were streaming in. An opportunity beyond their wildest dreams had come along at last.

When World War II started, Fr. Geraghty was working in Hunchon—which was later to be Fr. Philip Crosbie's parish. There, along with other Columbans throughout the area, he was arrested and in due course taken to the jail in Chunchon—from which some years later Mgr. Quinlan, Fr. Crosbie and Fr. Canavan were to be taken out to the Death March. The first two were among his companions in the jail on that first occasion.

He was in Chunchon jail for twelve months, then under house arrest at Hunchon until the end of the war. As senior in the community he was responsible for the others during that period. There were seventeen of them crowded together for the last four months and Fr. Geraghty never knew from one day to the next where the food for them was coming from.

"But the local Catholics were wonderful," he said. "They were not supposed to come near us, but they knew that we had no means of keeping alive and so they smuggled their own rations in to us."

For one period of two weeks they had nothing else but wheat bran. During that period, on August 6, 1945, six of their number were desperately ill with dysentery, of which one, Fr. Gillen, died. The other eight, including Fr. Geraghty himself, had malaria.

"I still shake with fear when I remember that time," he told me grimly.

At the same time, down in Mokpo, the priests of the Kwangju prefecture were under house arrest, crowded together in a tiny presbytery intended for a single priest.

Between the end of that war and the beginning of the next Fr. Geraghty and his colleagues were trying to build up again. But the peace was an uneasy one, with Communism triumphant just above the 38th Parallel and constant unrest in the South.

When the North Korean Communists started their invasion in June, 1951, he was away visiting. He managed to escape arrest, got back to Seoul and was among the last to leave the city. "I crossed that old bridge just three hours before it was blown up," he told me as we rattled over the temporary bridge across the Han River on our way back from Inchon. He pointed to the broken piers which still stood beside the temporary structure.

Taking his jeep, he joined the great mass of refugees on their way to Pusan. With him was his Korean cook—the one who had voluntarily gone to jail with him during the Pacific War— and the cook's wife and family. They crawled down the jam-packed roads by day, carrying as many refugees as could be got into the jeep, then slept in it by night.

In Pusan he stayed in the Maryknoll Sisters' clinic (the nuns had got out to Japan on the advice of the military but were the first white women to return); there he worked among United Nations' troops as they arrived in port, giving the Catholics among them the sacraments. For many of them they were their last, for they went straight into battle.

In September he returned to Seoul, where he remained, up against the battle area, until the Chinese came into the war and drove south. Again, in January, 1951, he was forced down to Pusan. But by March 21 he was back again. The Communists were driven out of the capital in the morning. Fr. Geraghty came in the afternoon of the same day. The city to which he came back was a desolated one. It had been fought over time after time. But he was 'home'.

As he went through the gates of St. Columban's in Don Am Dong, he tripped over a body. Walking through the yard, past the little Japanese garden, he passed two more. He had come back alone. Not a friend was near. Only two thousand people were in the whole of that great city of death and destruction, and each was preoccupied with his own burden of care. So he dealt with the bodies himself. It was clear that the Communists had shot them that morning, but who or what they were he never discovered.

When he went into the house he found that it had been used as the Communist Party headquarters for Seoul. In the base-ment Red troops had recently been making home-made hand grenades from old beer tins. A number of the finished articles were still lying around the place—for weeks he went on finding them in the garden and elsewhere—and a quantity of dynamite had been left there too. He went to sleep in the empty house that night not knowing whether he would be blown up before morning.

Apparently there had been some fifty or sixty people working in the house, and they had left it in complete disorder, even breaking the electric lamps before they went. A piano which the Communists had themselves brought in was, however, left intact, and it is still in the house to this day, a gift from the Communists to the Columbans. They also inadvertently left behind a number of documents, carefully rolled in oiled paper, and two truckloads of rubbish which he gradually cleared.

In the chapel inside the house (replaced now by the magnificent memorial chapel) the altars had been removed. On the walls hung three portraits—of Lenin, Stalin and Kim Il Sung. Someone had taken pot shots with a rifle at a statue of Our Lady, and the figure of the Crucified Christ had been prised from a crucifix.

Later, when the foundations for the new chapel were being dug, the figure was unearthed. The arms were broken where it had been wrenched away from the cross, but it had obviously been buried deliberately and with some care. Fr. Geraghty is still guessing whether it was buried reverently by some Catholic conscripted into the Communist forces or blasphemously by the Communists themselves. But the soiled and broken figure remains a treasured possession in the house.

From that day on, Fr. Geraghty remained in the house, whilst the fighting front moved to and fro, sometimes coming to the edge of the city, but for the last years of the war remaining some thirty miles away.

His job as Regional Director of his Society kept him on the move throughout the war, trying to trace the missing and the dead among its members and attempting to maintain contact with those who were carrying on, even though it meant going through occupied areas and being smuggled into districts cut off by guerillas.

That was the record—with a great deal more besides—which I managed to get from this front-line fighter, in scraps and by dint of much questioning, on the way back from Inchon and during subsequent trips, and which I confirmed later and filled in from the stories of his colleagues.

He had managed to arrange for me to travel to Mokpo on the following day. A telegram had been sent that morning to the Columbans who were to be my hosts, telling them that I would be coming on the 'Express' from Seoul and asking them to meet me.

The 'Express' was a train which normally carried only Korean passengers. Once upon a time it did the journey in some five hours or so. Now, because of the possibility of ambushes by guerillas, who still hung on in the hills through which it had to pass, it went slowly, with frequent precautionary stops, and usually took some thirteen hours.

When we got back from Inchon that night, word had come from the postal authorities to the effect that the telegram could not be sent.

"That probably means that the guerillas have cut the wires,' said Fr. Geraghty.

XI

MOKPO EXPRESS

I WAS up before five o'clock next morning and soon, along with Fr. Geraghty, I was going across the city by jeep to the station. Already there were queues at the shops. The day begins early in Korea.

The train was not due to leave for half an hour, but it was already full by Western standards when Fr. Geraghty saw me to my reserved seat. In my pocket, on a slip of paper, was the address to which I was going—written in Korean characters which I could not read.

"I haven't their telephone number," he said confidently, "but if you show this address to someone when you get there and sign that you want to phone, they'll find it for you."

I hoped he was right.

The compartment was entirely filled with Koreans, who continued to stream in until, by the time the train left, we were packed like sardines. Next to me, on the narrow, straight-backed seat intended for two, were two young R.O.K. soldiers. On the one facing me, so close that our knees touched, sat a young teen-age boy with an old man in long white coat and trousers and wearing a topee. He had a dark, lined, intelligent face, long whispy beard and immense dignity. He carried a small cloth money-bag on a cord at his waist, and had some sort of large semi-precious stone, the size of a bantam's egg, hanging on another cord round his neck.

Shortly before the train was due to leave, an R.O.K. officer arrived with his wife. They held reserved tickets and the old man and boy, with great charm, at once left theirs and were in turn offered others by some young soldiers.

The officer's wife was a typical Korean woman of the middle-class, wearing a lightly patterned pink silk coatee and white skirt.

From one of the many boys who came through the train selling packets of sweets and magazines the officer's wife bought several glossy papers. I noted that, because Koreans read from the back forward, the cover-girls were on the back instead of the front—which bore advertisements.

Outside, men sold bottles of brightly-coloured drinks and confections of various kinds, which they passed through the windows.

A little woman came along chanting her sales talk in half-notes as she sold flowers whilst the station announcer's sing-song voice came over the loudspeakers, making it a wonderful Oriental duet.

Then a man hurried through the coach selling breakfasts packed in two boxes. In one was rice with a few very tiny bits of meat in the other, some vivid yellow pickled turnip, red seaweed and other items to which I could attach no name. A pair of rough wooden chopsticks were provided with each two-box pack. Almost everyone bought a pack and eating and drinking began at once. It never for one moment stopped throughout the journey—which is the normal Korean social custom when travelling. On this occasion it lasted for some thirteen hours.

The train rattled out of the station with men and boys running beside the tracks, still passing in bottles and sticky sweetmeats and receiving their hwan in return. Then we rattled still more noisily over the temporary bridges across the Han River and on past shells of roofless factories inside which refugees had erected their tiny, flimsy shacks.

My presence, I noticed, now that everyone was settled, was creating a good deal of curiosity, which was renewed each time we stopped at a suburban station to take on still more people. The 'Express' was proving, right from the start, to be a stopping train.

At one such stop a man with a reserved seat ticket came on, checked the number of his seat and found two other men already sitting on it. He showed them his ticket and each produced another—made out for the same seat. They all laughed delightedly, the two already there closed up still more tightly and soon all three were squashed on to a seat intended only for one. When a ticket collector came to check our reservations, all three produced their tickets, he examined them and joined in the merriment.

It was a joke which kept the three occupants of the seat grinning widely for many a mile, and was for me yet another example of the Korean's ability to laugh at his own and others' discomfiture in situations where most Westerners would be irritated.

As we passed through one badly bombed village a barber was cutting a cumstomer's hair sitting out in the open air. Trains going in the opposite direction passed us frequently, packed exclusively with school children hanging on the sides and standing on the steps as well. At the end of the first hour most of the passengers in our train had slipped off their shoes and were sitting in stockinged feet. Korean stockings, incidentally, are made, not of knitted wool, but of padded white linen.

At one station two men came on selling yet more food. They carried between them a large hamper filled with wrapped cakes, dried raw fish and bottles of coloured drinks. Each time they put down their load, one would hold up a raw fish—small octopus as I later learned—and intone its virtues at great length.

The officer sitting opposite me, I discovered, knew some English, having undergone a six-months training course in California in 1952. He had seen from my 'flash' that I was a war correspondent, and we at once began to ply each other with questions.

He asked me what the British thought of Korea's recent elections. I guardedly answered that I was not there at the time but did not think that the return of Syngman Rhee would have surprised them. I countered by asking what he thought of them. Equally guardedly, he replied: "I am a soldier and must have no political opinions." His appetite for information was considerable, his range of interests wide. In particular he wanted to know more about British relations with Egypt, India and other countries.

I told him that I thought that the clothes worn by Korean

women, such as those his wife was wearing, were extremely beautiful. With great pride he replied that all such clothes were made in Korea—none were imported and that the materials are made there, too. He was transparently pleased at my very sincere admiration for the national costume.

At one point a blind beggar, with one arm just a withered, mutilated stump, came through the coach, led by a small girl of perhaps ten or eleven years of age. Almost everyone gave to the little girl, and it was revealing that both the beggar and his little guide were tidily dressed and decently turned out. There was no attempt at parading extreme poverty, and the child openly added the notes she was given to a thick handful she did not try to conceal.

At the next station, however, we encountered for the first time a different sort of beggar. A crowd of indescribably filthy little waifs, hungry, lousy, and in rags, came swarming on to the train. They were war orphans and children who had become separated from their parents in the great rush south. Each carried a stick, and would silently lie down on his stomach on the floor and prod beneath the seat in search of bottles. Bottles could be used to raise a few hwan, which in turn meant food.

After we were several hours on our way, a man who was clearly in the last stages of tuberculosis was led by his wife and daughter on to the train. At once the officer and his wife, who were sitting opposite to me, jumped up and offered him their seat. The dying man lay down, his wife put a pillow under his head, then stood at the end of the seat with the girl, tending his every need. From time to time he was convulsed with coughing fits which would end with his bringing up a quantity of sputum, which he spat into pieces of paper, a seemingly endless supply of which his wife had brought with her. He would then pass the paper to his wife, she would pass it to their daughter who then deposited it out of the window, or, rather, where the window would have been had it not been broken—or shot out —at some time. All down one side of the coach the window-frames were empty. The glass had gone, being replaced by pieces of wood and cardboard which in turn had been broken

y passengers in the interests of increased visibility rather than
f comfort.

At noon we stopped at a station, miles out in the country,
where women and children flocked out across the tracks to
reet us with large quantities of eggs, both raw and hard-boiled,
variety of cooked dishes, reminiscent of nothing obtainable in
he Occident, and even small tins and bottles of water, in all of
which they did a brisk trade.

One small girl, having failed to sell her bottle of water to
anyone else, shyly tried it on me, but I declined. Since there
appeared to be no sale for it, she very sensibly sat down at the
dge of track and washed her feet and legs with it instead. The
Korean rarely misses an opportunity of having a wash. As we
set off again, I discovered that the approved way of eating the
raw eggs is to knock one end off the egg on the back of a railway
arriage seat, suck out the white, fill the egg up again with
anned beer, shake it up with the yolk, then swallow it in a
single gulp. The result is something remotely resembling an
egg flip.

The real lunch stop came a little later, when everyone temporarily dropped their eating and drinking in the train in order
o alight and eat and drink outside instead. Bowls of steaming
noodle soup were on sale at a station stall. Almost everyone
bought one, followed it up with more solids, then bought two-
box lunch packs of rice, seaweed, squid and pickled turnip,
green onion and garlic, in order to be able to start up again
inside whilst they waited for the journey to be resumed. Even
my dying consumptive drank a little soup and played around
with chopsticks, taking little bits of this and that from a packed
lunch. Soon the air was even more heavy with the smell of raw
fish, garlic and canned beer and bottled cider.

At this station, too, the most incredibly filthy, uncared for
little waifs of all came on to the train, scrambling about under
the seats in search of empty bottles or bits of food. One little
seven-year-old, who hardly for one moment stopped scratching
the bare and filthy body which showed through the holes in his
rags, carefully scraped a piece of raw fish off the floor with a
stick. I had watched that particular piece of squid being

trodden around the coach for most of the journey until, by thi
time no more than a filthy, flattened, unrecognisable mess, i
had stuck to the floor under a seat. But for the hungry littl
waif it was food. Having removed it from the dirty boards h
quickly threaded his way through the crowded coach, dashe
out through the door, over the tracks and hid behind a freigh
wagon. From where I sat I could see him wolfing it ravenously
looking around furtively as he did so lest any other waif shoul
come and rob him of his find.

Before we left, a man came through with a watering can, with
which he swilled down the floor, then swept the piles of dus
and rubbish away in a sodden mass.

Another evidence of the Korean's preoccupation with certain
aspects of hygiene (possibly learned from the Japanese?) cam
when another man brought round a mysterious can of hot wate
in which was some form of disinfectant. Into it he droppe
small face flannels, which he picked steaming out of the can with
a pair of tweezers, then passed them to the passengers, who
carefully wiped hands and faces on them, later passing them
back to the man when he came round again. After eight and
half hours of crowded travel, accompanied in most cases by
non-stop eating, this was refreshing indeed.

In the late afternoon we approached the territory which unti
recently had been the most guerilla-infested in the land. Man
Communists took to the hills after the Pusan rising, which
occurred even before the Korea War began. They were joined
by others when first the North Korean and later the Chinese
Communist forces came south.

When the Red troops were driven back, guerillas stayed
behind to harass the United Nations and South Korean troops
Gradually, as a result of repeated actions against them, their
numbers were reduced. Some gave up the struggle and
surrendered, some made their way north, others tried to filter
back into Pusan. But a hard core remained to fight it out. The
area lying north of Pusan and Mokpo is perfect guerilla country
It is said that the Japanese, even after forty years of iron rule
still never fully succeeded in putting down the nationalist
guerillas who lived in those same hills.

It is not easy to discover how many armed Communists are still hiding there by day and coming down each night to raid farms and isolated villages for food. For its own reasons, with an eye to continued aid from the West, the Korean Government tends to exaggerate their numbers, hinting at the presence of many thousands. The view of generally well-informed people living in the area, I found later, was that there were probably no more than a thousand or two at the most in the immediate vicinity, and their numbers were steadily shrinking.

They certainly had a nuisance value so far as the Communists were concerned, helping to keep the country in a state of unrest, and to keep alive the feeling that the possibility of Communist victory did not end with the armistice. But for that very reason, though they may have helped the Communists in their war of nerves, they were a gift to Syngman Rhee too, providing him with an excuse for maintaining rigorous war-time restrictions over the population as a whole which would otherwise have had to be ended. And because they helped to give the impression that the Communist threat continued, they increased his bargaining power with the West. On balance, I would think that Syngman Rhee gains most from the situation.

Before rounding each hill in the guerilla country our train stopped for some time and a siren was loudly sounded. Then we nosed our way round. By the time we reached the other side armed guards were spread out along the foothills adjoining the tracks, with their guns pointed up to the peaks above in case of an ambush. On the tops of the mountains were stationed men with white flags who, when they had been given the all-clear, signalled us on from one hill to the next.

But, despite the guerillas and all the elaborate precautions against them, life went on much as usual in the little paddy-fields. Men still walked knee-deep in mud behind their ox-drawn ploughs, or transplanted the bright green young plants from the nursery beds, whilst children played and women washed their clothes in the heavily-guarded villages, much as though armed troops and pill-box defences were part of the natural order.

At one station, however, where an ambush was said to have

taken place not long before and, it appeared, another was expected, the usual crowd of people started to make their way towards us, laden with food and drinks for the passengers. But they were roughly driven back by the guards, who revealed their nervousness by their quite unnecessary violence. I saw one attractive young girl, for example, fall backwards when a guard hit her with great force in the chest with the butt of his rifle. The presence of guerillas in civilian clothes in an area inevitably creates not only nervousness but also an all-inclusive suspicion, where no one, least of all the guards, knows who may or may not be an enemy. Certainly they were taking no chances that day.

We steamed into Mokpo station just after seven in the evening. I showed a young Korean officer who was sitting beside me my precious little piece of paper, on which was the address, in Korean characters, to which I was to go and from which a jeep would be sent to meet me. The only man on the train who had known any English had left it hours ago. By means of signs I conveyed the idea that I wanted him to telephone for me, and we set off together into the town. There are no metal coins, only paper money, in Korea, and there can therefore be no public call-boxes on the Western model, so we walked to the telephone exchange from which public calls were made. The Korean was a stranger in Mokpo and had to ask his way. It was clear that he was helping me at some inconvenience to himself. At the exchange they told him that there was no telephone at the address written on my piece of paper. When he asked where it was one of the workers took us outside and pointed to a big church high up on a hill right on the other side of the city. I watched the young officer visibly flinch, and hurriedly look at his watch. He then produced the address to which he wished to go and the man from the exchange pointed to a spot far away in the opposite direction to my own destination. It was clear to me that the address I had been given was that of the Church, which naturally had no telephone, although the adjoining priests' house had. But I failed completely to get this point over to my companion. Nobly, he took my heavy bag, smiled wanly and set off quickly through the crowded, unpaved muddy streets with me at his side. We climbed up and up, often losing sight of the church, losing our way and being directed back on to it again. It was apparent that he was in a hurry to get to his destination and that we were every minute getting further away from it. It was also obvious that, since neither of us knew a word of the other's language, I could not even thank him for what he was doing. And he was not of the class that one could tip, even assuming that that would not grossly offend some Korean sense of propreity.

As we toiled together up the hill I thought of the injunction in the Sermon on the Mount: "If a man ask thee to go one mile with him go with him twain". This Oriental pagan, from the natural goodness of his heart, was doing precisely that—and more than twice over—with no hope of reward. I wondered how many Christians in the West would have done the same.

Both very tired and sweaty, we reached the church on the hill at last. The Korean bowed low, smiled, looked at his watch and disappeared down the hill again just as two young Columbans came out to see who and what I was.

XII

THE LEAVEN AT WORK

WHAT is the quality, the calibre, of the ordinary Christians who are in the front line of the battle for men's hearts and minds in Asia? At first glance it would seem wrong to generalise from those at Mokpo, since the story of Mokpo's Christians is in some ways an exceptional one. Yet their special quality derives from the fact that theirs is very largely a convert community of recent vintage. It may not, therefore, be unreasonable to hope that they are a pointer to what the Christian Asian of tomorrow will be like—if tomorrow belongs to the Christians. If it does not, then it is possible that there may be no tomorrow for any of us.

Let me say at once that my stay in Mokpo was one of the high spots, if not *the* high spot, of my life. It was a profoundly moving and unforgettable experience. I do not mean that the new Christians of that town have reached some unheard-of level of human perfection. Precisely because they are human they have their full share of failings. But, because they are almost all new to the Faith and have reached it by a hard road, they have together created something like what one imagines the atmosphere of early Christianity to have been.

My thirteen hours on the 'Mokpo Express' had been a thousand times worthwhile. When I boarded the train I was still an observer, looking at Korea and the Koreans from the outside. When I left it I felt that I 'belonged'.

Without knowing a word of each other's language we had none the less succeeded in making our minds contact. I had shared the suffering of my dying consumptive, exchanged sympathetic glances with his wife, now and again giving her a hand as she attended to his needs. I had shared bits of food (against all advice to the contrary) with my Korean companions.

192

I had laughed as extravagantly as they had done at the absurd—
for the extravagant laughter of a simple, unsophisticated people
is infectious. I had whiled away the long hours in their company. Finally, I had been helped, and helped quite selflessly, by
one of their number.

So when I took off my shoes at the church door at five next
morning, walked in stockinged feet to take my place with the
Koreans who were crowding in to Mass, then sat on the floor
among them, I no longer felt like an outsider, even though the
children—and some adults too, in this town where Westerners
are rare—did follow me wherever I went.

Most of the Koreans had been at the church since four
o'clock. Since then, led by Old Paul the catechist, they had said
their morning prayers aloud together. Throughout the larger
part of the time that the celebrant was at the altar they intoned
the prayers of the Mass in melodious sing-song voices. I came
to know well the pattern of their lives. When Mass was over
they streamed out into the cool morning air, a great throng of
men, women and children, exchanged hurried greetings, then
made their way down the hill.

For the men, in most cases, it meant going straight to a long,
hard day wading among the young swamp rice in the paddy-
fields. The women would later, much later, make a meal, which
they would take out to the men and share with them. They
would work till sunset, eat a quick evening meal at home,
then come up the hill again to say their night prayers aloud, for
perhaps an hour or more. Darkness would come, the curfew—
still maintained from the times when the guerillas were a direct
and constant threat to the townsfolk—would sound and they
would hurry down to their homes. All over the town the lights
would shine briefly in their squat little houses made of bamboo
and wattle, with thinly thatched roofs. Then the day was done.
And tomorrow, and all the other tomorrows, would be just the
same.

I stood that first morning profoundly moved as I watched
them making their way down the hill, up which I had climbed
the previous night, the women in their clean white, short
coatees, long skirts and blue rubber shoes with upturned toes,

the men in long white coats and big rice-straw hats. As I stood there, Fr. Sean Savage strolled up to me. He was a young Northern Irishman, dark, dour, slow-smiling, but with wonderful mastery of the Korean language acquired after only brief time in the country.

"Their work and their Faith, that's all they've got," he said as we stood together. "They're some of the poorest people of God's earth, but they are some of the richest too." Already knew that he was right.

No one could be less emotional than Sean Savage. He had met me in the mission compound the previous night with no sign of any sort of a reaction at finding an Englishman in uniform suddenly turning up unannounced in his churchyard. But now he added quite simply:

"You know, there are times, when I'm in the confessional hearing these people's poor little sins, when I feel like saying 'Let's change round. I've got no right to be here—it's you who should be hearing mine.' "

From having in the church already that morning felt something of the quiet fervour of these Korean men and women who could talk quite naturally and unaffectedly with their God for hours on end, and whose whole lives revolved around the Church, I understood what he meant. I nodded, feeling that words were unnecessary, then we turned and walked down the rough path round the side of the hill to the priests' house.

The church had been erected by the old French Mission pioneers years ago. The large house at its side had been built by the Columbans soon after they took over the Prefecture in the mid-1930s. Mgr. Thomas Quinlan had been one of the young priests there at the time.

It was a centre to which priests throughout the Prefecture could come, and be accommodated, for retreats and other diocesan gatherings. In addition it was the language school where young priests newly arrived in the country were taught the language before being sent out to the parishes, and it was the mission equivalent of the Bishop's Residence. But mission bishops in places like Korea tend to live simply, sharing the same life and quarters as the youngest and rawest of their priests.

At that moment the Prefecture was without its Prefect Apostolic, and the pro-Prefect, Fr. Harold Henry (later to become Prefect), who was carrying on the work until an official appointment came from Rome, was in America trying to raise funds for some of the most urgent of his projects. In his absence, Fr. Thomas Kane, a tall, broad-shouldered, quiet-voiced Chicago man in his late thirties or early forties, was taking his place. The Kwangju Prefecture, the most promising in the Korean mission, might therefore be said at that time to be in the care of a pro-pro-Prefect.

Fr. Kane's pale face and pale lips suggested the possibility of anaemia (or his condition may have been due to his years in jail during the Pacific war). But there was nothing anaemic about his Christianity, which was full-blooded enough.

St. Columban's House in Mokpo was the centre of an exciting movement towards the Church and from every part of the Prefecture were coming reports of people streaming in more quickly than the available personnel could handle them. As we ate our breakfast together that first morning I learned of these developments from the two priests who were running the Mokpo city parish and the others who were engaged in the administration of the diocese.

The following day, which was the day before Whit Sunday, I attended the baptism of a dozen converts, men, women and children. The seven lay catechists of the area were all present for the occasion and when the ceremony was over I plied them with questions for over an hour. There was Old Paul, the senior catechist, aged seventy-four, with four thousand converts to his credit; Louis, a peasant in his fifties, who took care of the surrounding villages; Simon, aged forty-five, who had been a lawyer, but had gone out of the profession to work for eleven dollars a month as a catechist. Simon was an intelligent, widely read but unassuming man, well versed in apologetics and theology and able to deal with any enquirer into the Faith who might come from among the town's students, university professors or professional men.

Angela, Veronica, Barbara, Margaret and Josephine, ranging in age from thirty-five to fifty-nine, were between them suited to deal with any women and children requiring instruction.

The Faith of all of them had been put to the test during the war and all had come out with flying colours. From them, with Fr. Sean Savage translating, I got a picture of the Faith in Mokpo as it is seen by the Korean Christians themselves.

The story of the Mokpo Catholics is a fascinating and heroic one.

There were only a thousand or so of them when the Korean War came. For fifteen years the Columbans had been trying to build up their number, but the abnormal conditions of the mid-1930s, caused by the Sino-Japanese War, and then the interruption of their work by the Pacific War, during which all the priests were jailed, had made it a slow business. The Catholics were but a tiny minority in this city of some one hundred and fifty thousand souls, but, like so many other Oriental Christians, they were tremendously loyal and firm in their Faith.

Then came the invasion by the North Korean Communists. Its full significance was not immediately appreciated in Mokpo. The 38th Parallel was some two hundred miles away, and in Korea that means two hundred miles of continuous mountain ranges. Down in the extreme south-westerly tip of their country the people of this typically provincial city, which still cannot boast a single surfaced road in the entire place, felt cut off from the disturbing happenings to the north.

But soon came news that the Communists were sweeping all before them and that soon they might even reach remote Mokpo. The Catholics there had been told something of the nature of Communism by the missionaries. They had acquired some practical knowledge of it too, from the activities of the Red guerillas who lived in the hills between Mokpo and Pusan. They realised that the arrival of the North Koreans might mean great suffering for them. But they stayed, prepared to see it through—and in any case they had little choice, since the town was on the coast and there was nowhere to which they might escape. The coming of the Communists did, indeed, mean suffering for them.

"They saw us as their biggest enemies," Old Paul told me as we sat together after the baptisms were over.

"And they had plans to get rid of all the Catholics in the town. They looked on the Church as an organisation of the imperialists and anyone who was prominent in it or worked for it was seen as a spy," added one of the women.

In Mokpo, as in other similarly compact cities, the local Communists had long ago listed the names and addresses of all the Catholics, in readiness for the day when their comrades in the North would come and 'liberate' the the town. Part of the process of liberation was to be the execution of every single Catholic.

When the North Koreans arrived, the lists of names were passed to them by the local Fifth Column and plans went ahead to destroy the entire Catholic community. There were many old scores settled in an unplanned way during those first days of Communist conquest, but the execution of the Catholics was to be done according to plan.

Mgr. Brennan, the Columban who was Prefect Apostolic, and Fr. Cusack and Fr. O'Brien, two of his priests, were arrested and taken away by the Communists when they retreated north. It is strongly suspected that they were among the victims of a mass execution in Taejon, where thousands of prisoners were killed by the Communists in cold blood and buried in communal graves before they pulled out.

I later learned how Father Brian Geraghty, the Columban Director up in Seoul, came down to Taejon when the graves were opened and spent hours among relatives of the victims, who with masks over their mouths and nostrils inspected the thousands of decomposing bodies. He found it impossible to identify any of his three colleagues. It was just one of many such jobs which have come his way during his years in the Korea Mission.

With the three Western priests out of the way, the Communists next quietly got ready to deal with the lay leaders. The catechists were seized, so were the Korean house-boys and cook at the priests' house. So, too, were many of the ordinary Catholics. They were all lined up, questioned, then told that unless they gave up belief in God they would be executed. Not one wavered.

Two days later, Old Paul was interrogated alone whilst the Communists were raiding the priests' house. But the old man had spirit and chided them even though he was their prisoner.

"You can't take that, it belongs to the missionaries and to the Church," he told them as he saw them preparing to remove the entire contents of the house.

"It won't make any difference to you, Granddad, you're going to Heaven today."

"That may be, and I don't care anyway. But I don't like the way you're giving this country to Russia. And I don't like what you are doing to the Church."

"You shut up and get ready for your wonderful Heaven. We're going to make a real heaven of this place when this war is over."

But soon the North Koreans got the order to pull out of the town. They appear to have decided, none the less, to deal with the Catholics before they left.

One man was charged with the job of executing Old Paul. Some others poured petrol on the house with the idea of burning it down. Another group packed all the Catholics already under arrest into a garage and sprinkled that with petrol too. John, the cook, was made to dig his own grave and stood at its side awaiting the fatal bullet.

But neither Old Paul nor John died. Nor were the Bishop's house and the garage-ful of Christians sent up in flames. For at that very moment some South Korean troops arrived on the scene, supported by American aircraft. The man who was about to execute Old Paul was himself killed by an American bomb as he ran away. The Communist who was preparing to shoot John the cook, down into the grave he had been made to dig, died on the little path from the house to the church with a South Korean knife in his back.

The Communists went away, the women who had gone to hide in the country outside the city came back. The little Catholic community got together again, minus its three spiritual leaders.

Then came the bombshell. The North Korean Communists had been driven back, the United Nations had gone sweeping north, but now the Chinese had come into the war. Already, according to rumours, they had a reputation for being even harder on Catholics. And they were heading straight for Mokpo.

The news sounded like a death-knell to the townsfolk of Mokpo in general and to the Catholics in particular. This time there were no Columban Fathers to whom they could turn for help and guidance. But the rank and file Catholics, quite spontaneously, began to make their way up the hill to the church. More remarkable, some of the pagans joined them.

The church filled to the doors, it overflowed, and soon there were people, pagans and Christians alike, packing the big yard outside. Led by the lay catechists they began to say the Rosary, asking Our Lady to save Mokpo from the Communists or, if that was not to be, that God should give them the grace and strength to die as Christians should.

As the Chinese Reds drove deeper and deeper south, this great, curiously mixed congregation prayed all night, storming heaven with their prayers. Whilst the enemy made towards the city their great unbroken battery of prayer continued. And then, at the last moment, when it seemed that the city must inevitably soon fall, the United Nations' forces arrived, drove the Communists back, away from Mokpo and on and on up the country right to the 38th Parallel. Though the war dragged on for years after that, the Communists never again came near Mokpo.

You can say, as I have done, to people in Mokpo: "The United Nations' forces came just in time to save your city, didn't they?" But even the pagans will reply: "It was Our Lady who saved Mokpo."

In the circumstances, it is hardly surprising that the catechists I met that morning had a heartening story of great progress to tell me.

In terms of cold statistics the story is impressive: over three thousand Catholics in that parish and an additional thousand and more down in a recently-started one in another part of the town run by a Korean priest, Fr. Victor Kim. Another couple of thousand converts had left the town for other parts of the

country, taking the Faith with them. And six hundred out of the
original Catholic community had not been accounted for since
the Communists came to Mokpo. There had been over seven
hundred baptisms last year and many more were certain during
the current one. In Fr. Kim's new parish two hundred and
eighty-nine converts had been made in the past twelve months,
and four hundred and fifty catechumens were under instruction
at that moment.

In other words, the figures showed that a snowball action had
started. Significantly, and important for future development,
those coming to the Church were a reasonable cross-section of
the populace as a whole. There were peasants, townsfolk,
professional people; they ranged from intellectuals to illiterates,
from little children to venerable old men and women. The
appeal of the Church was to all sections, not either just the
privileged or the under-privileged, the educated or the un-
educated. One of the parish's latest converts, whom I was to
meet later, was head of the local university and had just been
elected to the National Assembly, representing a Mokpo
constituency and returned as a member of a party in opposition
to the Rhee Government.

That was the side of the catechists' progress report which
could be told in figures. The other side to the new and promising situation was something one sensed as one mixed with the
people. It could be felt if you went into the church, at any
time from four in the morning until long after dark, for there
were always dozens, and sometimes hundreds, of Koreans there
at their devotions. It could be heard in their songs and prayers
and their endless saying of the Rosary. It could be witnessed
during Mass as they crowded down to the rail for Communion.

Here was a largely convert community, a large body of people
who had newly come to the Faith through appalling hardship
and suffering. It was as near to New Testament Christianity as
one can get, two thousand years after the death of Christ. It was
Pentecostal in its fervour, but that fervour was not of the Holy
Roller type, it was not wildly or emotionally demonstrative.
Yet it could be felt unmistakably. It was very real and went deep.

Each of the catechists in turn—and this included Old Paul,

who for forty years had been a catechist—declared, in answer to
my questions, that they had never at any time known so many
people coming as converts to the Faith and so many others
wanting to know more about it.

"If we started another church in another part of the town
tomorrow we could get another four hundred converts within a
year," said Old Paul. "The next year you would more than
double that number, for every convert here is convert-minded
and gets at least one new one in a year. At the moment most are
getting many more than that."

Said Simon Kim, the one-time attorney: "There is really no
limit to the number we can get. As soon as men and women
become Catholics today they go out and start telling all their
friends and neighbours about what they've got. And because
Koreans everywhere at this moment are asking the questions
which really matter and to which we alone have got the answers,
they quickly get converts as a consequence."

"How does this compare with the Japanese times?" I asked.

The catechists talked it over together.

"It is nearly one hundred per cent better. In the last years of
Japanese rule our people were under pressure to practise
Shintoism. There was not real freedom of religion. Now there
is religious freedom—the first that most people alive today have
ever known. Shintoism went when the Japanese went. So
there is a big gap left and, coming at the same time as the new
religious freedom, that has given us a great chance."

One after another they told of places of which they knew,
where to be given a catechist, or a priest, or a little church,
"even as small as a house," would lead inevitably to the
immediate conversions of hundreds.

One shrewd-looking elderly woman catechist had been
quietly thinking it over whilst the others talked. "In twenty
years we could have this Province Catholic if only we had
enough priests," she said with quiet confidence. The others all
agreed.

I brought them round to the subject of Communism again.
Simon Kim had grown up in North Korea before the Communists took it in 1945. For more than five years he had lived

under Communism. He left when the United Nations' troops withdrew, after their first big push into the North. As compared to what the Communists did in the North their treatment of Catholics in the South was relatively mild, he said.

Simon had been well-known as a Catholic catechist up there. He soon discovered, when the Communists first came, that if he talked to anyone in the street they were invariably arrested that night. Soon the Communists were forcing all the able-bodied youths and men into the Army. He had no desire to fight for Communism nor to endanger his friends, so he hid in some caves along with large numbers of other Catholics. He later learned that most of those local Catholics who did not similarly hide were sooner or later taken out and shot.

Thirty-three-year-old Fr. Tjun, the Korean priest in Simon's own parish, refused to obey the Communists' orders when they told him to stop his work. He was taken out of the town, his lips were sewn together with wire so that he could say no last word of encouragement to his people, and then his head was bashed in with a stone.

"For five years I lived under Communism," Simon Kim told me, "and the recollection of those years from 1945 till December, 1950, are still a nightmare to me."

The way in which Communist policy was applied, he said, had tended to vary from one area to another according to whether there were few or many Catholics there. In the area from which he came, where the Faith had been strong, if there were now any Catholics left at all, they would be only the old grandfathers and grandmothers. All the young ones had long since either been killed or had got out.

When I met Fr. Victor Kim, the Korean pastor in the new parish in the town, I found that he too was a North Korean. He had been taught by the German Benedictines of Wonsan. They had trained this intelligent, smiling-faced man well.

Like Simon Kim, Fr. Victor had had to go into hiding after the arrival of the Communists. He had already escaped to the South and was in Seoul when the Communists got there. He knew that he could expect no mercy if they found him, and was prepared for the worst. Three times they came to the house where he was hiding and each time they missed him. In the end he managed to get to Pusan, where he served as a chaplain with the R.O.K. troops, going with them right up into his native North again, prior to the big Chinese push south.

The converts, he reported, were already streaming into his newly-established Mokpo parish, and he expected that their number would shoot up spectacularly when this new church, which was just being completed, was opened. Already the crypt was being put to good use, and was yielding its crop of converts, even before the building above it was finished.

For in the crypt he had established a kindergarten, which was now being run by a small group of North Korean nuns (also trained at Wonsan) who had escaped to the South and lived in a little house by the church. There were some one hundred and ten children, most of them from middle-class homes. The kindergarten had been established only three weeks, but already a handful of parents were coming for instruction. The nuns thought it probable that all would come in due course.

"If we had accommodation for twice the number of children we would have twice the number of parents as converts," one of them told me.

When I called on them, the children were playing an organised game. One nun was sitting at a harmonium, playing a dance tune and singing lustily. Another was crawling round and round the floor, along a white circle which had been painted on it, and followed by one half of the children, also on their knees. The remainder of the children crawled in the opposite direction round another circle inside the first. A third nun, keeping time with the music, stood rhythmically clapping her hands.

They insisted that I should sit in the centre of the two circles, to the great amusement of the delightful Korean infants, but to the detriment of the game, for they all wanted to stop and look at me. Many Korean children are very lovely and all are quite fascinatingly unselfconscious. One after the other little five-year-olds, boys and girls, stood up to sing me solos.

In his presbytery I got Fr. Kim to talk about his work. He was, he reported, having particular success with the students and intellectuals in the town. Three dozen students were at that moment under instruction.

I questioned him about the movement of intellectuals towards the Church, and about the reasons for the present progress. Fr. Kim is a man of great intelligence—which in part accounts for his success with the intellectuals—with a striking breadth of outlook and a clarity of thought. The reasons he gave me for the Church's headway are therefore of some interest and value, the more so as they were subsequently endorsed by the Columbans at the priests' house and by the keenest educated laymen I could find as well. These latter included the town's Catholic naval commander and the head of the local university, to whom I have already referred. The same, or similar, reasons were subsequently given to me over and over again in every part of the country.

Firstly: For a long period, despite the fact that Catholics had done the pioneer work for Christianity in Korea, most people who became Christians went to the Protestants, who, having more money, had schools, colleges, hospitals and orphanages, all of which the Catholics lacked. Today pagans who grow interested in Christianity note, and are put off by, the growing disunity and fragmentation of Korea's Protestant sects and turn instead to consider the claims of the Catholic Church.

Secondly: They admire immensely (Fr. Kim used the Korean triple affirmative) the celibacy of the Catholic clergy. Koreans traditionally have identified sanctity and scholarship with celibacy, but it has usually been in relation to people long since dead. They found it difficult to believe it possible on the part of people they knew. Fifteen years ago few people believed that the Catholic priests' celibacy was genuine, or, at the best, they doubted it. Today it is accepted, and that acceptance has been aided indirectly by the fact that Catholic missionaries, unlike their Protestant opposite numbers, had no families to think about and were therefore generally in a better position to 'stick it out' with their people when the Korean War came.

Thirdly: The war and the tremendous loss of life which came with it, leaving hardly a family in the land without someone to mourn, brought home to the people a conviction that there must be something more in life than just the things of this world; that there must be a God, a soul and a life after death. For the same reason it made them re-examine their own paganism and realise its inadequacy in time of stress and suffering, and its inability to provide the answers to the tremendous fundamental questions which were worrying them.

Fourthly: Koreans have been greatly impressed and influenced by the way in which Catholic G.I.s attended Mass. "These are the Christians who really take their religion seriously," they have said as they noted the packed churches and regular attendance at Mass by Catholics.

Fifthly: They have seen proof of the extraordinary generosity of American Catholics in the enormous quantities of relief goods sent and distributed through Catholic war relief agencies. They have also noted the way in which those goods were handed out without any hint of discrimination, according to the needs and not according to the beliefs of the recipients. And they saw that there were no 'strings' attached to the gifts.

During the weeks that followed I met a number of Korean priests in different parts of the country. Almost all had an exceptionally difficult time during the period of the Communist occupation, and now had exciting stories to tell of how, although marked men, they had none the less somehow managed to survive.

For example, with Fr. Tom Kane and Fr. Savage I went one day to see Fr. Paul Kim at Hampyong. We travelled for most of the way along rough roads which only a jeep could take without breaking a spring or getting bogged down. At one point we reached a river which was normally crossed by a bridge. But the bridge had collapsed, and we had to drive straight through the water instead, nosing our way cautiously across, testing its unknown depth as we went. We knew in advance that just a few yards to our right, at any rate, the water was deep enough to go right over the jeep, for a huge, high army truck was stuck there with the water far above its wheels, waiting for the level to drop when the tide changed further down the river.

Fr. Kim's story was typical of what Koreans in his position have endured in recent years. He was a small, round-faced man with glasses and greying hair. He had been jailed by the Japanese because of his connection with a 'foreign' Church—that is part of the story of most of the priests of his generation.

When the Communists arrived in his parish in July, 1950, they told him that there would be religious liberty for all. For just one week he practised that liberty, celebrating Mass each day unhindered.

But then, during Mass one day, an armed party of Communists came in, ordered the people to their knees and began to interrogate him. They put him on a charge, but not, of course, for being a Catholic priest. Instead, they faked a reason which allegedly had nothing to do with his religion.

The Communist chief looked around the newly-built church and asked how Fr. Kim had got the money to build it.

"My people helped me to build it."

"Who carted the sand you used?"

"My people."

"How much did you pay them?"

"Nothing. They did it voluntarily."

"Then we charge you with being an exploiter of the people."

The Communists began to try to intimidate the people by firing shots above their heads, there inside the church. They took pot shots at a statue of Our Lady and put a bullet through the Tabernacle on the altar. Then they tied together the entire congregation of three hundred and took them off to the police station.

Later, most were released, but Fr. Kim was kept in jail along with thirteen of his lay leaders. Among these was Fr. Kim's own brother, a builder who had been engaged in the construction of his church. One night, just before the North Koreans were told to pull out of the town, they took him away and riddled him with bullets. They would have done the same to Fr. Kim, but the order for the evacuation of the town came just in time to save him.

There was an interlude of some three weeks between the departure of the North Korean troops and the actual arrival of the South Koreans. Throughout the period, as in Mokpo, the local Communists went around killing all the opponents of

Communism they could find and settling some old personal scores at the same time. Fr. Kim heard what was happening and managed to escape from jail. He went back to see his church. There he heard that the Communists were looking for him, and hid under the floorboards for twenty-five days, until the arrival of the R.O.K.s.

Some of his people who knew that he was there managed to get sufficient food to him to keep him alive. Once they came and told him that one of his parishioners was thought to be dying. It was a case for Extreme Unction, and he decided that it was his duty to take a chance. He dressed in woman's clothes, went out, anointed the dying Christian, then returned to his hiding place under the boards. On another day he crept out and baptised a family of converts. Whilst he was away, the Communists came and burned down the church. Taking a chance had this time saved his life.

The local Communists were driven into the hills, from where for some time they continued to raid surrounding villages, killing those who would not help them. In 1952 the authorities gave them two months in which to surrender and be pardoned or take the consequences. Many came back. "But the die-hards are still there to this day," Fr. Kim told me.

He estimated that at that time (June, 1954) there were probably some three to four hundred Communist guerillas in his district, some three thousand in the whole area and at the most ten thousand in the country as a whole.

His progress report was typical of those I was given in every part of the country.

When he arrived in Hampyong nine years before, there were sixty Catholics in the entire area. Now there were one thousand six hundred, despite all the upheavals during that period. Before the people had experienced the Communist invasion he averaged some one hundred converts a year. But now the figure was shooting up. Last year it had been three hundred; this year it would be many more, for he had three hundred people under instruction at that moment.

"If you build a church, or put a catechist, in any village around here you could be certain of at least two hundred converts in the first year—after which the number would go up and up each year."

We lunched with Fr. Kim and his young Irish Columban assistant, then pushed on to Naju, where a young Korean priest, Fr. Lucius Chang, had a picturesque little Church built in attractive Korean style. In his small town he had had two hundred and seventy converts in the past twelve months, and, with two hundred and thirty currently under instruction, was expecting more in the next year.

In the area for which he was responsible there was a State leper colony with some four hundred lepers. At Easter he had baptised some thirty of these into the Faith. One of the lepers was trained and given responsibility for instructing others, and at the moment some sixty were receiving instruction from him.

From Naju we bumped along more rough tracks, through open country and on to a remote spot in which was a Catholic leper colony, started a few months previously by Fr. Harold Henry, the Columban pro-Prefect Apostolic.

Crowds of lepers, men, women and children, gathered around our jeep to welcome us as we arrived. There was a boy of perhaps fifteen or sixteen years of age with an active ulcer on one ankle, so large and deep-seated that it looked as though his foot might fall off at any moment. An elderly man who constituted himself one of their spokesmen had not a finger left on either hand. His face was a mass of ulcers, and his sight was failing. There were mothers with small babies on their backs, children of all ages, and several teen-agers, who included a very attractive young girl of perhaps eighteen or nineteen.

I asked to see the doctor. There was none. Instead, a thirty-year-old leper named Moses An came forward. Moses had a scarred and somewhat twisted face. But despite the ravages of the disease it was also clearly an intelligent and sensitive one.

He was not, he explained, a trained doctor, but before coming to the present camp he had had years in a big State leper colony, and there had learned something about the administration of drugs, and had picked up some rough surgery. At present he was doing amputations with a penknife and a small axe. Could I get him a bone saw? he asked earnestly. I promised him I would try. In fact, thanks to the generosity of my fellow Catholics, I did quickly raise the money for one soon after my return to England.

Accompanied by Moses An, and followed by some fifty or sixty lepers, I went around the camp. It was, to all intents and purposes, a newly-built village in which the villagers supported themselves by growing their own food in the surrounding fields. They were doing almost everything for themselves. They had built their own houses, and were still building more and had just finished a little bamboo and mud chapel, into which they proudly took me.

They took me, too, into the dispensary they were just completing. It was pathetic. With great pride they showed me its various rooms. "But where are the drugs, dressings and surgical instruments?" I asked. The answer was that there were none, literally none at all.

Everything depended, it seemed, upon the outcome of the tour which Fr. Harold Henry was making in America, where he was appealing for funds to carry on his work, of which this was a part.

Being in the leper camp meant in practice that they were segregated from society, but apart from that, for lack of funds, nothing was at that moment being done. They had had drugs but had used them all and were patiently waiting for more. Meanwhile, for want of more drugs, the old man's sight was steadily being destroyed, the young boy's foot was fast approaching the stage where it would go entirely, the disease was getting an ever greater hold on the attractive teen-age girl. . . .

I thought back to the huge leper camp I had visited a few months earlier in Africa. There a steady supply of modern drugs was coming in and the Franciscan Missionary Sisters of Africa who ran it were getting spectacular cures as a consequence. I recalled the series of photographs the two nuns there had shown me, tracing case-histories from the time of arrival at the camp to the cure and dismissal. Then I looked again at the boy with the hanging foot, the attractive girl, the mothers and fathers of families and the little children crowding around them.

"It seems to me," I told Fr. Kane and Fr. Savage, who were accompanying me, "that when possible cures for leprosy exist in the world, we in the West have a responsibility to see that they are somehow made available, if it is at all possible, to those who would benefit by them wherever they may be." They agreed, in principle, but reiterated that everything depended upon the response that Fr. Henry got to his appeals for help. Nothing could be expected from the near-bankrupt Korean State.

I found myself thinking, too, of some of the Western Christians I had met who, so far as one could see, were just as materialistic as the modern pagans around them. I wished that they could see that empty dispensary, or hear Moses An's anxious pleas for a bone saw with which to do his amateurish amputations.

Meanwhile, the one hundred and twenty lepers were at least getting back their self-respect in this Catholic camp by living a decent community life together, making themselves self-supporting, and by being treated not as pariahs but as in-dividuals of incalculable worth.

That was, indeed, something, as I could appreciate from an experience I had had in Mokpo a few days earlier. There I saw a group of begging lepers who for some weeks had been going around the town blackmailing tradesmen and others into giving them money. Their technique was to go into a shop, ask for money and then, when they were given something, to demand some vastly larger, and often quite ruinous, sum. If the shop-keeper refused they simply took up positions around the door-way of his shop, if necessary for days on end, until he gave in. This sooner or later he was likely to do, since Koreans have a great fear of the disease, which is widespread throughout the country, and as a consequence no customer would be likely to push past them into the shop. Trade would cease and sooner or later the shopkeeper would have to admit defeat, for usually the police refused to drive the lepers away, because of their own fear of leprosy.

In theory, all lepers were supposed to be isolated in State or other leper colonies. But in the existing disorganised state of

ιe country bad types among the lepers (who are of course a
ιross-section of a community which, like any other, contains its
ιrooks and blackmailers as well as its saints) were constantly
ιscaping, banding themselves together and terrorising the
ιopulace.

In Kwangju next day I was to learn that no less than four
ιundred had that very morning been rounded up by American
ιroops and run out in military trucks to the nearest big State
ιprosarium.

There was no doubt, therefore, of the moral good which Fr.
ιlenry's colony was already achieving by helping the people
ιhere to live a decent and relatively normal life. Spiritually, its
ιinety-seven Catholics were benefiting greatly too, by having
ιheir own chapel, in which they themselves organised daily
ιrayers together, and by living in the company of fellow
ιCatholics.

But their need for proper medical supervision and supplies
ιvas urgent none the less. Fr. Kane told me that Fr. Henry was
ιoping that, in addition to getting cash during his tour, he
ιnight also be able to find a small community of medical nuns
ιvho would volunteer to look after them, in which case the
ιumber of lepers in the camp could be increased almost
ιndefinitely.

As it was, I left the colony, despite the friendliness and cheer-
ιulness of the lepers themselves, deeply troubled by the
ιnowledge that they were missing so much that modern
ιnedicine could do for them.

I was still depressed when we got to Song Jong Ni. All the
ιvay from the leper camp, as we had bumped along over rough
ιracks for mile after mile, I was fretting over that empty
ιlispensary. As we got nearer to Song Jong Ni, I gloomily
ιecalled that it was at the station in this town, on my journey
ιrom Seoul down to Mokpo, that the largest numbers and quite
ιhe most neglected of all the homeless waifs I had seen invaded
ιhe train. The recollection of the hungry boy dashing across
ιhe tracks with the scrap of raw fish made me still more
ιlepressed.

But that gloomy side of the picture was balanced by another

after I had met Fr. Mangan at his church in the town. A children's catechism class was in session when we arrived, and soon I was sitting with Fr. Mangan on the floor in the middle of scores of delightful little tots of both sexes, who answered our questions with a complete absence of self-consciousness.

Fr. Mangan, like Fr. Philip Crosbie, was a Columban from Australia. And like Fr. Crosbie, who was the first Columban I ever met, he was not given to advertising his own achievements. I will confess that I allowed myself to be deceived by his appearance, putting him down in my own mind at first as one of the less dynamic personalities of his Society. Then, with great difficulty, I began, despite his reticence, to extract scraps of information from him, which I was later able to check with others.

Making Christians in the town was easier now than ever before, he said. When I got him to produce his figures it was clear that this was so. Once again it was the story of the 'snowball'. Four years ago there were just thirty Catholics in Song Jong Ni. Now there were four hundred, in a town of ten thousand people, making them already, as an organised minority, a force in the place. But the graph was sharply rising and at that moment there were another hundred under instruction. It could be three or four times that number had he the forces available to instruct them. Fr. Mangan was actually having for the time being to turn away would-be Christians because with the forces he had available there was no means of satisfactorily teaching so many the Faith. Yet still they crowded to his Masses in such numbers that often the baptised Christians themselves could not get into the church, and he had reluctantly to ask pagans to make room for them.

Beside his present church a new one was being erected. It would hold four hundred at each Mass—and he expected to be able to fill it over and over again. His great need was for catechists. But lay catechists, even though they gladly accept the minimum on which to live decently, cost money.

"For fifty cents a day I could ensure a hundred souls for God each year," he told me wistfully, "for every catechist would get at least a hundred converts in the course of a year."

"At the rate he is going he'll have the whole town Catholic before long," Fr. Kane wrote me four months later, after I had returned to England. Fr. Kane was writing to tell me that the new church had just been officially blessed and opened and that Fr. Mangan, assisted by Fr. Philip Crosbie, had baptised a great new batch of converts.

At Kwangju, where we arrived as night was falling, it was much the same story. As we ate our evening meal with Fr. Rafferty, the local priest, the background to our conversation was the sound of forty pagan children in an adjoining room learning the catechism by rote. I was coming to regard the sound of voices repeating the catechism as a normal part of life in Korea's presbyteries. I met it wherever I went.

The most exciting personal story I heard in Kwangju came from Sister Rosa. She was a tiny Korean nun, probably no more than four feet eight or nine inches in height, who looked not a day older than eighteen. But she assured me that she was thirty-two. Koreans, and their women in particular, tend either to look young or old. There are a few, but only a few, who look middle-aged.

But even by Korean standards Sister Rosa was still extra-ordinarily young-looking. With each hand tucked into the opposite sleeve of her habit, only her youthful, smiling face was visible. One's first reaction was that here was someone quite unformed by any notable experiences of any sort—small, innocent and perhaps over-sheltered, whom you would instinctively want to protect, just as you would protect a helpless child. It was difficult to think of her as a 'front-line fighter'.

Sister Rosa came from North Korea. Her father was a shopkeeper-cum-farmer, a small proprietor. She became a nun whilst she was in the North, joining a congregation started by the German Benedictines at Wonsan.

During the Pacific War the Japanese drove the twenty or so nuns out of their convent in order to house some of their sailors there. When the Japs were driven out by the Russians the Sisters found it impossible to continue community life of any sort, and so went out into the parishes to work as priests' housekeepers. But soon the priests were all arrested or obliged to flee and the nuns one by one made their way back to the convent. There for three years they were put to work by the Russians making clothes for the women who accompanied their troops.

With the departure of the Russians, things became still more difficult. The North Koreans who took over regarded the nuns as imperialist spies, and subjected them to constant surveillance and interrogation. Gradually they turned the heat on them, putting up their taxes bit by bit until there was no hope of their being able to pay.

Finally, at one o'clock one morning, Red troops came to arrest them. They were all put in jail. A week later the Koreans among them were told that they must go back to their families. Their nuns' habits were taken from them and they were given ordinary Korean clothes and sent packing. Some German nuns arrested at the same time were kept in jail and have not been heard of since.

Five of the Sisters managed to make their way across the border and down to the South. In 1950 another group filtered through, following in the wake of the United Nations' forces as they were driven back over the Parallel. Little Sister Rosa was ill at the time and so unable to accompany them. But she, too, was planning to escape from the Communist North into the part of the country where she could continue her life as a nun unhindered by persecution.

At last, in 1952, this tiny woman with the childlike expression set out on her own to make for the South and freedom. The Communist forces in the North and the United Nations in the South were dug in along a front which stretched from one side of the country to the other and ran through wild and mountainous country. Moreover, the front was fiercely active.

At that time there were lawless adventurers, natural bandits, who made a living by smuggling people down to the South. They probably still do. Often both the guides and their 'clients' were caught, cross-examined and shot, or else just shot out of hand by some guard who came across them on his night watch. To undertake this journey one had to be as fearless as the bandits—perhaps more so, since they were often as dangerous as the Communist soldiers themselves.

Sister Rosa collected the necessary cash to pay the high fees demanded, then set out one night with a group of desperadoes as her guides. For weeks they slowly made their way through the Communist lines. They slept by day, hiding in caves and forests, and by night they made their way south, wading rivers and climbing perilous mountain slopes and evading enemy patrols. They found a spot where the Chinese lines were thin, in a high mountain region, and managed to slip through. Then they made their way across no-man's-land, but for days could make no contact with U.N. or South Korean forces and so remained exposed between the lines.

Some smugglers who should have met them from the South had failed to arrive. Money began to run out, the gang Sister Rosa was with demanded more money and, since she had not got it, they said they could wait no longer and must go back. So back they went to the place from which they had set out. All the risks and all the expense had been for nothing.

Again she saved up, and in due course approached the smugglers again. They said they would make another attempt to get her through. This time, she decided, there would be no going back. She would push on, if necessary alone, until she was killed, rather than return to the Communist North.

It was the period of the last big military push before the truce and the whole front was alive with bombing and shelling. But again they got through the Chinese lines by night. Once a Communist guard challenged them in the darkness and they had to run, expecting to be shot at any moment. But at last they reached the U.N. side of the front. There, although they failed to contact the smugglers from the South who were to guide them, they fell in with some friendly American and South Korean troops who undertook to get Sister Rosa through the fighting lines and on through the area in which no civilians were permitted.

After two months of continuous night travel she got to Inchon. For much of the journey she had been ill and without

H

food. Now, having got to relative safety, she collapsed. But ten days later she was off again, making her way down to Taejon, where, she had heard, some of the other Korean nuns of her congregation were now working among Communist prisoners of war. When she joined them at last she learned that fifteen out of the Korean Sisters had succeeded in getting through to the South, many of them suffering hardships on the way similar to her own. Eight of those who had set out were unaccounted for. Her own sister, also a nun, had got down to Mokpo, and was the Superior of the little group I had found running the kindergarten there. Sister Rosa and three of the others were now running their own kindergarten in Kwangju, and also instructing converts.

As we sat together on the floor of their little convent I asked them how the results of their work compared today with those of the past.

"In Wonsan in the old days life was easier," said one of them. "We had a fine convent and monastery, and we thought the number of converts we got was good. But it was nothing compared with what we get here now."

"We never dreamed of such numbers," said another, backing it up with figures: one nun had instructed two hundred and fifty families, another two hundred, another travelled regularly to help in a village where just one convert had gone to live and had already made forty others.

I asked what they thought had brought the change. They gave me the answers with which I was growing familiar.

They are coming because of the suffering during the war. . . . Because of the evil things done by the Communists, who they knew were atheists. . . . Because they feel that there must be some explanation for so much suffering and that all those who have died cannot just be finished. . . . Because no one outside the Faith can give any satisfying answer to their questions. . . .

The answers came back like the responses to a litany, first from one, then from another. But they added up to substantially the same as those I had got from the American nuns, the priest in Pusan, the Columban Fathers, the Korean priests, the naval commander, the member of Parliament, from the old

Korean priest in the guerilla parish and the young one in the small town.

Yet the extraordinary thing was that, such is the life of a priest or nun in a mission country and, in particular, in one like Korea where communications are bad, each thought that he or she was wrestling with a purely local phenomenon, and was usually not only delighted but also genuinely amazed when I told them that I had now heard the same story over and over again in other areas.

No one, of course, mentioned the small matter of their own rôle in helping to produce this great opportunity. Yet from the stories I had extracted from them, of their own loyalty to the Faith they proclaimed, their heroism and refusal to be put down, it was clear that their example must in itself have made a profound impression upon the people about them.

In Kwangju, too, I met officials of the United Nations Civil Assistance Commission, which had a large headquarters in the town. They took the view that, although it was admittedly still far from perfect, the work of rehabilitation was steadily improving.

"We're over the hump," was how they put it. The previous year, they admitted, grain had been kept in storage whilst people starved. That situation had now ended. The relief supplies which came in went out again, although they could not be certain that they went where they were most needed. K.C.A.C. had built one thousand five hundred houses in the province; a fertiliser plant would soon be going ahead, although it was not ready yet; a child research department was needed to 'break the orphanage racket', but that was a project still to be started.

K.C.A.C. (pronounced 'Kaykak') had the limited aim of keeping people alive during the immediate post-war period. U.N.K.R.A. was the one which was really concerned with rehabilitation.

I met good men in the K.C.A.C. offices in Kwangju, sincere, humane men who were anxious to do a good job and who, seeing so much human suffering around them, were ready to do all they could to ease it. But I came away with a strong feeling that they were very frustrated men, too, who were afraid to look too far into the future. So far they were still laying foundations and there was no guarantee that the United Nations might not in time grow tired of hearing of the troubles of Korea and forget their responsibilities. There would then be little to show for their work apart from first-aid measures, grand plans, and patiently laid foundations—with the Korean nation, after having its land made a battlefield, left at a new low level of poverty, suffering and bitter disillusionment.

Whilst I was at Kwangju I heard that Mgr. Thomas Quinlan, whom I had last seen in Ireland, soon after his return from captivity on the Yalu River, was shortly due to arrive in Mokpo. It was likely, I understood, to be something in the nature of a great home-coming, for Mokpo had been his first Korean parish.

I heard of this when I was waiting at the American military airstrip in the hope of getting a lift on a courier plane to Seoul. So I switched back to Mokpo again, going down by jeep. I was glad I did so.

On the afternoon that Mgr. Quinlan arrived, the church on the hill was already festooned with paper streamers in the colours of the Irish Republic. Crowds of Koreans were waiting, hours before he was due, holding paper flags, bouquets, and garlands of flowers.

Then, an hour or so before his train was to come, they set off in procession to the station. They were still waiting when I got there, and with them was a band equipped with an extra-ordinary assortment of instruments, some identifiable as having once been of Western origin, others, of Korean type, wildly unfamiliar. The bandsmen were all good pagans. But what did that matter? The name of Thomas Quinlan, hero of the Death March to the Yalu River, was known to all.

The train came in, the bandsmen gave him a rousing blast on serpents, trumpets, gongs and other instruments, the crowd surged forward and soon the smiling Monsignor was walking along with a garland round his neck, a second garland in one hand, a bouquet in the other. Somehow we got him through

e crowd, who followed along behind. But soon the press
f people in the streets was such that he could make no
rogress and we had to get him into the jeep in which I was
ding.

Before us, clearing a way, went another jeep, filled with
.O.K. military police. Attached to its radiator were three
ags, Korean, Irish and Vatican, and, a superb touch, at the back
at a straight-faced Korean military policeman wearing 'snow-
rop' helmet and holding aloft the Papal colours.

Mgr. Quinlan took one look at it, and then at the surging
rowds, and his eyes filled with tears. "Before the war, when we
orked for years and saw very few results for our pains, I never
hought I'd live to see this day," he said. "And I never thought,
hen I was up there in the prison camp, that I'd come back to
his either," he added.

The big Monsignor was now Papal Regent, having taken the
lace of Bishop Byrne, who had died on the Death March, as
he Vatican's representative in Korea. As such his home was
ow in Seoul, but he was doing a tour of all the dioceses and
ain centres in order to be able to get an over-all picture of the
Church's progress and problems. He was also still Prefect
Apostolic of Chunchon, where he had been at the time of his
rrest, but had little time to go there, and the Prefecture had to
e left in the hands of the sub-Prefect, who had worked wonders
hilst he was a captive of the Reds.

That night, up in the house on the hill and with priests from
very part of the area sitting around, I asked him to sum up the
mpressions he had gained on his tour. Mokpo was the last
lace on his itinerary, and so by now he had got the picture he
ad wanted.

"People were never before so receptive to Catholic teaching,"
e told me. "Never before were there so many converts or such
nterest in the Faith. In every diocese the story is the same. I
m more edified than words can express at the state of the
Church in Korea."

And then, a little wistfully:

"We must ride on the crest of the wave or the moment of
pportunity will pass."

In the room were a score of Columban Fathers from scattered mission centres on the mainland and from the little islands, also part of Korea, which lie between South Korea and Red China. They included old Korea hands who had lived through years of imprisonment, first by the Japanese and later by the Korean Communists; some of them had been having encounters with the Chinese Communists in the 1920s, before they were switched to Korea. There were young men fresh out from the seminaries, who had come to a different Korea from that to which the old hands had come; materially poorer, but spiritually richer, because of the recent war. It was becoming a more settled Korea, now that the guerillas had been got in hand and Communism was, apart from a small remnant of Communists in the big towns, sealed off behind a strong defence line on the 38th Parallel. There were half-a-dozen or so Korean priests too. Some of these were grizzled old men, trained by the French Fathers years ago, with a great knowledge of Latin and theology but rendered a little breathless by the speed at which events were now moving. Others were the first products of the promising new situation. And all these very different types who probably knew Korea and the Koreans better than any other body of men in Korea that night, agreed with the Monsignor in his estimation of the possibilities and opportunities which had now come so unexpectedly to them.

The stories they exchanged together as the evening wore on all took on a striking similarity in that they each tended to illustrate Mgr. Quinlan's impression of the possibility of great undreamed-of progress. And of the danger of the moment of opportunity slipping through their fingers for want of sufficient helpers.

XIII

ABOVE THE PARALLEL

THE journey back to Seoul from Mokpo was less eventful than that going down. I had seen much more of the Koreans since that day I had set out on the Mokpo Express with my scrap of paper bearing the address of my destination in Korean characters, and so was at home with my travelling companions from the start.

Again I was the only Westerner on the train, but I did not lack company. By a coincidence I found that sitting behind me was a Catholic who had been trained by the Benedictines at Wonsan and was now a teacher on the island of Cheju, where the Columbans have a flourishing mission. Sitting next to me, on the same seat, was a university professor who had once taught in the school at Wonsan. Both spoke English and so I pumped them with questions for hours on end. At the end of a thirteen-hour train journey together you know an English-speaking Korean better than the average resident in a London suburb knows his next-door neighbour after thirteen years.

On the day I had travelled down, the authorities had been expecting an ambush. This time things were quiet, and the same elaborate precautions were not being taken. We went through the hills in the South without a sign of a guard anywhere.

After an hour or two, when the train was already crowded, a student and his young sister boarded our coach. The student managed to find a corner on the end of a seat, but when the guard came checking reservations he brusquely sent them both, along with a great many others, down to the third-class section, which was even more crowded than ours. As soon as his back was turned the student and the small girl came back. Half an hour later they were sent packing again, and so it continued for some time.

The little girl began to show signs of wilting, so I edged up closer to the man sitting next to me, made a corner for her to sit on and then by means of signs persuaded her to occupy it. Soon the officious guard came round again and, before I had guessed what he was saying to her, had bundled her down the gangway and into the third-class coach, which by now was more like an overcrowded cattle truck than a railway carriage intended for human beings.

Five minutes after he had gone she was back again, and again I signed to her to sit on my seat. Next time, as soon as the guard began to shout at her I quickly asked my neighbour to tell him that she was my daughter and that I wished her to stay. For a moment the guard looked as though he was going to relent. He grinned, traced her almond eyes against his own, then my straight ones, and shook his head. But his bad temper got the better of him and he roughly dragged her out.

We did not see him again, but some time later another guard, who had taken over from him, came through, attempting once more to reduce the number of people in the coach to more reasonable proportions. This time I was ready for him. As he approached us I took her arm firmly and asked the man next to me to tell him that she was my wife. The new guard looked somewhat startled, looking from the little child to me and back again questioningly. Then he burst out laughing and from then on left us alone.

By means of signs I established that she was twelve years old (thirteen by Korean reckoning, since they include the day of birth), and was going with her brother to visit her grandmother. She had the Oriental-type fringe across her forehead, and was wearing an orange silk muslin coatee and long blue patterned lace skirt, in the typical Korean style, with rubber shoes, which she took off during the journey. Soon we were exchanging sticky Korean sweets I had bought from a vendor at one of the stations and others which her brother passed back to us. Towards evening, when air in the stuffy compartment grew more and more rare, she dropped off to sleep, and we finished the journey with her lying with her head on my shoulder whilst my neighbour and I talked quietly in order not to wake her.

The Koreans on the crowded train had long ago decided that
a Western officer who voluntarily chose to travel Korean must
be strange indeed, and there seemed no reason why they should
not be made to think he was even stranger.

My general impression was that, as in Africa, parents in
Korea tend to spoil both boys and girls, letting them in their
early years do just whatever they please, and then, in the case of
girls, in particular, on their eleventh or twelfth birthday,
suddenly cease to treat them as playthings, stop spoiling them,
and project them without preparation into an adult world.
Certainly no one had shown the slightest inclination to make
room for this particular small girl and had seen no reason to
protest when the guard rough-handled her. I felt that in the
circumstances it was all the more necessary that I should take
her part.

I had promised Fr. Brian Geraghty that I would join him in
Seoul on June 10, so that I could accompany him on a trip he
had to make to the Chunchon Prefecture. I had not gathered just
why we must set out on that particular date, but knew that our
trip would take us through some of the wildest country in that
part of the Orient, right over to a town one hundred and eighty-
six miles to the east. There he would leave me in the hands of
other Columbans who were going over the 38th Parallel and
later on to Chunchon city, where Mgr. Quinlan had been
Prefect at the time of his arrest.

We set off early next morning after another warning from
Fr. Geraghty that the journey would be 'a bit rugged'. Because
of the mountainous nature of the country and the bad condition of the roads, the one hundred and eighty-six miles
would mean at least eight hours' continuous driving. And at all
costs, he emphasised, we must get to Kangnung before nightfall,
since it would be impossible to drive after dark through the
precipitous mountain passes we had to follow.

We were a party of five. Fr. Patrick Burke, who was returning from Seoul to his parish of Kangnung, drove one
jeep, Fr. Geraghty the other. In the first was a Korean girl
who worked in Seoul, but whose home was in Kangnung.

H*

Transport there was difficult and so Fr. Burke was taking her back to see her parents.

In the second there was, in addition to myself, a twenty-one year-old girl student from Seoul University, named Johanna. Her home, too, was in Kangnung, and she, like the other girl, was taking advantage of the opportunity to pay her parents a brief visit. When Fr. Geraghty returned to Seoul next day he would take both back with him.

It was mountains, mountains all the way. The road took us through some of the wildest and most magnificent scenery one could wish to see. One mountain range joined the next right the way from the west coast to the east. And they got higher and rougher the further we went.

At first the villages were relatively close together, then they began to thin out as the mountains became higher and steeper and fertile valleys more and more infrequent. As we climbed one particularly magnificent pass beside which ran a noisy stream, reminiscent of the trout streams in the Highlands of Scotland, Fr. Geraghty turned to me and said: "This is the Kang-Won-Do Province, where I worked for years. This is the Korea I love." One could understand why. It is the wildest and most scattered mission country in the land, with parishes which stretch for a hundred miles or more of mountain country. It is full of character and so are its people, who are of a particularly tough and independent type.

The strength of that characteristic emerged when Fr. Geraghty persuaded Johanna, who sat bumping about in the back of the jeep, to tell me her story of the early days of the Communist invasion of the South.

Johanna was already a B.A., and was now studying for her M.A. But when the war began she was still a senior girl at a high school in the capital. Her parents were in Kangnung, right up against the 38th Parallel.

So, when the attack started, Johanna's thoughts naturally centred on her parents and her home. Were they still alive? Was the home up there, on the other side of the one hundred and eighty miles of mountains which separated them, still standing or had it been destroyed?

The Communists reached Seoul. She remained in the city and saw what life under their rule was like. And the more she saw of it, the more she fretted over the fate of her family. No news was coming through, there was no transport, and there seemed no means of getting to know what was happening. Her home was sealed off as part of the great Communist Empire which stretched now right across into the very heart of the west itself.

Finally, she decided that there was only one thing to do and that was to walk there, put her mind at rest—or learn the worst —then walk back again. Since Communist troops and transport were pouring down the road, it meant taking the untracked mountains, immensely lengthening the journey and making it far more exhausting and dangerous.

So for ten days this Korean schoolgirl, averaging more than twenty miles of stiff climbing a day, made her way across those same mountains which, as she told me her story, we were skirting in our jeep. They were heavily wooded all the way, except where they became too high and bare for any but the scrubbiest of trees to grow there. In those woods there were wild boar, bear and the occasional Manchurian tiger, a huge and notably ferocious fellow. And all the time she was dodging the Red Army and Communist guards who were scattered everywhere. Korean hospitality, however, is such that never once did this young girl passing through strange country want for a friendly roof over her head at night and never once was she molested.

When she got to Kangnung she found her parents still alive and attempting to carry on with their work. Satisfied that they were as safe as they might reasonably be expected to be in the circumstances, she turned round and made the return journey to Seoul on foot.

Looking at the small, modest, quiet-voiced girl, in the white blouse and navy blue skirt, it seemed almost incredible that she could have faced the journey alone. But when Fr. Geraghty told me another side of her story, I realised the strength of character which she possessed.

She had been born of pagan parents, but at the age of twelve had come to Fr. Geraghty, who at that time was pastor of Kangnung, asking to be baptised. Following the usual custom in Korea, he told her that he could not do so unless at least one of her parents was converted too. Without that, there would be no guarantee that she would be permitted to grow up in her religion, and she might later even be made an unwilling party to a polygamous marriage.

When she was fourteen she again came and asked for baptism and again got the same reply. Then she proceeded to work for her parents' conversion and was still doing so when the Korean War began. With the Communists hammering at the gates of Seoul and death everywhere, she came to him once more. This time Fr. Geraghty felt that he could not withhold baptism from her. In due course she brought her mother and all her brothers and sisters into the Church too.

We ate our lunch sitting together at the side of the road, some five thousand feet up among the pines. Then, with our two jeeps making what speed they could, we climbed into country where the paddy-fields became ever smaller and more rare, and the rice growing in them had less and less grains to the ear—at the highest point at which rice could be cultivated there were as few as four. We passed places where peasants were engaged in ladling the precious water for their rice uphill from one tiny paddy to the next. Then the rice-fields stopped altogether, stones replaced soil, and for miles we travelled through country where lumbering, not farming, provided the means of life for the poverty-stricken people.

The last big mountain, Ya-Kol-Yeoung, which we reached after more than seven hours of incessant bumping over stony tracks, was by far the worst. As we approached it we saw that it disappeared way up into the clouds. Our track went right over the top.

The road was barely wider than the jeep itself. On one side was a deep ditch, dug in order to break landslides from the towering rocks above it. On the other was a sheer drop of hundreds of feet. For miles, as we climbed higher and higher, it continued like that.

Here and there the remains of vehicles could be seen which

had gone over the side. At one point we had to pass on a sharp bend an R.O.K. Army truck which was stuck in the ditch with its wheels wrenched off. The Korean driver still sat in his cabin philosophically waiting for the help which a colleague had set out to find, unable to leave his truck and prepared if necessary —and as seemed likely—to spend the night on the mountain-top.

We drove into a thick mist through which it was possible to see only a few yards ahead and just over the precipice at our side. Once a truck, coming from the opposite direction, loomed suddenly out of the gloom. Providentially at our side there was a break in the cliffs, cut by a stream, into which we backed. When we got out I found that the mud surface of the road had been turned by the dripping mist into the consistency and depth of, say, four inches of half-melted snow. It was so slippery that it was almost impossible to walk on it!

As we took the worst bend of all, Fr. Brian, who for miles had been alone with his thoughts, said very quietly: "Last time I did this journey I had a trailer behind the jeep."

"That must have been rather unpleasant."

"It was. I had my best friend, Tom Neligan up behind—in his coffin."

And then I learned for the first time why Fr. Brian Geraghty was making the trip that day.

He was going, he said, for Fr. Tom's 'month's mind'—an Irish Catholic custom by which, thirty days after a death, a Requiem Mass is celebrated on behalf of the deceased.

Forty-six-years-old Fr. Tom Neligan was a native of Youghal, in Ireland, who went as a student to St. Columban's, Dalgan Park. He was ordained in 1932, and went to Korea the following year. Fr. Brian Geraghty went to college with him, and became his closest friend. They were ordained together and set off together for the Korean Missions. All through the years that friendship continued. Neither was demonstrative in his friendship—that is not the Columban style—but each had a deep respect for the other.

"He was my best friend. He was the best I ever had and the best I ever will have," said Fr. Brian, whose thoughts were clearly on the journey of thirty days earlier. "He was a great class-mate, and he was a great pastor. People did not look forward to his coming, because he had a reputation for sternness, they didn't immediately appreciate him, but they always regretted his going tremendously. He was strict, but he never deviated one iota from the law."

They worked in the same Prefecture—one which is as big as all Ireland—meeting just occasionally and exchanging experiences. Throughout the Japanese War they were imprisoned together. Then Fr. Geraghty was put in charge of all the work in Korea (protesting that he much preferred to remain the pastor of his mountain parish of Kangnung) and Fr. Neligan took his place.

But Fr. Tom fell ill during the Korean War, which was no time to be ill, for transport and medical treatment were both difficult to get. There came the day when he was told that he had only a few months to live. He decided to work for as long as he could and to push on, in particular, with the construction of a much-needed orphanage he had just started to build.

He saw the orphanage completed, then, a fast-dying man, cleared up the affairs of his parish so that the next man moving in should find everything in order. Then he left for a military hospital in Seoul.

But first he went to St. Columban's in the Don Am Dong, to make his last report to Fr. Geraghty.

In appalling agony from heart and kidney trouble, he discussed his forthcoming death with a calm which his old friend found it impossible to maintain.

"I have found a lot of kindness and love in Kangnung," he said, "and I have found some hardship too. I will couple both together, with my life, and offer them up for the propagation of the Faith in Korea, and in particular in my own parish."

Then he contentedly went off to the austerity of a military hospital to die.

He had already told Fr. Geraghty just what he should do when he died. He had chosen the spot for his grave. It was to be in the grounds of the convent orphanage which he had just completed. "Tell the nuns," he said, "that I want the children to play around it and to say a Rosary for me each day. And when you go back to my parish tell Fr. Pat Burke to ask his people to go and say a prayer there sometimes too."

"He suffered greatly, but he never complained," Fr. Geraghty told me, reminiscing as we rambled on over the mountain passes, with Fr. Burke going on ahead of us.

"He was the Society's best conversationalist in Korean. He really enjoyed carrying on conversations with the people in their own language. He was only forty-five when he died and twenty-one years of his life were spent in Korea. It was his first and only mission, and he never wanted another."

When Fr. Geraghty was giving Tom Neligan the last Rites, anointing him for the last time, he showed signs of his own nervousness and distress.

"Now, Bernie, don't get nervous," said the dying missioner, "keep quite cool. For me this is the ringing of the bell."

But 'Bernie's' thoughts were in a whirl and he made mistakes. It was the dying Tom who reminded him that he should anoint a fellow priest on the back of the hands.

When the end came, Fr. Geraghty carried out his promise. He celebrated his Requiem Mass in the Memorial Chapel at St. Columban's, in Seoul. Then he set out in his jeep on the dangerous eight-hour journey that we were just completing, over the high mountain ranges, along the precipitous passes, round the one hundred and fourteen hairpin bends, through the slush and mud and danger on the top of the great Ya-Kol-Yeoung. He made the journey alone with his thoughts, and with his best friend's body on the trailer bumping along behind.

Tom Neligan's wish was granted. He was buried in the orphanage grounds, and we were travelling up for his 'month's mind'. Fr. Brian would celebrate the Requiem Mass tomorrow.

I was beginning to understand the unusual quality which was reflected deep in the pale blue eyes which had struck me so forcibly when first I met Fr. Geraghty.

We reached Kangnung, a muddy little town, as it grew dark, dropping Johanna at her parents' home, a middle-class place in the centre of the town, and then going on to the presbytery.

Two of Fr. Neligan's closest associates, Fr. Hubert Hayward, the pro-Prefect who had supervised the work of the diocese during Mgr. Quinlan's years of captivity, and Fr. Frank McGann, the Society's pro-Director there, had already arrived, along with some younger men newly out from Navan and still busy learning the language.

The talk that night, until we went to bed, was of building and rebuilding in this diocese which had been cut in two by the 38th Parallel, and which had inevitably suffered so much during the fighting.

Coming up that day we had travelled for much of the time close to the Parallel and here and there had crossed it. One mountain, in particular, Fr. Brian had pointed out as having been for years a Communist strong point. It was Mount Odae, which the Communists used from the time they first arrived in 1945 as a base for frequent probing actions.

"They used to organise skirmishes from there, with eighty or a hundred men," Fr. Geraghty told me as we passed it. "They were always beaten back by the South Korean Army. The result was that many people were fooled into thinking that that was about their strength."

Next day I was to go with Fr. Hayward and Fr. McGann to a place high up above the Parallel, into territory which had known Communist rule for more than five years.

I went to bed that night with a pain in my back. My nearly two hundred miles of continuous shaking as the jeep bumped over the rough mountain passes had let me know, for the first time in my life, just where my kidneys were situated. I remember going to sleep wondering philosophically to myself whether one of them, perhaps, might not have become detached from its base.

Next morning I went to the earliest Mass in the adjoining church, to be with the Korean peasants before they left for their work in the fields. Then, a little later, came Fr. Tom Neligan's 'month's mind'. The black-draped catafalque and the empty coffin stood in the centre aisle, calling to mind the man who had so calmly prepared the way for his successor. Fr. Brian Geraghty, in the black vestments of the Requiem Mass, seemed to linger on each word as he celebrated it, and the little group of Columbans and still smaller group of Korean nuns from Tom Neligan's convent-orphanage tried valiantly to make it the best possible sung Mass. It was certainly the most impressive I have ever attended.

Later I went up to the new orphanage, and there, around the even newer grave, the children, who were the victims of the recent war, had already said their Rosary that day.

At noon I set out with Fr. Hayward and Fr. McGann for the 'liberated territory' north of the Parallel. When the truce came at the end of the war, it was agreed that the new border should follow the lines already occupied by the contending forces—or rather, that they should each draw back three thousand yards leaving a demilitarised corridor between them. The lines roughly followed the Parallel, which had first been made the *ad hoc* border when Russia and America both went into Korea, the one from the north, the other from the south, in 1945. But at this point, over on the east coast, it happened that the United Nations had driven a wedge up into the Communist territory and had managed to hold it. So there they stayed when the truce was signed, and one tiny bit of the Communist Empire— the first on earth—was liberated and its people returned to life in the free world. It was into that narrow wedge, surrounded on three sides by the Communist world, that we travelled that day, making Sok-Cho-Ri, which lies some thirty miles north of the Parallel, our destination.

On our way we stopped, some ten miles inside the liberated territory, at Yang-Yang, where the two Columbans inspected a site on which a new church was soon to be erected. The foundations were there already, for a church had stood on the same spot until a few years ago. Its pastor had been a saintly old Korean named Fr. Timothy Ri. His death is a commentary on what has been called this 'Age of Suspicion'.

One day during the war an American aircraft crashed near-by. Fr. Ri, along with the other local people, went out to see it. Out of the crashed plane stepped a startled U.S. pilot, who, seeing Fr. Ri in his priest's Western-type clothes, came forward to greet him.

Immediately, the Communists demanded to know how it was that the American imperialist knew the old priest. No explanation of Fr. Ri's would satisfy them. He was never permitted to leave his presbytery again until the day he was taken out and shot.

An elderly Korean priest had been at our small party in Kangnung and we were now giving him a lift home. We dropped him at his little church built of bamboo in Korean domestic style, with upturned eaves and tiled roof.

Some time earlier he had been moved there from another parish. Like old men everywhere he preferred to remain where he was. So when he was next officially visited by the pro-Prefect, he gravely declared that he feared that he could not continue at the new parish.

To understand the reason he gave one must recall that 'night soil' (the product of the country's primitive sanitary system) is a highly treasured commodity there, being extensively used in cultivation. The conversation between the old priest and the pro-Prefect went somewhat as follows:

"Well, how do you like your new place? Are you settling in all right?"

"It's not bad, but I can't stay. I shall have to go back to my old parish."

"Why?"

"The money I get never was enough to live on. But at the old place there was a water closet attached to the church and my parishioners, who came from miles around, used it regularly. This place hasn't got a W.C., so I have lost a valuable source of income and I just can't carry on."

His point was accepted as a real one, and a compromise between East and West was achieved. He did not go back to his old church. Instead, a new toilet was built beside his present one.

Sok-Cho-Ri proved to be a coastal town with a population of some ten thousand. In the centre of this outpost of the free world stood a huge, newly-erected memorial, consisting of a towering woman and child, cast in concrete, who with heads erect looked out over the slave empire beyond.

But dominating the town still more, as one approached it, was the newly built Church of Our Lady of Fatima, which likewise faced out over the Red-ruled territory.

Beside it was a squat, square presbytery in which lived Fr. Patrick McGowan, from County Tyrone, in Northern Ireland. Living against a hated border in a country partitioned into mutually hostile areas was not a new experience for him.

Most of my 'front-line fighters' for the Church had looked anything but that—diminutive nuns and quiet-voiced reticent priests who just carried on with living Christianity. But Fr. McGowan looked and acted the part.

Early in my quest I had discovered how the Almighty uses a great variety of types and qualities for His work, baptising the Irishman's *wanderlust* and love of adventure, the German's sense of duty, the Frenchman's lightheartedness. If he had not been a priest, and had he been born into a different age, Patrick McGowan might possibly have been a swashbuckling buccaneer.

As he talked, he paced restlessly up and down, with a slightly swaggering gait, his thumbs stuck into the wide leather belt around the army officer's knee-breeches he wore. Some men might not have chosen to be the pastor of this church on the edge of a hostile world. Pat McGowan clearly loved it. To him the building of the Church of Our Lady of Fatima was a challenge to the Communists to do their worst. An act of faith, yes, but an act of defiance, too.

He had sought, and been given, the permission of his superiors to move into the 'liberated wedge' as soon as the United Nations' troops arrived there. At that time the battle was still fluid; territory won from the Communists today might be back in their hands tomorrow. He went in at his own risk. And when he asked permission to start building a church there, whilst the war was still raging around the spot, he was told that he might, provided that he raised the money himself.

He got on with the job. He collected amongst G.I.s, scrounged unwanted materials and persuaded the town's Mayor, who, providentially, was a Catholic from Wonsan, to give him the site for a church, right on the top of the hill. To the land he had been given he added a similar area on which to build a presbytery of his own design, and some day, he hoped, a public hall as well.

The local Catholics had lived under the Russians for five years without the Mass, been driven down to Pusan by the Communists and lost everything at least twice. Now they came to him and offered to do the building, even whilst the town was still being shaken by the Communist guns just across the way. They put up their own flimsy little shacks in the church compound to be near the job, then started erecting a brave new stone church—right there in the front line.

Fr. McGowan lived with them in a shack on the site, and he worked with them too. Fortunately the Communists did not again enter the town and the church was completed by September 1953. The parish it serves stretches from the Parallel up to the front line between the two worlds. It includes eighty miles of magnificent coastline. Within it lie the Diamond Mountains in which were the famous thirteenth-century Buddhist monasteries, and the place which Kim Il Sung, the North Korean Communist premier, made his summer residence. It covers several hundred square miles of mountain country.

Even before the war was over, Catholics living in isolated spots in the parish (and, incidentally, well inside the area from which civilians were supposed to be excluded) walked as much as eighty miles each way to church in order to get to confession and Mass at Easter. Sok-Cho-Ri, its priest and its people, all have character.

We had just finished dinner in the little mission house.

"Do you mind if I take a stroll?" I asked Fr. McGowan as the others began to get out pipes and cigarettes.

"Why not? We've just fought a war for freedom, so you're free now to go when and where you please," he cracked back.

I stood for a minute or two in the compound at the top of the hill looking north. For an ex-Communist like myself the place had a peculiar fascination. There was nothing between me and Moscow, which once had been for me a magic name—or for that matter between me and Budapest, Prague, Bucharest, Warsaw, East Germany and Peking, too. Nothing but Communist-ruled territory, stretching across nearly a quarter of the world, ruling more than a quarter of its population.

The soil I stood on had for more than five years, and until so recently, been part of that Communist Empire.

Now, liberated, it was one of the few towns which have known Communist rule and are now back with the West. This area was the only one in the world of which that could be said. And Fr. McGowan's church, at that moment, was the only one on earth standing on soil over which a one hundred per cent Communist Government had ruled.

Some day, presumably, there would be whole countries and peoples freed from Communism. Meanwhile, Sok Cho Ri was the guinea-pig of guinea-pigs, the place where life in the free world could be demonstrated, a working model of what it was like, a shop window facing towards the millions who dreamed of better things and watched by those who, having known both ways of life, were inevitably making comparisons.

So my thoughts ran as I walked down the hill to the town. Then they were interrupted by someone tugging at my elbow and saying "O.K.?" in my ear. It was a 'moose'. In other words it was a Korean girl dressed in American clothes, wearing an American hair-style, talking what she imagined to be the American language, but pursuing a business which is international.

With her slinky two-piece suit, her smart sling-back shoes, her lipstick and permanent wave, she was at once quite hideous and absolutely pathetic.

I brushed her off and walked on in the dusk. Within the next three or four hundred yards I was accosted again and again. As I walked to the sea-front, groups of American Service men stood talking to other 'mooses', all equally made up, equally spoiled and equally pathetic products of the war which had swept away their moral defences.

So far as I am aware, Sok-Cho-Ri is neither better nor worse than most other places where G.I.s or other U.N. troops are stationed in Korea today. Certainly my experience there was one I had already had in other places and which was many times to be repeated. But its setting was different. The 'liability' side of Korea's profit and loss account had disturbed me from the day I arrived in the country. I knew what a tragic break this sort of thing represented with all Korea's best traditions. But here, in this town whose people had longed for liberation from atheistic Communism, and had got it, it seemed peculiarly disturbing.

I went back up the hill in a cynical frame of mind.

"This," I told myself, "is the freedom for which men fought and died—freedom to accost and be accosted in the streets, to get V.D. and then have it cured again with a regulation 'shot' as a matter of army routine. The newfound freedom which comes to unsophisticated girls when they meet men in possession of officially-distributed contraceptives."

Still in the same frame of mind I went into Fr. McGowan's grey stone church.

Up in the loft the choir were practising the music of the High Mass. They were singing the *Asperges*. As I took my shoes off at the door they sang *Lavabis me et super nivem dealbabor*—"Thou wilt sprinkle me with hyssop and I shall be clean; washed by Thee I shall be whiter than snow".

"*Lavabis* me," I said to myself. "And it's necessary. For preference put some disinfectant into the holy water. This whole place could do with a wash."

I sat on the floor among the Koreans who had come to say their night prayers, pondering the stupidity which permits a place which by any reckoning ought to be one where the way of life of the 'Christian' West can be favourably contrasted with that of the atheistic, totalitarian East, to become just the opposite.

"They are absolute idiots not to see the symbolic significance and tragedy of all this," I told myself bitterly. "We have done a dreadful thing to the Korean people. Far from securing Korea for the Christian West we have disintegrated a way of life which, pagan though it was, was morally superior to that of most of our own modern pagans."

Then, as I looked around the church, I cooled off. For I

recalled what Fr. McGowan had told me about it and the manner of its building.

I knew that with my sweeping generalisations I had been libelling to myself thousands of good men who had made possible the building of that church, and so many others in Korea, too. For it had been paid for out of the generosity of American Catholics in the Forces.

This fortress of the Faith which stood on the edge of the Communist world was a living proof of their determination to give reality to the West's claim to be Christian. It was their sacrifices, coupled with the faith and energy of Fr. McGowan, the other Columbans and the Korean Christians, which had erected it.

It has still to be shown whether the evil which we have taken to Korea has outweighed the good, but it will be our own fault —the Christians' fault—if this is so.

Even there, where the people had been subjected to continuous propaganda by the Communists for years on end, the flow to the Church was the same as elsewhere, as Fr. McGowan's figures, which we went through together before I turned in for the night, proved beyond doubt. But more revealing than any statistics was his account of something which had happened just a few weeks earlier.

He had gone one day to take the Blessed Sacrament to some Catholics in the furthest point in his parish with which he had any contact. Whilst he was there he was met by the civic head (approximating to the English chairman of a rural district council) of a place some six miles further on. He came with a remarkable story and a request. During the war his people, like so many others in Korea, had been trying to find answers to the fundamental questions which their sufferings and experience of Communism in practice had prompted. Then a demobilised R.O.K. soldier came home, bringing with him a copy of the Catholic catechism. They read it together and there found what they sought. Together they learned it by heart. Now nearly three hundred of them wanted to enter the Church. Would Fr. McGowan please send a priest at once,

to baptise them and to take charge of a church which they
would build?

Sadly, Fr. McGowan had to tell them that he was the only
priest in the whole vast area covering hundreds of square miles,
and that no more were available. When the rice harvest was
over he would try to find a layman to come as catechist. That
was as much as he could offer.

By the time we had rattled next day along still more miles of
mountain road in our jeep I had no doubt whatsoever as to the
exact position of my kidneys. My back ached and something
inside quite definitely seemed to be in revolt. But the rugged
mountain country through which we passed more than made
up for my minor discomforts.

As the crow flies, we covered no more than seventy miles that
day, but as we twisted and turned through mountain passes, we
doubled and trebled that distance. We were making more or
less due west to Chunchon, following the Parallel most of the
time, and also for a good deal of the way travelling within the
militarised zone. As we went along one long straight valley
between parallel mountain ranges, American gunners were
lobbing shells along beside us. They whined down the valley,
then exploded on a hillside behind us. I hoped that those
American gunners knew their job.

In that same sector of the front, too, we came to a church
which was under construction, and had already a history which
is unique. In fact, one might say that in its fabric it symbolises
the battle of our time as does probably no other building on
earth today. It was in a place called Inge.

When the Korean War began the Columbans had already
bought a site for a church there and had laid its foundations.
Then Inge, along with all the other towns and villages on the
Parallel, disappeared behind the Iron Curtain.

Later, when it was freed, the Columbans went back. They
found that upon the concrete foundations which they had
constructed for their church the Communists had built a great
cinema in which they showed their propaganda films. For
several years the site which had been intended as a means

for making Christians was used to make Communists instead.

Then Inge was freed, and in the fighting the roof and the tops of the walls of the cinema were destroyed by a shell. Now the Columbans were in process of putting up a small temporary chapel at its side, to meet the immediate need. At the same time they were building straight on to the Marxist cinema, to complete their original, permanent church. Thus the foundations were those of a church; the lower part of the walls and the ornate front, complete with 'classical' concrete columns in the worst Western cinema style, were those of a Communist propaganda movie house; and the tops of the walls, the roof and, of course, the interior fitments would be those of a church again.

As we tramped around the site a huge American Negro soldier got up from the pile of building materials amongst which he was sitting and greeted us. He had been put in by the American Army to guard the property against pilfering. On the shell-pocked walls of the cinema-cum-church were scrawled the names of other G.I.s, from Wisconsin, from Kansas and from the Philippines.

Well into the afternoon we reached Hunchon, whose name I had first learned when Philip Crosbie told me his story, the story which had brought me out here to Korea.

On a hill just at the back of the town stood the presbytery. From it a young Korean priest, the same one who had been assistant to Fr. Crosbie before his arrest, came out to greet us. Near-by, Korean building workers, supervised by a big American from one of the rehabilitation agencies, were busy rebuilding the bombed church, of which nothing at all had remained by the time the war was over.

Fr. Crosbie was reported to be even now on his way back from Australia. He would find a splendid new church well on the way to completion by the time he got there. We stood talking for a while with the big American. He was a keen, genial type of young man who talked enthusiastically of his work. No frustration there, at any rate.

He accompanied us as we crossed the compound. I enquired

about Fr. Crosbie's famous cellar, the one he had dug himself in order to teach his people by example how to preserve their vegetables throughout the winter.

"The cellar and the remains of his pump are all that are left of the place as he knew it," I was told. And then I heard the story of what had happened to that cellar, which had been his pride and joy, since last he saw it.

After Fr. Crosbie had gone off to jail and his Korean assistant had been smuggled off to safety, the Communists rounded up a number of his parishioners and, lacking jail space, threw them into the cellar, which was partly filled with water. And from that cellar many of them had been taken out to execution. The cellar which was to have aided them became their jail and, for some, their tomb.

Behind the compound a bulldozer, driven by a G.I., was levelling off a shelf on the hillside in readiness for a hospital to be built there. The big American supervisor had a grim story about that, too.

"The R.O.K.s were put on to flattening it with bulldozers at first," he said. "But then one day one of them saw the machine he was driving turn out something white. He peered over the front and saw it was a human skull. He jumped down and looked behind, the way he had come, and all along the surface of the soil were broken human bones which he had churned up. He took one look at them, and ran off scared. From that day on the R.O.K.s refused to work the bulldozer on that site, and we had to put G.I.s on to it instead."

"Whose bones were they?" I asked, and I half anticipated his answer.

"Fr. Crosbie's Catholics, as far as we can make out. A lot of them were taken from his cellar, led up the hill and then shot. They must have been buried in shallow graves just where they fell."

Philip Crosbie was certainly going to find some changes when he got back. But his work would have as its foundations the blood of the local martyrs.

Not all the changes were grim ones. His Korean assistant, put in charge of the parish until his return, was able to give me the same picture of progress that I had got elsewhere, even though the whole area had been literally razed to the ground and its people were later preoccupied with starting their ordinary material life all over again.

From the hill I could see the little town laid out down below. Almost every house was new, most of them built of timber provided from American sources.

My thoughts were with Philip Crosbie as we jeeped down to the town's centre and out on the road to Chunchon. This was the road he had taken under guard in a Communist army truck on the night of his arrest. The next stage of my journey, to Chunchon, would be the one he did as the prelude to the Death March. My thoughts went back to the radiogram in my home in the London suburb and Fr. Crosbie playing Tchaikovsky's Pianoforte Concerto No. 1 as he tried to delay having to tell me the story of his experiences. I had not thought that I, too, would ever make that journey.

It was, I found, a twisting road which rose and fell over steep, wooded hills, along which he had been taken, typical of those I had been travelling for the last few days and of all that mountainous area adjacent to the 38th Parallel.

Three-quarters of an hour later we swung round a corner and I saw Chunchon sprawled out below us. The town, though quite high, none the less lay in a hollow, formed by a wonderful circle of hills. And right in its centre gleamed a great new metal roof.

"That's the new cathedral," said Fr. Frank McGann, with pride in his voice. "It is the one Mgr. Quinlan dreamed of and had got going at last when the Reds invaded. It was smashed up, but in his absence we've built it. It is the best church building in the land."

And so, indeed, it was. It was the centre of a large compound which had been bulldozed out of the top of a hill. On the one side stood a fine diocesan house; on the other a big new dispensary which the builders were still completing. Below was the little Korean presbytery where Mgr. Quinlan used to sleep on the floor. Now it was the house of some lay catechists whom I was able to visit and who showed me every corner, with the usual Korean courtesy.

"All we want now is a group of nuns to run the dispensary. We'll build them a convent, too, you can tell them, if you find any for us," said Fr. Hayward.

Behind the cathedral stood three graves with new crosses. They were those of some of Chunchon's martyr-priests, who had died at the hands of the Communists. There was Fr. Anthony Collier, first Westerner to die in the Korean War. He had been tied to a young Korean, Gabriel Kim, and shot. Both were left for dead. But Gabriel though sore wounded was still living. He had later been able to assist in the finding of Fr. Anthony's body.

Buried with Fr. Collier were Fr. Patrick Reilly and Fr. James Maginn, both shot by the Communists in the first days of the war. From this same area, too, had gone Fr. Francis Canavan, who had shared the Death March with Mgr. Quinlan and Fr. Crosbie, then died in the internment camp on the Yalu River as a consequence of the hardships he had endured.

Some months after my return to Europe I was staying in Dundalk, in County Louth, Ireland. Whilst I was there I called at the Colliers' farm, the one from which the young Anthony had set out to become a Columban Father. It was large by Irish standards, and had a reputation for being one of the best in the county. He had, one could see at a glance, left considerable comfort behind when he set out for the Korean mission.

I went to see his mother, who lay sick in bed. She talked to me of those graves behind the big new cathedral and of Gabriel Kim, the boy who was tied to her son when he went to his death.

I was able to tell her that during my stay I had seen the way in which the local Catholics stop on their way to and from Mass to say a prayer at the graves of the men who stayed with them in their time of trouble and gave their lives in doing so. And I was able, too, to add that over and over again when I talked both to Columbans on the mission and to the Korean Catholics, too, they had put the missionary-martyrs high on the list as they enumerated the causes for the big new turn to the Faith. She told me how her son had come home on leave just before the Korean War began and added that before he left he had a strong presentiment that he was going to his death, and so, as a consequence, had she. She told me, too, how she had another son who was also a Columban stationed in North Burma.

Old Mrs. Collier was magnificent in her bereavement. For her the front line of the battle of our time had reached right into a farm in peaceful, Catholic Ireland and claimed her boy.

"Would you have it any different?" I asked her as I left. The fact that I could ask the question at all testified to her spirit.

"You mean for Anthony?"

"Yes."

"No. I wouldn't have it any different at all. I am glad that he did what he did. If I had my time over again I would still be proud to let him go."

The following day was Sunday, and the great cathedral was packed to the very doors with Koreans attending Mass, for Chunchon numbers its recent converts in hundreds and those taking instruction by the thousand.

They were a gay, light-hearted, resourceful lot, despite all that they had endured. Only a few weeks before, when I had first arrived in Korea, fire had swept the new wooden town, making hundreds of families homeless. Now all was patched up again, and every narrow street was the scene of enormous activity.

Reminders of the recent war were everywhere. Even the big truck which stood in the mission compound was Moscow-made, still bearing the Soviet Star from the days before it was captured from the Reds.

As I set out again in the inevitable jeep for Seoul, I took a backward glance at the big cathedral with the shining roof. Through all his years of captivity Mgr. Quinlan had fretted about the fate of the one that he had built. That one had gone and this magnificent one had taken its place, bigger and grander than he had ever dreamed possible. It reflected the huge possibilities which had come so unexpectedly. The Monsignor was himself miles away from his Prefecture, the honoured representative of the Holy Father, but looking back a little wistfully, I would guess, to the days when he lived Korean, with the people he loved.

I could well understand how he must long to be back in his parish in the hills, reaping the harvest for which he had worked and suffered, and for which his colleagues had died. And I understood, too, why it was that Fr. Geraghty had said as first we crossed into this mountainous province: "This is the Korea I love."

XIV

OPPORTUNITIES AND DANGERS

THE days in Seoul were full. There was the night when Mgr. George Carrol, the Maryknoller who directed relief work throughout the country, showed me a film he had made before the war. In it I made the acquaintance of Mgr. Bryne, who had died on the Death March, and got a glimpse of what poor battered Seoul had looked like in the days of its magnificence, before the Communists turned it into a battlefield.

There was the day, too, when I went to lecture to a great hall full of young Koreans in Bishop Ro's seminary—the native clergy of tomorrow, into whose hands the Church in Korea will be passed. Their college had been used as a barracks by the Red Army, and the walls of the lecture hall were covered with slogans and still filthy from the mass of men who had slept there.

In particular, there was the visit to Bishop Germaine Mousset, an old Frenchman with more than half a century in Korea behind him. Once he had been Bishop of Taegu, but he had stood down when the Japanese wanted Korean bishops, and so was now without a diocese.

He lived alone with his seventy-two-year-old priest-secretary, in a decaying old house which once had been the centre of great activity. Beside the house was what had been the seminary of the Paris Foreign Missions. It was slowly collapsing, partly from bonb damage, partly from dilapidation. Its roof was sagging and weeds and even small trees grew up through its floor-boards.

When we rang the bell the seventy-eight-years-old Bishop himself came to the door. He had a forked white beard which covered his chest, a stained and threadbare soutane, mauve socks of thick wool, sandals, and a skull cap covering his close-cropped grey hair. But his face was bright and alert, and his mind as active as ever.

He showed us into his room. Its floor was bare and with broken boards. The ceiling was peeling. Its only furniture was an iron bedstead, a wash-bowl, a desk and an almost empty bookcase. In a corner were some old leather valises which clearly had not been used for many years. The air was heavy with the smell of stale strong tobacco.

He had come to Korea in 1900, he told me, fresh from seminary. Ever since he could remember he had wanted to be a priest and by the time he was twelve he was already in a junior seminary. There he read about the need for men in the missions and the suffering that members of the Paris Foreign Missions had endured in Korea. He thought he would like to help, so joined the P.F.M.s, and in due course was appointed to Korea at a time when the pioneering work was still being done.

"If I was twelve years of age again I would do it all over again," he commented with a chuckle. In the fifty-four years he had been in Korea he had been to France only three times. The first was after twenty-four years, the second was to have an operation.

"In 1950 I and the other French priests thought there would be no more converts for years. Thank God we were mistaken," he said.

As he talked his secretary came into the room. He was a mere seventy-two years old, but his beard was even longer than the Bishop's. He was a bright-eyed little priest with a face which was for ever breaking into a smile which somehow took in the whole of his face. He had come to Korea in 1905 and looked forward to many more years there.

Together they took us around the great barn of a place, which echoed to our footsteps as we went down its long corridors past one empty room after another.

There was something sad and yet something quite magnificent, too, in these two old men who had given their lives to Korea, hanging on in the remains of what had been the main-spring of the Seoul diocese in the days before it was passed over to a native bishop and clergy. In one sense they symbolised the decline of a great pioneer effort, but they symbolised also the progress of the Church in a land which was moving away from mission status and in which the Faith was spreading fast.

His Society had today just thirteen priests and two bishops in Korea, although it was still responsible for large areas of the country. Once it had been the foremost Society in the land. Now it was short of younger men, and vocations from France were few. Gradually younger societies like the Columban Fathers and Korean bishops and clergy had taken over much of their work, but the fact remained that the Paris Foreign Missions had been the first to break, at enormous cost, into the Forbidden Kingdom. They had laid the foundations for all that had followed. The signs of their achievements were everywhere.

"Would you part with this property?" asked Fr. Geraghty as we left the two old men. It was clear that he was wondering whether the house might not yet be saved from collapse, and turned into a school, and the tumbledown seminary, perhaps, be rebuilt into a hospital or orphanage.

Bishop Mousset shook his head.

"I wouldn't care to say," he said cautiously.

It was clear that the old French pioneer was still desperately hoping for a spiritual revival at home which would bring eager young missionaries out once more, ready to work and if need be to suffer as he and his generation had done. Maybe he had his dreams, too, of some day using again the collapsing buildings amongst which he was living out his last years, proud of the job that he and his countrymen had done and still believing that France would once more send out her sons to every corner of the earth.

In his palace adjoining the Anglican cathedral in Seoul I met Bishop Cooper. He was as English as Bishop Mousset was French. In his home he had created a tiny bit of England. Korea might have been on the other side of the earth.

Bishop Cooper, a gentle old man of culture and great courage, had been on the Death March with Mgr. Quinlan and Fr. Crosbie. He spoke little of his own heroic rôle in those dreadful days. But he paid great tribute to Mgr. Quinlan in particular.

"There was never a moment on the March," he said, "when that wonderful man was not carrying someone."

On the day before the Feast of Corpus Christi I travelled up by jeep to Chunchon again. Next morning, on the Feast itself, the church was packed at six o'clock and again at seven. Many of the local Catholics were treating it as a holiday. They set off in trucks, straight from Mass, for Pung Su Won, over in the east, to which I was going, too.

Pung Su Won was a Catholic village, converted by the Paris Foreign Missionaries years ago. It was now in the spiritual care of Korean priests and the Catholics there celebrated Corpus Christi with a great procession which I wanted to see.

We went out through Hunchon, then into wild country where in places the road over the mountains was so narrow that R.O.K. police equipped with radio had to let traffic through in single file. If vehicles moving in opposite directions should meet, there would be no going forward and probably no going back either.

The church at Pung So Won was built in the Gothic style and its high steeple, poking out from among the trees, made the place look from a distance like some English village in a particularly lovely setting. When we got there we found that it was packed for a High Mass. Outside and in, it was festooned with brightly-coloured paper flowers and streamers.

When the Mass was over the people streamed out of the church, formed themselves into a procession before the Blessed Sacrament, which proceeded up the steep hill behind the church. As we wound our way up the hill the people sang their hymns, with pagans from surrounding villages standing reverently by or actually taking their place in the procession and joining in the singing. When Benediction was given at an altar set up on the top of the hill, pagans and Catholics alike dropped to their knees.

In the presbytery later, Korean women gave us plates of boiling stew ladled out of the great earthenware bowls in which all their cooking is done. Here was not a new convert community, but an old-established one, strong and solid in its Faith, which had stood up to life under the Communists, endured the upheaval of the war and remained as Catholic as ever it was.

It was my last trip in Korea. It was one which gave me confidence in the country's future. Koreans are not subject to passing whims. When they get the Faith it sticks.

In Chinhae, down in the south, the first meeting of the Asian People's Anti-Communist Conference was gathered, in response to a call from President Syngman Rhee and Chiang Kai Shek. In every street in Seoul through which the thirty delegates from eight Asian countries would pass when they came to visit the capital, long streamers stretched from side to side, bidding them welcome. The cynics said that South Korea's one thriving industry was that which produced streamers for welcoming important personages from abroad. Certainly new ones seemed to be up for different reasons almost every week.

To welcome the delegates, too, and to impress them, the people had been ordered out on to the streets to cheer. The work of schools and colleges was brought to a stop so that the students could swell the crowds.

Down in Chinhae, President Rhee made the welcoming speech. He called for a campaign which would include the organisation of anti-Communist societies, the 'investigation of Communism and its nefarious plots', and the 'exposure of the enemy and the enslavement which he is planning for all of us'.

As always, he was for battle.

"You, who are patriotic citizens," he declared, "may have to risk your lives by organising revolutionary movements or anti-Communist fronts. In doing so, profit by the example that the Communists have set in their own intended conspiracy."

It was grand, heady stuff, but hardly a positive contribution to Asia's real fight against Communism.

In what had once been the home of a rich Japanese family in the diplomatic quarter of Seoul, and was now the Apostolic Delegation, I had dinner one night with Mgr. Quinlan.

The rooms still kept their Japanese character, reflecting the gracious mode of life which had been lived there. Outside was a delightful Japanese garden in which the bull-frogs croaked noisily. The big, smiling Monsignor once again talked to me of his hopes and fears for Korea.

The impact of Western ways upon the morals of the people saddened him. The fear that the country might not get the aid that it had hoped for when it was being laid waste made him anxious. The enormous opportunities of the moment he found heartening and exciting. But he was troubled by the thought that perhaps the opportunity, which had arisen out of events connected with a particular period, might pass because of the lack of sufficient available forces to make the most of it. Such opportunities may come only once in a nation's life.

In all Korea there was not much more than half the number of foreign priests of fifteen years ago. Then there were one hundred and twenty, now perhaps seventy. Of these forty were Columban Fathers, half of whom had been in the country for not more than three years, and so had hardly finished wrestling with the language. Then there were forty-nine foreign sisters, now only thirty. Today there were some two hundred Korean priests, as compared with one hundred in 1939, but hundreds more were urgently needed. There were now nearly five hundred Korean nuns, but the country could do with thousands.

South Korea now had twenty-one million people—only two million less than in all Korea fifteen years ago. Catholics were only one per cent of the total population. But they were ones with a solid faith in a land of people looking for precisely that. Given the forces to instruct the would-be converts, that tiny minority could quickly be made into a decisive one. "In twenty years all Korea can be ours," Mgr. Quinlan said, "provided that we have the men and women out here in time to give the lead."

A minority which is only one per cent of the population is a very small one. But the Catholic minority in Korea could immediately and enormously multiply its size, given the additional aid from outside. The possibilities of the snowball growing are plain for all to see, but someone must be there to keep it rolling.

In any case even a very small but united minority, in Korean conditions—and anywhere else for that matter—can exert a great influence upon a disunited majority.

The Communists, of course, were never more than a small minority in Korea. Ironically enough, in the 1930s there were more Communists in the South than there were in what is now the Communist North.

It is interesting also to note that although there are still underground Communists, who live in Seoul, Mokpo, Taijon and other Southern towns, it is only in Pusan, the one which never knew Communist rule, that you find any large body of active Communist sympathisers.

The Communists who came down from the North were not, most of them, Korean-born at all. They came from the Communist groups which had been carefully cultivated and trained among the Korean émigré population in Manchuria and in Russia itself.

Russia had had its Korean colonists since 1861, and by the time of the Bolshevik revolution of 1917 they numbered some fifty thousand. A big immigration which followed the revolution brought the total in Russia's Far Eastern Republic up to three hundred thousand, making them, after Russians and Ukrainians, its third largest ethnic group. In 1926 a quarter of the population of Vladivostok was Korean.

The Bolsheviks put in years of work among them. They built up the Communist Party and the Young Communist League, purged them time after time, moulded them and made them according to the Marxist pattern.

From them were drawn the 'shock troops' for the spread of Communism in Korea. They were backed up by others from the Korean minority in Manchuria, who, from 1945 on, were trained by the Chinese Communist Party for the same purpose.

These were the 'foreign missionaries' of Communism. When the North fell into the hands of the Russians they were ready and available to be used. From the time the Pacific War ended to the moment of the invasion from the North they were

I*

infiltrated into the South, joining up with local Communists, providing them with a trained leadership for their political activities, and sharing their experiences with them they staged risings or took to the hills as guerillas.

They had, of course, the tremendous advantage that they were Koreans, even though their speech betrayed their foreign origin.

The Korean Communist Party to which they were sent was not without experience. In 1927 the number of Communists in Korea was greater than in Japan and Formosa combined. Following the pattern elsewhere, it had its deviators, was disbanded by Moscow and re-formed. It was persecuted by the Japanese-Korean police. Not less than six thousand party members were arrested between 1928 and 1934. In 1939 there were already a few Communist-led anti-Japanese guerillas, living in the mountains and forests.

Communism was never a mass movement in Korea, as the Soviet Encyclopædia itself admits. It was imposed upon the North. The South has seen enough of it of late to fear it and to react away from it.

The one thing which—apart from military invasion—could make Communism a serious danger in the future would be if, with Japanese rule ended and the ancient pagan ethical codes disintegrated by contact with the West, the Korean people drifted into modern materialism. Then they would have no defence against it and the 'Marxist missionaries', who could be infiltrated from the North in their thousands, would have an easy time covertly spreading their influence. That would be a tragedy indeed after all that the people have suffered in recent years as the result of Communist activities.

XV

FAITHS AND JUNGLE FIGHTERS

AFTER weeks in Korea, with battered, desolate Seoul as my base, Tokyo somehow seemed all wrong. The bright lights, well-dressed people, shops bursting at the seams with goods of every sort, jarred so that it hurt. I found myself longing for my poor Korea again.

I had flown over in a big army transport plane which got me to Japan just after dark. At the airfield an Australian sergeant, an old sweat, was waiting to drive me to the camp in Tokyo. Speeding along well-made roads through villages in which large coloured paper lanterns hung outside the houses, and women in silk kimonos did their last bits of shopping, was like going through fairyland. It was lovely, but it all seemed unreal.

Tokyo was unmistakably real. There was the constant search for entertainment, everywhere. Pin-table saloons—'pinocheoes' —which have become a major distraction and soporific in Japan—thrust themselves at me with huge paper rosettes on sticks decorating their fronts and music blaring from within. The nude shows and strip-tease theatres were doing as brisk a trade as ever. Asakusa Movie Street, 'the street of cinemas', was packed. From one end of the great street to the other are nothing but big cinemas, theatres and other places of entertainment, out of which were pouring thousands of people when I toured the city next day with Fr. Roggendorf, S.J., the dean of studies at Sophia University.

Fr. Roggendorf has lived in Japan for years, speaks its language with a perfection quite exceptional among Westerners, has a deep understanding of the country and its people and has earned their respect. He was an excellent guide.

"It is this materialism of the Japanese, which expresses itself today in a mad pursuit of pleasure unequalled anywhere on

earth, which is the most difficult thing we are up against here,'
he commented.

That difficulty, at least, was largely absent in Korea. Fr. Sea.
Savage's words that day in Mokpo, as we watched the loca
Catholics going home from their morning prayers, came back to
my mind: "Their work and their Faith, that's all they've got."

Someone suggested that it would be a good idea to go to a
Japanese theatre. There I would see what attracted so many
people and, after all, I was reminded, the Japanese theatre has a
reputation for artistry.

I was told that there was a recommended choice of three
shows which, each in its own way, could be called typically
Japanese. But one was a modern play in which there was no
scenery or costumes and in which everything depended on the
spoken word. I would not understand it. There was another
the puppet theatre, which was good to see, but drew only a
dilettante public, not in any way representative of the ordinary
Japanese. If, first and foremost, it was the crowd I was interested in, then this was not the best for the purpose. And
there was the great International Theatre, one of the largest in
the world, to which the masses poured each night. The second
appealed most, but I decided that it was more important that I
should go to the third and see what was really drawing the
Japanese masses.

Present were some five thousand people; approximately two
hundred of them, at the most, were Americans. The remainder
were Japanese. Yet, although all the artistes were Japanese, the
entire show was American-style. There were Japanese cowboy
(and girl) singers, a Japanese 'Hawaian band', Japanese crooners
singing American songs, Japanese comics, the whole of whose
patter was in English. It was an impressive evidence of the
Japanese flair for copying—which ranges from the manufacture
of 'Swiss' watches and 'German' cameras to 'American'
entertainers.

The Americans in the audience applauded enthusiastically
the Japanese politely. I sat wondering what could possibly have
persuaded me to come to this place when I might have been at
the puppet theatre. Yet it quite possibly taught me more

bout the people of post-war Japan than the other would have
done.

But not all the people of Tokyo had thoughts only for their
own amusement. In the afternoon I had gone with a Japanese
university student to visit one of the capital's famous tea shops,
where we drank powdered green tea, reminiscent of cocoa in its
consistency, and were waited on by a very well-bred and entirely
arm's length' geisha girl (as, contrary to a popular mis-
conception in the West, are most geisha girls).

Police cars and foot police with walkie-talkie radio sets were
at every crossing as we came away, and soon we ran into a huge
Socialist demonstration which, in a life-time of demonstrations
of one sort or another, was one of the most orderly and well-
organised I have ever seen. Twenty-five thousand trade
unionists, intellectuals and students marched in formation
through the city streets.

Each contingent had its own loudspeaker van relaying
Socialist songs, which the marchers sang with impressive
earnestness. Both the intellectuals and the workers showed that
same combination of determination and idealism that one found
in Socialist May Day demonstrations in England twenty-five
years ago. But there was no banter and joking as there would
have been had the demonstrators been English. The Japanese
take their pleasures, and their crusades for social justice and
democracy, too, with great seriousness.

I handed in my uniform at the Ebesu camp next day and got
back into 'civvies'. Then, an hour before I was due to set out
for my aircraft to Singapore, I gave a lecture to the girls at a
college run by the Madams of the Sacred Heart. The questions
which followed, and which were all asked in excellent English,
showed not only that the girl students had followed the lecture
closely but were clearly already interested in, and well-informed
upon, world affairs.

Fr. Joe O'Brien and Fr. Hanson, with whom I had been staying again at St. Columban's, went out to the airport to see me
off. I left them knowing that these men who make the conversion of Japan their goal have a tough job ahead of them. But
it is a tremendously important one, very worth doing, and, if

they succeed, the repercussions throughout all Asia will be enormous.

We flew all night to Hong Kong, just making a short stop at Okinawa on the way. The airport at Hong Kong was packed next morning with Chinese families who were seeing off some of their men. Among them I noticed a cretinous boy of the type we in the West call 'Mongols'. What, I wondered idly, do the Chinese call them?

The airstrip, like everything else in Hong Kong, is near the sea.

Whilst the aircraft was being refuelled I strolled out on to a jetty to get a moment to myself. As I came back again a little Chinese nun in a brown and black habit approached me. She was almost as small and young-looking as Sister Rosa, the tiny Korean who had herself smuggled down from the North through the Chinese lines.

To my surprise the little nun greeted me with: "Excuse me, but aren't you Douglas Hyde?"

"I am, but how did you know?"

"Oh, a month or two ago I saw in our Hong Kong Catholic paper that you were here but I didn't know you were coming back again. They published your picture, that's how I knew you."

I had imagined that most Westerners must look the same to an Oriental, just as do the majority of Chinese to us. She, at any rate, could distinguish between us.

She told me that she was flying alone to Singapore and asked if she might accompany me. Whilst we waited to leave, and on the aircraft later, she told me her story.

Mother Cecilia, despite her youthful appearance, was forty-two years old. When she became a Carmelite twenty years ago she was the first Chinese girl in all South China to do so. Her father was a pagan who sent her to a Catholic college. There she was converted, and in due course became a nun, although her parents remained, and are to this day, pagans.

At first she was in a convent in Canton, but there were difficulties with the Chinese authorities, who had little understanding of or sympathy for a convent full of contemplatives, and so they moved to Hong Kong to find the peace and quiet they wanted.

Now she was prioress of the Hong Kong Carmel and was flying to Singapore with the purpose of starting another there. Her brother, a pagan, who had been looking out for suitable sites and buildings for her in Singapore, was going to meet her.

She last left her convent when she set out to look for the site for a new one in Hong Kong. Apart from that she could not remember when she was last out, it was so very many years ago. Now, straight from the sheltered enclosure of one of the strictest Orders in the Church, she was about to fly across the South China Sea.

I asked her what were her impressions of flying.

"Before I met you I was watching the aeroplanes coming and going," she said, "and I thought to myself: 'If man can do such wonderful things as this, what cannot God do?'"

But though life in her Chinese Carmel might be remote from the modern world, she was certainly not cut off from its thought.

Like so many enclosed contemplatives who have few distractions, she seemed to remember everything she had ever read. Between Hong Kong and Singapore our conversation ranged as freely around the Catholic world as it might have done with any well-read, knowledgeable Western laywoman who was completely 'in the world'. It was difficult to realise that she was a Chinese woman whose only contact with the outside world for the past twenty-three years had been through a grille.

She was in touch with events inside Red China, but, more surprising, she was familiar with religious developments in America and Britain, as well as Korea and Japan. She knew my own conversion story in detail and was *au fait* not only with most of the leading Catholic writings of today but with the lives of the writers too.

Against the background of her experience in China she had good reason to know the nature and ferocity of the Communist attack. But her job, which she saw quite clearly, was to maintain a great battery of prayer for the salvation of a world adrift, believing that by her prayer and penance she could aid others who were out in the battlefield. And all over Asia there are men in the front line who agree with her and who believe that the source of much of their own strength is to be found in the cells of holy monks and nuns who have sacrificed all for the Faith they have in common. That is something which no modern pagan reader who has come this far with me can be expected to comprehend. It is something which the Communists would deride. But it is something about which few in the front line have any doubt whatsoever.

The weapons used by Christians and Communists in the fight for the heart and mind of modern man are indeed as different as the philosophies they hold and the gods they serve.

We flew across troubled Malaya to Singapore. The fight against the terrorists in the jungles seemed very far away from the Raffles Hotel, where a considerate air line company had accommodated us. The hotel, with its huge suites of rooms, belonged to an age which has gone. It will probably never again be possible there to build such vast places and with such contempt for the amount of space occupied. Between them, the decline of colonialism and the skyrocketing of land values make such places things of the past.

But although the jungle fighters might seem remote from the Raffles, there were people in Singapore who were becoming increasingly concerned at the evidences of the growth of Communism among the city's teeming Chinese population. They feared that terrorism might just as surely reach in time into Singapore as the blood-stained hand of Kenya's Mau Mau has reached into the heart of Nairobi.

In Singapore, too, were men whose job it is to supervise the operations against the Communist guerillas 'up-country' in Malaya.

For the moment, at least, the military measures taken against the terrorists has reduced the Communists' strength and effectiveness. But the example of China shows how fatally wrong it is to assume that when you have weakened a Communist guerilla force and reduced it to little more than a band of irreconcilables all is over bar the shouting. Malay's Communist guerillas may be defeated, but this does not mean that they are therefore broken.

The Chinese Communists took one 'defeat' after another over a period of twenty-seven years; they were forced to abandon all the territory which they had dominated, trek across an enormous country and start all over again. Superior arms were not sufficient to prevent their ultimate victory. The experiences of Mao Tse Tung and his followers, and the lessons learned from them, are being absorbed with benefit by the Malayan and other Asian guerillas today.

The first thing to grasp if one is to understand the difference between the Communist conquest of power by guerilla tactics (Chinese-fashion) as opposed to the seizure of power by insurrection (Russian-fashion) is that in the latter case everything must be gained in one great blow or all is lost, whereas in the other the fight may go on over the years, losses of men and territory may be enormous and still victory remains a possibility. An ideological guerilla army is never defeated so long as the idea that prompted it continues to live.

For this reason it is far too soon to assume that we are now on top of the situation in Malaya, as too many complacent politicians in Westminster are ready to tell one.

What I think is clear from the experience in Malaya is this: the Chinese Communist leaders are not at this moment taking any great risks on behalf of Asian guerillas armies which are not within sight of possible victory. In other words, they were prepared to send in arms and experts to Ho Chi Minh in North Vietnam and take all the risks of world war which were involved, but are giving no such support—or certainly not to any decisive extent—to the Malayan and Filipino Communists. But if and when these, too, can make the early conquest of power seem a genuine possibility, then all the arms and aid they need will be theirs for the asking.

Meanwhile, the fight in the jungles for the extermination of Communists continues side by side with another for their rehabilitation. And from that second fight there are certainly lessons to be learned.

In the course of years of fighting, many Communist guerillas have been captured and, in the last year or two in particular, others have surrendered. Too little is known about the attempt to reform these men and women and to turn them into useful, peaceful citizens.

Early in 1949 the authorities recognised that the attempt to rehabilitate the Communists who had come into their hands must be made. Those detained fell into various categories. There were the adventurers, the professional bandits of the type well known in the Far East, and young men and women who had been press-ganged into joining guerilla bands. If these had been all—as the anti-Communist propagandists had always said was the case—the task of the rehabilitation officers would have been relatively easy.

But the most significant group was precisely the one that the blimps had claimed did not exist. They were the hard core of indoctrinated Communists, those combinations of idealism and immense toughness whom the Communists call the 'steel-hardened cadres'. And they, of course, are the intractables, the irreconcilables. Some of the guerillas needed only a full belly to wean them away from Communism. Others could be taught a trade in the detention camp, and found a job, or perhaps a bit of land to cultivate. Thereby they were given a new interest, along with their first self-respect, and soon they, too, were forgetting their Communism. Still others responded when they were put into positions which made them feel important, where their flair for leadership and action could be utilised for something better.

More than this, however, was needed to win the hard core away from their Communism. For them Communism was a faith, an ideal, the most dynamic thing they had ever known. Having tasted it, they had to be offered something still more dynamic if they were to be 'rehabilitated'.

But what 'counter-dynamic' had the authorities to offer? This was the question to which conscientious and thoughtful officers working among them had to try to find an answer.

These men and women had already rejected their own Oriental religions. The Western democratic idea could not be expected to fire men who had never seen democracy in action or, if they had, had never seen it applied to their own country, to themselves. Western democracy is at this moment no counter-dynamic to Communism in most of Asia. Still less is the attempt to create a British public-school spirit, complete with Old Boys' Society, likely to impress its dedicated followers.

The experience of those responsible for the rehabilitation work has tended to drive them back to the conclusion that only a firmly held and well understood religious faith, of a type which provides a complete philosophy of life and claims the whole man, can offer such a counter-dynamic. But Christianity in general, and least of all a particular branch of it, may not, and should not, be used by Government officials just as a political weapon. To do so would be to degrade religion and also to guarantee an outcry at home from all the other Christian sects, and from the organised freethinkers, rationalists and others, and in Malaya from the organised Moslems. It would be both unseemly and unwise. That is the dilemma with which those who work for the rehabilitation of Malaya's Communist detainees are faced.

I do not wish for one moment to suggest that there have been no successes at the Taiping and Morib rehabilitation centres. There have. A good job, in the face of much discouragement, has been done. But very, very few of their successes have been among the real Communists. So the essential problem remains. No real answer to it has been found. The idea which, if still left undefeated, may yet mean the conquest of Malaya by Communism still lives on among its hard core, and those who hold it are largely untouched by the best attempts to 'rehabilitate' them.

A British Government White Paper, issued in 1953, discussed this work and the results it has achieved. It reported that out of a total of one thousand two hundred and eighty detained persons who up to March 1953 had successfully completed the course at Taiping, only eight were known to have again become supporters of the terrorists. "One hundred and three persons," it continued, "have been returned without release to normal detention camps as *being irresponsive to rehabilitation*" (my italics).

But it is precisely that just-under-ten-per-cent of 'irresponsive' ones who are the people of real significance. They represent the minority upon whom international Communism pins its hope of certain victory. They are the mainspring of the revolution. So long as their faith remains unbroken the revolution will still tick on to victory. They are the ones who challenge us.

What are we to do? Do we keep them in jail until they die? Do we physically exterminate them because they stubbornly refuse to be convinced that we have something better than the Communists to offer? To do so would be to admit our own defeat—and to provide their movement with a welcome gift of martyrs.

The Taiping experience seems to me to underline my contention that you will stop the spread of Communism only by the spread of a better faith—the Faith. And that is not the job, as such, of the politicians, nor of Government officials, although if these bring with them a living Christianity they can help the work enormously by their own example. It is the job of the missionary and the apostolic layman. They are the decisive men.

We flew out from Singapore across the Malay Straits, then along the coast of Sumatra in Indonesia. There the Communists are making significant headway. They have, of course, their armed guerilla bands. But there are others upon whom they place their hopes too. They are digging themselves into strong positions in the trade unions. The amount of industrialisation is so far still small, but it is growing and the power of the unions, in which the Communists are already established, will grow with it.

The second centre of Communist influence is the Chinese community, which, like those all over Asia, contains many who are sympathetic to Mao Tse Tung.

The third is the hatred of Dutch colonialism. Above everything, Indonesians today are anti-Dutch. Mohammedanism is the strongest religion in Sumatra, but when the Communists offer their aid in breaking the Dutch influence the Moslems take it. But the Moslem cannot afford to associate with the

Communist, for Communism contains almost everything that Islam lacks. And for the semi-Westernised, educated Moslem to do so—and he is the man of tomorrow—will almost certainly prove fatal.

Islam places its emphasis only on the externals of religion. It sees ritual observance as being more important than an appeal to the intelligence or loyalty to a creed. That has been the source of its strength among illiterate peoples. It must prove to be a fatal weakness among those who become literate and in due course are drawn into the battle of ideas. For the moment, particularly in the case of business men or Government officials, dependent upon 'the masses', they continue to put up some show of observing the minimum practices demanded of them by Islam. It would be bad business not to do so. But when their materialism and loss of faith filters down to the masses even this will no longer be necessary.

The largest concentration of Catholics in Indonesia is on one of its smaller islands, the picturesquely named Flores. A majority of its one million people are Catholics, practically all of whom can read and write. The remainder are mostly animists. The impoverished, frustrated, literates of Asia, as of Africa, tend to provide particularly fertile soil for Communism, but, although Flores is poor and the economic level of the life of its people is low, Communism has so far not got a foothold there.

The possibilities for quickly raising the standard of life of its people are reasonably high, but Indonesians, like others in South-East Asia, do not trust Western agencies—which is what makes the work of U.N.E.S.C.O. and similar bodies so difficult.

To an outsider there would appear to be a strong case for the native Christians of Flores being given every possible assistance with the formation of their own producers' co-operatives and credit unions so that they themselves may, under Christian inspiration and guidance, make their country at once better to live in and a 'shop window' for the application of Christian social teaching to Indonesian conditions. The effect upon the whole of turbulent Indonesia might well be

considerable and would help, among other things, to demon-
strate that there is an alternative to Communism for those
newly 'liberated' people who seek a higher standard of life
and whose old faiths are weakening under the impact of
Western ways.

XVI

TWO WORLDS

THE scene from the balcony of the Mount Lavinia Hotel, just outside Colombo, in Ceylon, is all that one imagines the Orient to be. There is the bluest of blue seas and a wonderful beach on which a blazing sun shines from morn till night. The bathing, including the surf-riding, is excellent. Hanging out over the sea grow tall palms with feathery tops.

And up one of these palm trees, for the benefit of the idlers on the balcony, ran a small dark-skinned boy dressed only in a loin-cloth. Then he came sliding down again and ran straight into the sea, mounted a piece of wood on a wave, shot straight past the white-skinned bathers, and landed neatly on the beach at my side.

The bathers showed their appreciation of his performance by coming out and passing him their loose change. Then they settled down to eating the big pineapple they had just bought from a beautifully slim, erect Ceylonese woman, with dancing black eyes, a wide, white-toothed smile and immense natural charm and dignity. At the gateway to the beach stood or sat a small group of beggars. One persistently touted the hotel guests, asking to be allowed to take them to see "old women making lace for young girls. Very pretty." Another offered strings of beads made from coloured beans and little shells. This was life in the East as the Victorian Englishman thought it should be and always would be.

A barefooted page-boy came to tell me that I was wanted on the telephone. It was the editor of Ceylon's Catholic weekly paper. He told me that, learning that I was staying just outside Colombo, he had already taken the liberty of getting the Young Christian Workers' Movement in the city to call a meeting of its members. Would I mind addressing them? And perhaps, whilst I was there, I would address one or two other gatherings too?

The hotel was only a few miles outside the city, but the world of the tall palms, the bathers, the idlers on the balcony and the small black boy entertaining them was very remote from that of the young men and women who formed my audience that night.

The meeting was held in a disused church which had been built by the old French missionaries years ago. Since a new one had been erected near-by, it was now being used as a public hall.

The audience was composed of young workers, both manual and 'soft-collar', keen, intelligent and clearly accustomed to expressing their views in a sharp, forthright manner. Their questions, which came thick and fast, ranged from the rôle of the Christian in the trade unions and political parties to the difference between Stalinism and Trotskyism and whether it was wise in any circumstances to associate with either. They were questions arising from the problems confronting the Christian in an industrial society and might just as easily, given the different background, have come from a similar group in any Western country.

Sitting in a semi-circle around me, with a group of girls in colourful sarongs grouped together at one side, they talked of the attempts of the Communists to influence the youth, the workers and the intellectuals of Ceylon. As in the case of the country's big neighbour India, delegations to Russia and China were constantly coming and going. Printed propaganda material was pouring in from Moscow and Peking. The Trotskyites, who had had a curious vogue there for some years, and had even constituted the official Parliamentary Opposition, were losing something of their grip, but to the advantage of the Stalinists—not, so far, to their opponents.

The cultivation of the people of Ceylon by the Communists was taking interesting forms. For example, a prominent journalist, not a member of the Young Christian Workers, told me of Communist doctors who were getting supplies of modern drugs which were much sought after, but in short supply, free or at greatly reduced cost, from Eastern Europe. Thus they were given an advantage over their non-Communist competitors and the chance to get an easy popularity with those who were sick and with their grateful families.

I gave three lectures that night, meeting three very different groups of people—young workers, students and the Ceylonese religious community responsible for the running of a big college. In each case the questions reflected a preoccupation with the problems which are typical of any modern industrial society. They were naturally coloured by their Ceylonese setting but might otherwise just as easily have come, say, from young workers in France or Belgium, students at the London School of Economics, or a community running a college in New York.

This was the world of mid-twentieth-century Asia and of its tomorrow, just as that on the beach near the hotel was that of yesterday.

It was, despite the elephants in the city streets, the bazaars and the rickshaws, more like the one to which I returned a few days later in London than was that of the Asia of the peasants in the paddy-fields. It was a world dominated by the minority who make and break social and political systems today. We may not like it. We may look back nostalgically to that other world. But we cannot deny its significance.

What will the Asia of tomorrow be like? Will it be, at the best, materialist and, at the worst, as a consequence of its materialism, Communist? Or will it, on the other hand, be dynamically Christian? It is possible that there is no other alternative, for the other faiths are quickly corroded by the creeping materialism of our day.

Will Communism with its trained, indoctrinated, steel-hardened minorities triumph? The chances of those minorities getting their way is greater at this moment in Asia than anywhere else on earth. Only now is a glimpse of the full significance of the Communists' victory in China being seen by the instructed few in the West.

All over the colonial world today Red China's propaganda is

penetrating and doing its work. The appeal of China in Asia is already vastly greater than Russia's was at any time.

And her message is, firstly, that any country which has a land-hungry peasantry and a national liberation movement can make a Communist revolution, provided only that it has its hard core of trained Communists. Secondly, in a semi-feudal, semi-colonial country, such as China was, it is not necessary to wait for the moment of the collapse of the old system before you strike. The armed revolution, conducted by Communist-led guerillas, can be started at once. It can lose ground here, gain it there, until at last the existing system is destroyed from within. Thirdly, although the Communists have taken the view that where possible, as in Russia and other European countries, such democratic forms of struggle as can be used should be utilised to the full right up to the moment for insurrection, in the semi-feudal, semi-colonial countries of Asia and Africa you may, and should, use the gun from the start.

Mao Tse Tung said: "We are the advocates of the omnipotence of the revolutionary war . . . the whole world can be remoulded only with the gun."

In other words, a difference, of great significance to the West, between Chinese Communism and Russian Communism is that the Chinese variety is even more dangerous, more impatient and far more quick on the gun. The Communists of the Moscow school take to the gun only at the very end of their struggle for power. Those of the Peking school use it right from the very beginning.

This is the Communism which will guide and inspire Asia's Communists in the years ahead. They will depend even less on majorities than the Western Communist Parties have done in the past.

The question is fundamentally not just one of combating today's Communists but of saving potential Communists from themselves, winning them for a better faith and creating material and spiritual conditions in which Communism cannot flourish.

Between the Communists' front-line fighters and the Church's there is a world of difference. Communism's dedicated men are consciously in the fight. They are carefully prepared for it and understand just how they are to conduct it. They can use any methods, including deception, coercion and brute force. All these are denied to the Christian.

The dedicated Christian in the front line fights Communism in the main by spreading something better. Sometimes, as I discovered, he is conscious of the battle and the nature of that battle, but more often he is only partly aware of it. In the past he has had little special training for this modern battle. Today, since the fall of China, there is probably more such special preparation than before, but even so it is doubtful if it is what it should be. His weapons cannot be those of the Communist. That gives the Communist an immediate advantage although the weapons are ones which will sooner or later break in his hands. The weapon of the Christian is the sword of the spirit. Yet his purpose, to win men's hearts and minds, and to change the world, is the same.

Some of Christianity's front-line fighters see the thing on the world scale. Most see only their own small sector of the front, the one where they labour for the cure of souls, which absorbs all their thought and time. Yet if there are enough of them and if they are given sufficient support, they will yet stop the spread of materialism. Thereby they will rob the highly trained Marxist men of their best hope for tomorrow, for they are tackling the problem at its roots.

They are confronted with opportunities which are quite unique today. The chances are there if the men are available to take them. If they are missed, a materialistic Asia will be vastly more difficult to convert.

An enormously heartening factor is that at the present stage, where men have experienced Communism, as in Korea and among the refugees in Hong Kong and Formosa, there such post-Communist populations are reaching out their hands for the Faith. The sobering thing is that there is a real danger that they may reach out in vain, because the number of men and women available to give them what they yearn for is too small.

If that should happen we shall deserve the fate which will

assuredly be ours. We shall have failed, not only to help them but to help ourselves as well.

For in saving the soul of Asia, the West may well save its own soul too.

I went back to Navan, in Ireland, a month or two after my return to the West. I was greeted by Fr. Aedan McGrath, newly arrived from Hong Kong after his expulsion from Red China. He had come straight from three years in a Chinese jail. Three years of unbroken physical and mental torture. And already this game little man was impatiently agitating for his superiors in the Society of St. Columban to send him back to Asia again.

Once such a man might have surprised me. But I had now seen the Church's front-line fighters in action, wielding the sword of the spirit regardless of the consequences to themselves. I knew their calibre. I knew the strength which is given to even the most human of human material. So I was no longer surprised.

"This," I said, "is where I came in."